Violence against Women in Medieval Texts

Violence
against
Women
in
Medieval
Texts

Edited by Anna Roberts

University Press of Florida

Gainesville Tallahassee Tampa Boca Raton
Pensacola Orlando Miami Jacksonville

Copyright 1998 by the Board of Regents of the State of Florida
Printed in the United States of America on acid-free paper
All rights reserved

03 02 01 00 99 98   6 5 4 3 2 1

Library of Congress Cataloging-in-Publication Data

Violence against women in medieval texts / edited by Anna Roberts.
p. cm.
Includes bibliographical references and index.
ISBN 0-8130-1566-9 (cloth: alk. paper)
1. Literature, Medieval—History and criticism. 2. Violence in literature. 3. Women in literature. I. Roberts, Anna, 1966- .
PN682.V55V55 1998
809'.93355—dc21 97-48732

The University Press of Florida is the scholarly publishing agency for the State
University System of Florida, comprised of Florida A & M University, Florida
Atlantic University, Florida International University, Florida State University,
University of Central Florida, University of Florida, University of North
Florida, University of South Florida, and University of West Florida.

University Press of Florida
15 Northwest 15th Street
Gainesville, FL 32611
http://nersp.nerdc.ufl.edu/~upf

Contents

Figures

Introduction

Violence against Women
and the Habits of Thought

Anna Roberts

This collection originated in sessions devoted to the study of violence against women in medieval texts, organized by Linda Rouillard and Anna Roberts for the International Medieval Congress at Kalamazoo in 1995. The collection's most distinctive asset is the broad range of contexts explored by the contributors, from Anglo-Saxon hagiography (Horner) to the Spanish Inquisition (Ellis). Because of the wide geographical and genre distribution of the articles, we have arranged them chronologically, tracing in the introduction the conceptual links between the essays, which suggest other (nonchronological) itineraries of reading. Although the contributors recognize that the purpose of a text (hagiographic, narrative, or historiographic, for example) shapes the rhetoric of violence against women—that is, violence is constructed differently in different categories of texts—the sum of these studies reaches farther than the individual analyses, bringing answers to general questions concerning violence against women and its textual encoding: can we detect similarities in different retellings of violence against women, across such divides as genre, geography, and chronology? Do the texts we study indicate the presence or the elaboration of a code of violence operating beyond the boundaries of a text? Are the (narrative, physiological, ideological) rationalizations of violence against women in these texts cumulative, successive, or mutually exclusive?

The earliest context presented here is tenth-century Anglo-Saxon hagiography; by including the discussion of Anglo-Saxon texts, we contribute to filling an important gap left by previous collective discussions of body and gender. In Ælfric's *Lives of Saints*, Shari Horner studies "a key paradox in medieval hagiography," the ominous presence of erotic and tortured fe- male bodies in "texts that purport not to be about the body at all." Ælfric's own theories of interpretation are exploited by Horner in a reconstruction of the hermeneutics of the *Lives of Saints*. The question of female subjectiv- ity is crucial as Horner refines Katherine Gravdal's conclusions on rape in medieval textual tradition.

Gravdal argues that diversion (reorientation of the text from the sexual violence as apparent subject toward a transcendental, often spiritual or political meaning) is the primary strategy for making sexual violence ap- pealing. While Gravdal's hypothesis is essential to many essays in this collection, it serves as a starting point of the analysis rather than as its conclusion. For instance, while Horner shows that hagiography sexualizes the violated female body—as Gravdal suggests it does—Horner reminds us that Ælfric "anticipates" Gravdal's analysis by positing distinct levels of reading, transcendent (*gastlice*, or spiritual) and immanent (*lichamlice*, or bodily). More important, in Horner's analysis, the bodily and spiritual readings are not as distinct as both Gravdal and Ælfric suggest.

Gravdal invites us to see the violated female body without the distrac- tion of a metaphysical principle, be it spirituality, virility, or power; she shows the functioning of rape as a trope for military prowess, social hierar- chy, and political hegemony. Gravdal's definition of rape as trope then al- lows us to see rape where it is in medieval narrative. Thus, Gravdal undoes the exegesis that Ælfric proposes when he invites us to read the martyr- ology spiritually (*gastlice*) instead of bodily (*lichamlice*). Indeed, Gravdal and Ælfric occupy the opposite poles of the same exegetic procedure. Ælfric explains the formalism and encourages the reader to practice it, to focus beyond the female body in pain to see the intended meaning (spiri- tual victory). Gravdal launches the archaeology of this formalism in order to recover the female body, allowing us to hypothesize in turn that the interpretive procedure is heavy with social consequences: the habit of overstepping the female body in pain in order to access transcendental, spiritual, and social meaning may be linked to a wide spectrum of cultural phenomena, from submission to torture.

Horner offers an approach that differs from both Gravdal's and Ælfric's when she argues that "the saint's body acts as a text displaying the ten- sions between the practices of reading literally . . . and spiritually." By fo- cusing on the tortured body as a locus of interpretation, Horner under- scores the mechanism that renders female saints (and their mutilated bodies) dialectically indispensable in medieval cult. The female body is not only the vehicle of deeper meaning, a transparent subject matter from which the reader is diverted toward the spiritual significance; it also stands for the reading procedure. The silencing and erasure of women's bodies through exegesis, a narrative violence, complements the narrative of violence.

The saints' lives explored by Horner (those of Agatha, Lucy, and Agnes) are also emblematic of essential trends in genres other than hagiography. To the extent that hagiography is a narrative of torture, it does fall into the same category as the texts analyzed in Jody Enders's and Deborah Ellis's studies of the Inquisition in the present volume. Perhaps more unexpectedly, Horner's hagiographic examples illuminate some crucial aspects of the romance tradition, specifically because of Horner's interest in bodies as tropes, "reading bodies as texts." The case of St. Lucy is perhaps the most directly pertinent to the romance tradition, her fate prefiguring that of the romance heroines. As Lucy remains unscathed in spite of being covered in oil and pitch and set on fire, so the romance heroines emerge alive and intact from the hands of incestuous fathers, violent husbands, rivals, and uncouth villains. As Lucy becomes rooted to the soil when dragged to a brothel, so her romance counterparts inevitably return to the niches they occupied before the initial transgression marking the beginning of the narrative. The hyperbolic resilience of women protagonists, characteristic of a number of genres, results in a heroi-comic depreciation of women's suffering (on the comic quality of violence, see also Weisl's essay in this volume).

More than a century and a distinct, political purpose separate Ælfric's hagiographies from Orderic's chronicles; yet acts of violence against women provide the historiographer with a subject matter as gruesome as the martyrologist's. Jean Blacker introduces Orderic Vitalis's *Historia Ecclesiastica* (c. 1114–40) as a work typical of its time and genre with respect to its content and ideology. As in other comparable works, the narrative space accorded to women in the *Historia* is limited. The author's interest is not in women but in the monastic community of Saint-Evroult and, in later layers of the *Historia*, in Norman and ecclesiastic politics. However, as Blacker argues, a degree of "even-handedness" in the representation of women sets the *Historia* apart from similar works of its period. References to women are both more frequent and more qualified than we come to expect. Blacker shows that instead of a polarization between male (good) and female (evil), the common denominator is "the use and abuse of power."

If the phenomenology of reading does not coincide entirely with the purpose of writing (as is most frequently the case when reading about women in medieval texts), the critical apparatus must be finely tuned.

Blacker's analysis demonstrates particular sensitivity to this circumstance. She shows how the representation of women in the *Historia Ecclesiastica* is predicated upon literary and philosophical traditions as well as the communal politics of the author. In a number of cases, she shows the *Historia* as a crucible where literary representations of women are brought into being or recombined, in covert references to literary paradigms, negative or positive (Mabel of Bellême as a perverted *alma mater* poisoning with her milk or food; slaying of Mabel recalling the death of Agamemnon), old or new (the first appearance of the motif of a Moslem princess saving a Christian hero).

Blacker argues that the literary paradigms in the representation of women are far from ornamental—instead, they are powerful enough to preempt reality (as is the case with Mabel's poisoning an infant with her milk). Following Natalie Zemon Davis's argument about "women on top," Blacker emphasizes that the literary paradigms are often polyvalent, and she adds a new dimension to Davis's discussion. Davis argues that while gender reversals serve as a safety valve in a system of oppression, these reversals also inevitably provide models for change. Davis thus qualifies the argument proposed by Mikhail Bakhtin in his study of reversal rites (Bakhtin emphasizes their role in stabilizing and thus preserving the oppressive system). Both turns of the argument, Bakhtin's and Davis's, are based on the unintentional functioning of the text. Blacker focuses on a point that Davis and Bakhtin do not anticipate because of the general (not text-specific) scope of their argument: the author's intent in presenting the reversals. Thus, she brings us one step closer to the understanding of violence in medieval texts.

Blacker first demonstrates that the portrayal of women and violence in *Historia Ecclesiastica* is guided less by the author's misogyny than by his ecclesiastical allegiances. She gives the example of an aristocratic wife goading her husband "between conjugal caresses" to rejoin the crusade; this, according to Orderic, is not advocating violence. On the other hand, she reminds us that the most ignominious and violent woman Orderic depicts is a wife who induced her spouse to be "hostile to the monks in many ways." In great simplification, we may be witnessing in Orderic's text the victory of the clerical ethos over the feudal warrior ethos.

Yet Orderic's loyalty does not lie exclusively with the ecclesiastic institutions but also with the narrative coherence of his story, the literary viability of the noble heroes of his *Historia*. Here, the "constructive," myth-making role of violence in the historical, aristocratic, empire-building narrative must be recognized. As Blacker notes, violence bestows heroic qualities only on those whose name is great enough for the record: Mabel of

Bellême, Orderic's antiheroine, is incidentally "the only named female figure . . . to die by the sword," distinguished from among the many unnamed women and children slaughtered in the wars; the echo of the epic tradition gives her death a heroic dimension. At this and other junctures, narrative functionality overrides Orderic's political and institutional loyalties, which otherwise dictate a more conservative, moral distribution of heroic qualities.

Still other incompatible sympathies break through Orderic's predominant ecclesiastical and feudal allegiance, this time suggesting that his definition of violence may not always originate in institutional and narrative interest but also in a principle overriding these narrow loyalties. The objection to gruesome abuse of children and women, going against the grain of the historiographer's allegiance to Henry I, creates a medieval simulacrum of modern humanitarianism. Blacker concludes that the "ability to transcend gender and rank is central in Orderic's thinking."

If Orderic's incoherences in apportioning praise and blame reveal traces of compassion and charitable principles, Laurie Finke and Martin Shichtman effectively dissuade us from identifying Arthur's punishment of the Mont St. Michel giant's rape as altruism. In their study of Wace and Laʒamon, Finke and Shichtman conclusively interpret the rape sequence as an essential element of the myth of foundation of empire. They demonstrate that the narrative of sexual violence—male on female violence—is constitutive of historical writing as a whole, as it articulates the three principal objects of historiography: military prowess, social hierarchy, and political hegemony. In the analysis of three episodes (assembling armies, dream, and Mont St. Michel's giant), Finke and Shichtman provide a careful assessment of the reconfigurations that transform the history into legend, an assessment attentive to the social and political context (with sustained discussion of social stratification, political aspects of nascent and triumphant Norman imperialism, and of Wace's, Laʒamon's, and William of Malmesbury's political circumstances). Most important, they identify rape as a symptom or trope "in the writing of history," a 'quilting point' ([Lacan's] *point de capiton*) binding together the floating elements that make up ideological space, thereby creating and sustaining a particular ideological formation." Finke and Shichtman's essential contribution is identifying the Mont St. Michel rape episode as pivotal in the economy of the Arthurian legend, as it serves to "transform Arthur from local to world historical hero" and to "legitimate imperial ambition."

Three foci of ideological anxiety marking the twelfth-century "aristocratic diaspora" are important for Finke and Shichtman: imperialist expansion, military prowess, and aristocratic privilege. These three ideological dimensions correspond to three functions of rape episodes in the medieval literary tradition (of the five functions identified by Gravdal in *Ravishing Maidens*): rape as an emblem of political hegemony, as a trope for warfare, and as a means of distinction between the aristocracy and the lower classes.

Finke and Shichtman point out that women are vehicles of political alliance, economic power, and, as Duby suggests, of "blood," that is, a promise of masculine prowess. Therefore, both their exchange and *raptus* (abduction and/or rape) in the imperialist society bring the legitimation of power, just as the sexual violence in fiction establishes the hierarchies of virility, class, and supremacy (see also Jed, *Chaste Thinking*, quoted by Enders in this volume). If Mary Douglas noted that "violations of physical bodies can be metonymies for violations of the political body" (as quoted by Finke and Shichtman), Finke and Shichtman show that, rather than a metonymy, rape is a political metaphor in which female (no)bodies are used to stage the conflict.

In discussing three functions of rape in the episode of the Mont St. Michel giant, Finke and Shichtman also note that the rape scene produces "a certain excess (Žižek calls this 'surplus-enjoyment') that exceeds the rape's ideological and structural function." Thus, the rape episode is not only functional but also nonfunctional. The "obsessive and symptomatic repetitiveness" of rape in the process of mythmaking may derive both from the functional aspects and from the "surplus-enjoyment." Combining such theoretical tools as Douglas's and Eliade's reflection on the sacred, the profane, and the taboo with the historical approach of Boswell, Bartlett, and Moore (among others) and with Žižek's and Greenblatt's reflection on genre, literature, and ideology, Finke and Shichtman build a powerful case for reading rape as a symptom, "a particular, 'pathological' feature . . . an inert stain resisting communication and interpretation . . . a terrifying bodily mark which is merely a mute attestation bearing witness to a disgusting enjoyment" (Žižek, quoted in Finke and Shichtman).

Contemporary with the rewriting of Latin *historiae* into the vernacular by Wace and Laȝamon is the *translatio* of a fundamental myth linking sexual violence and cannibalism, the story of the nightingale, in Chrétien de Troyes' *Philomena*. Formulating an essential connection between the medieval versions of the eaten heart story and the nightingale metaphor, Madeleine Jeay shows that in the medieval rewritings of the nightingale myth, "the distancing and ironic character of literary representation has produced its normalizing effect by comparison with the direct expression of violence." She exposes the process of "normalizing violence" in the text on two levels, "in both senses of the word: attenuating the unbearable cruelty of the myth but also presenting as acceptable, and unavoidable, the violence of desire." Jeay traces two complementary processes: the medieval development of the nightingale/eaten heart myth into a metaphor and the "normalization" of violence. Her study is a timely addition to the discussions of other aspects of Philomela's story by Dinshaw (in this collection) and Burns (in *Bodytalk*).

Jeay opens by noting the exceptional status of the nightingale/Philomela myth, which in its twelfth-century *translatio* by Chrétien "stands alone like a *hapax* in medieval French literature." She points out that the exceptional cruelty of the story (rape, incest, mutilation, infanticide, cannibalism) prevented direct imitation, being incompatible with the dominant tendency of medieval courtly style, which instead effaced the distinction between seduction and aggression in "a process of aestheticization" analyzed by Gravdal. This process makes the medieval French posterity of *Philomena* almost unrecognizable, and Jeay's article is the first to posit the kinship between Chrétien's close rewriting of Ovid's *Metamorphoses* and the more remote, euphemized versions, including the *lai* of *Guiron* in Thomas's *Tristan*; the *vida* of Guillem of Cabestaing, the vida's longer version and related *razo* version; the *Lai d'Ignauré* attributed to Renaut de Beaujeu and its analogue, the vida of Raimbaut d'Aurenga; and the *Roman du castelain de Couci et de la dame de Fayel* (here abbreviated as *Couci*) by Jakemes. The focus on avian rivals (nightingale, kite, hawk) also allows Jeay to bring into her discussion such analogues as Marie de France's *Laostic* and Jean Renart's *Escoufle*, and she completes her reading by comparisons with Boccaccio's tale of Rossiglione and references to John Peacham's *Philomena praevia*. Drawing evidence from classical, medieval, and early modern contexts, scanning myths, lyric topoi, and mystic traditions, Jeay presents a conclusive, groundbreaking case for the reading of the nightingale figure and the rites of spring as ominously violent metaphors of the brutality inherent in French courtly love tradition. Moreover, by remaining attentive to the role of social status in the fictional relationships she explores, Jeay creates a basis for a political reading of sexual violence, similarly to Finke and Shichtman's study of the episodes of sexual violence in historical narratives.

Jeay's analysis of the polysemous metaphor of the nightingale allows the refinement of Gravdal's hypothesis concerning "the cultural habit of conceptualizing male violence against women as a positive expression of love." In the texts Jeay analyzes in the light of *Philomena*, the poet usurps the metaphor of the nightingale (in Ovid and Chrétien, the metamorphosed female victim of rape, incest, and mutilation) to represent himself, the "singing subject." The poet/secret lover/nightingale, the lady, and her murderous husband form a triangle—on one hand suggesting Girard's conclusion that desire is primarily mimetic, with the lady as the accessory to the contest between the two men, and on the other hand exemplifying Huchet's hypothesis about the "dissatisfaction inherent in sexuality" as the source of the literary figure of the successful rival. As Jeay notes, by adopting the metaphor of the nightingale, the medieval poet complicates the "men on women" schema of violence proposed by Gravdal: while the lady is for Jeay both "the stake and object of [her] legitimate partner's aggressivity," the poet/nightingale is the "designated victim in a world [of] knights."

However, as Jeay demonstrates, the poet's ambiguous figure is susceptible to yet another reversal. He is ambiguous since the control he exercises over the power of words is self-defeating; as Huchet suggests, the poet—disseminator and narrator—is a double of the figure of the *losengier*. Still, the poet gains credit at the symbolic level through narration, ultimately eluding punishment. Following Huchet, who concludes that courtly literature uses violence against women as a substitute for control among men, Jeay shows that the woman is "the only partner in the love relationship who can be reached," violence against her compensating for the lack of control over the words wielded by the poet/lover or by the losengier (both male rival figures).

The fundamental metaphor of violence against women is the image of the wounded bird. Jeay says "men want to believe that the woman's body keeps the mark of their embrace in blood drops," as in Huchet's central example of Chrétien de Troyes' *Conte du Graal*, where three drops of blood on the snow ravish Perceval into the vision of his beloved Blanchefleur. In an unprecedented critical proposition, Jeay places this oft-interpreted scene in the context of avian metaphors of sexual possession, pointing out the folkloric and medieval association of birds, bird chase, and virility (including in her discussion *Erec and Enide, Couci,* and *Escoufle*). The destruction of the opponent is here an act of sexual aggression (the bird is disemboweled through the pelvis, a substitute for rape) as well as of cannibalism (eaten heart motif): "the assimilation of the rival is not mediated through the woman's body."

At the heart of Jeay's analysis is the diversity of configurations involving the female figure. She points out that in the love narratives of the romance, unlike in their lyric analogues, the lady "cannot be the pure—but absent—object of a phantasm; she becomes an acting subject whose attitudes and decisions affect the outcome of the contest between the two rivals." While the lady/lover is "the object and playground of . . . violence" between male rivals, Jeay demonstrates that in a number of versions, the woman is granted a measure of narrative autonomy, allowing her to "subvert the violence aimed at her so that she does not become its passive and powerless victim."

Thus, Jeay shows that while the avian metaphor contributes to the "normalization" or euphemizing of male violence against women (through the aesthetization of the "unbearable cruelty of the myth" and by casting violence as narrative necessity), the polysemous nature of the nightingale metaphor allows "breaches in the univocity of the expression of male culture," as each narrative configures differently the autonomy and symbolic worth of the participants: the jealous husband, the poet, and the woman.

Jeay's article and Anne Laskaya's study of the Middle English *Emaré* (late fourteenth century) both place medieval *fabulae* in the rich context of their multiple retellings. While Jeay discusses links between the nightingale/eaten heart stories from Chrétien's early romances to Boccaccio, Laskaya proposes a reading of the Breton lai in the light of other retellings of the "Constance-saga," well known from Chaucer (*Man of Law's Tale*), Gower (Book 2 of *Confessio Amantis*), or (in French) Philippe de Beaumanoir's *Manekine* and other versions. Going beyond the comparison with Gower and Chaucer, Laskaya also emphasizes the similarities with the tales belonging to the "female worthies" tradition in *Gesta romanorum*, Chaucer's *Legend of Good Women*, and Christine de Pizan's *Livre de la Cité des Dames*. Like other stories of worldly "worthies," the "Constance-saga" is dependent on the motif of female sacrifice, "the narrative's emphasis on *passio* (suffering and acceptance stemming from faith and its consequences in a fallen world)," Laskaya notes.

As Laskaya and Salisbury point out in their edition of Middle English romances, *Emaré* and other lays are preserved in manuscripts containing devotional, didactic, and hagiographic texts. Moreover, the fabula of the "Constance-saga" appears in two important collections of exempla—Jean Gobi's *Scala coeli* (1322–30) and Heunannus Bononiensis' *Viaticum narrationum*—as well as in Marian miracles. The story is also found in historiography (*Vita Offae primi* is generally regarded as the first medieval occurrence), in *roman d'aventures*, and in the late epic. This suggests that the medieval audience recognized the ideological homogeneity that we note in the representation of violence against women in the romance on the one hand and the didactic genres on the other hand, a similarity which belies gestures calculated to draw distinctions between the genres, such as the frequent condemnation of the romance by the moralists or the use of the unworthiness topos by romance narrators. Laskaya's discussion of gender violence may therefore be applied to more than the romance tradition.

As does Dinshaw's essay in this collection, Laskaya's study explores strategies through which, while overtly condemning incest, rape, and murder, the texts (here, analogues of the "Constance-saga") insidiously authorize violence against women. Three main strategies are analyzed: effacing of violence through narrative structure (happy ending); the narrative paradox of the patient (passive) heroine; and the elliptic representation of violence in the microstructure of the romance. Laskaya also points out auxiliary strategies: the gravity of father's attempted incest effaced by the focus on mother-in-law's attempted murder of her son's spouse; downplaying of father's crime by the prominent "seductive daughter and collusive mother" motif; and others.

Emaré presents the threat of incest but strikes down the heroine's rejection of incest by a reversal—her reinsertion into the patriarchal order. While the story presents the disruption of the family by the father's incest, it nonetheless posits the reunion with the father and husband as the ultimate goal, thus privileging the continuity of father-daughter relationship over the daughter's autonomy and the continuity of husband-wife relationship over the wife's autonomy. Laskaya parallels Horner in showing that the narrative of violence does double violence to women, first torturing them and then showing that they cannot be raped, mutilated, and killed—either (in romance) because all violence can be survived and compensated or (in hagiography) because torture is ineffectual and death illusory, overcompensated by a spiritual reward.

The patriarchal theft of women's suffering—what Horner calls the violence of the exegesis and Laskaya terms the social rhetoric of violence against women—produces a paradoxical narrative, its subject being also its blind spot: "although Emaré is appointed heroine within the title, she will rarely occupy the narrative's subject position" (Laskaya). On the level of narrative microstructure, the text diminishes the woman's suffering by ellipsis or distortion of woman's experience. While Laskaya notes that romance fictions feature violence against women much more frequently than historical records do, this fictional representation is conflicted; violence against women is represented not as it is suffered by women but as it is recognized by men. Laskaya follows Gravdal's hypothesis that the focus on the man's suffering has a diversive function: it diverts from rape to raptus, shifting focus from rape to class, from rape to political expansion, from raptus to nationalism (since man is party to, or subject of, the economic, political, or social exchange of which the woman is the object).

Foucault shows in *Discipline and Punish* how medical jargon and incarceration marginalize the mental states that are defined as pathological and are therefore inaccessible directly through the patient's experience, so that they are best handled and only definable by "professionals." Similarly, the narrative of violence establishes a lexicon and a rhetoric relegating the woman's suffering to a sphere that cannot be accessed by the woman victim, a sphere where the language of suffering is male. However, as Laskaya suggests (following Tanner), feminist readers are "less likely to be implicated by any textual naturalization of violence"; awareness of the text's coercive dynamics prevents the perception of violence as natural. Calling on Bal, de Lauretis and Brownmiller, Laskaya herself proposes a "resisting reading," bringing to the fore "a continuum of violence that stretches from threats of violation and death to absorption into the culturally endorsed roles of daughter, mother, wife," a continuum latent under the "surface rhetoric of the text."

Finally, Laskaya's analysis leads far beyond the reduction of textual representation of violence against women to ellipsis. If, because of the distance between the body and the focus of the narrative (spiritual, class, or national), we may discuss violence against women in terms of erasure, as Gravdal did, this basic concept is problematized by the recent interest in the textile in the text, in the covering which reveals, like mute Philomela's cloth. In a reading destined to become canonical, Laskaya focuses on Emaré's cloak—a narrative way of obstructing our perception of her body, as well as our perception of the father's incest (provoked by the love charm woven into the cloth), and finally an obstruction in defining family and social relationships. The prominence of the cloak in the negative as well as positive crises of the plot, its ambiguity "as both protection and heavy burden," results in "a potential disruption of the text's moralizing framework, a disruption created by structural repetition and a subtle equation of violence with social system." For Laskaya, Emaré's cloak serves the same purpose as Philomela's cloth, demonstrating the inherent inconsistencies of the system and its hypocrisy.

As Laskaya evokes Tanner's and de Lauretis's discussion of the representation of violence and rape in order to raise the question of the relationship between literature and the ideology of the dominant culture, so Angela Weisl in her treatment of *Canterbury Tales* relies on Anette Kolodny's proposition that art and life are codependent parts of a cultural continuum, and therefore "the critical examination of rhetorical codes becomes . . . the pursuit of ideological codes." Weisl circumvents the question of auctorial intent or predominant trend by arguing that, while Chaucer may be "sympathetic to gender concerns" as some recent critics demonstrate (including Dinshaw, Mann, and Weisl herself), these sympathies arise "against a background of violence." This background is the focus of Weisl's typology of violence against women in the *Tales*.

Weisl suggests that violence in *Canterbury Tales* has an essentially non-functional value—in Žižek's terms, "surplus-enjoyment"—of a profoundly pathological nature (see Finke and Shichtman's essay in this collection). She evokes the pattern of male "quiting" (from Middle English *quiten*, "to requite, repay, or reward") in the narrative frame of the *Tales* as a parallel to the "quiting of Eve," derived from the theological concept of woman's fault, to be quited and held in check by violence (Weisl refers here to Warner, Duby, and Klapisch-Zuber). She enumerates different aspects of quiting in the *Tales*: reminders of the biblical Eve, classical references, and comic representation of violence in *fabliau*-like tales, where "humor . . . covers up horror." These instances add up to a literary game of tag, where violent abuse of women is reduced to literary, social, or erotic currency in exchanges between men.

Weisl focuses first on the comic genre, which separates violence from its consequences—suffering and death—and normalizes violence "by turning it into the punch line of a joke." Unlike the heroines of romance, the abused women in the fabliau do not gain sympathy; however, in similarity to romance, they serve as objects in the quiting game.

In turn, romance-based tales recount violence for a variety of narrative purposes. Violence frames the tales (*Knight's Tale*); it also provides a disturbing alternative lurking on the horizon of expectations in nonviolent tales (Franklin's, Sir Thopas's, and Squire's). The negative alternative may be provided by the resonance of the plot, lexicon, or themes within the collection (Dorigen's fate compared with that of Emelye and Criseyde; lexical and thematic resonances in Sir Thopas's tale); the violent reading may also be made overt, inscribed in the narration (Dorigen's catalogue of dead virgins and wives). Indeed, the absence of violence may be marked as exceptional by the narrator.

Weisl suggests that the narratives' kinship with hagiography, "the Middle Ages' most brutal genre" (quoting Warner) allows more overt inscription of violence. The story of Constance is that of "a model saint who 'quites' the evil women by remaining good, Christian, and alive," says Weisl. She focuses on the three women who perish in the course of Constance's *passio*: Sultaness, Donegild, and Hermengyld. Interestingly, the first resounding epithet Chaucer lays on one of his antiheroines, the Sultaness, refers to her exemption from the patriarchal rule of quiting, requital, and reward ("O Sowdanesse, roote of iniquitee!" 2.358). In turn, the

Physician's, Prioress's, and Second Nun's tales resonate as exempla "of the ideal life for women—perfect virginity followed by a violent death."

Finally, in the *Wife of Bath's Tale,* Weisl notes a series of reversals: a rapist punished by a dishonoring marriage (the usual fate of rape victims); a wife granted autonomy and choice. While episodic, these reversals challenge the paradigm of violence against women. Combined with the central metaphor of quiting, Weisl's focus on reversal traditions, from the Wife of Bath to Christine de Pizan, elucidates the essential ambiguity of the *Tales*— "support for woman's autonomy and woman's voice" against a background of gender violence. Weisl concludes that violence against women in each of the *Canterbury Tales* connects Eve's fault, classical and medieval tradition, other tales, lexical and thematic clichés, and the ideological paradigms of the dominant culture, into a game of narrative references— quiting, or tag—which necessitates no rationalization beyond its own automatism.

In the choice of texts, Carolyn Dinshaw's study of sexual violence as currency of literary canonization is germane to Weisl's. Dinshaw's study also articulates an essential theoretical direction followed by all the essays in this collection in their specific and distinct modes: identifying habits of thinking as means of institutionalizing violence against women. The article, previously published in a collection on Chaucer and Gower, is thus indispensable in the economy of our volume.[1] Moreover, Dinshaw's analysis of the process of historical-literary appreciation of Chaucer and Gower provides close analogies to Chance's history of diminished reception and hostile translation of Christine de Pizan in England; analogies theoretical as well as derivative of the common literary and historical context analyzed by the two contributors. Finally, both Dinshaw and Jeay evoke the myth of the nightingale—Dinshaw in its English rendering by Gower, Jeay in French by Chrétien de Troyes.

Dinshaw traces the legend of the quarrel between Chaucer and Gower, pausing to remark on its "strange currency that consists mostly in its negation"; she asks what critical purpose may be served by differentiation between the two poets, "what desire might it fantastically fulfill?" The question of desire is directly pertinent, since rape, incest, and other sexual transgressions constitute the basis for distinction between the two poets in the literary legend. Aside from the terms of the comparison, Dinshaw emphasizes the general necessity that underlies the process of literary canonization: "aggression is necessary to the articulation or assertion of a strong, coherent character, an identity." Dinshaw also convincingly demonstrates that the difference between the two poets is "gendered feminine." Reading

Girard's argument on scapegoating and ritual violence through the lens of Joplin's feminist interpretation, Dinshaw proposes that the myth of rivalry between Chaucer and Gower served the Romantic (and later) need to reassert the virility of the poet (a literary-historical construct). In this process, Chaucer "was purged of Gower's femininity"; the place of both poets in the literary canon was established. Of primary importance to Dinshaw, however, is the remainder of the equation—the vehicle that mediated the rivalry and provided the measure of identification—the feminine.

Dinshaw remarks that "we have been trained out of seeing structural connections between minor habits of thinking, on the one hand, and sexual violence, on the other"; her argument goes against this tendency. The historical-literary confection of "quarrel" between Chaucer and Gower fails to recognize "the threat of violence to women's bodies." Dinshaw proposes to reorganize the relationship between Chaucer and Gower by bypassing the elusive decoy of quarrel and targeting instead a quite demonstrable parity, reading Chaucer's *Troilus and Criseyde* in the light of Gower's "Philomela" in *Confessio Amantis*.

Gower characterizes the rape of Philomela as bestial and demented; the rape itself, incest, infanticide, cannibalism, are all "spectacularly anomalous." This abnormalcy obscures resemblances between rape and other transactions illustrated in the tale. As Dinshaw points out, these transactions are all between men; participating women are conspicuous by their silence. Simultaneously, casting rape as the effect of an abnormal, "single, even inhuman desire" makes the other elements of the continuum of violence against women inaccessible from the angle of analyzing sexual violence.

Beyond the silencing of women in rivalry between men and the ideological continuum of rape as one of many gender-asymmetrical acts, the third point made by Dinshaw is germane to Jeay's thesis on the nightingale as a polysemous sign, potentially signifying cruelty inherent in the courtly love tradition. Dinshaw emphasizes that all three main figures of the myth (Philomela, Procne, and Tereus) gain "an immortality of an unexpected kind, and the horrors of violation and mutilation are recast as sweet amorous suffering," as Philomela is metamorphosed into the nightingale. Dinshaw points to the ironic nature of Philomela's song, incongruous with the conventional love song. She then focuses on Chaucer's *Troilus and Criseyde*, highlighting its Ovidian echoes. After she is lulled to sleep by the nightingale's song, Criseyde has the violent yet sweet dream of having her heart torn out; the erasure of violence is enacted in the figure of the bird (rape song to love song), reenacted in Criseyde's dream (violence to sweetness). Criseyde's dream is expressed in paradoxical language, as is the raped Philomela's song. Paradoxes are, as Dinshaw argues, "breakings of logic, yoking two things that cannot be yoked together except by violence." Courtly discourse, constituted by such violent language, is grounded on "the violation of the woman's body," Dinshaw maintains. Deconstructing the paradox, reading Chaucer's text with Gower's can in fact reveal this misogynist ground and "resist the violent obliteration of the feminine," thus working against the habits of thought that produced the rivalry legend in the first place.

Resistance to the "socializing glare" of literary tradition and revealing the "obliteration of the feminine" are among Jane Chance's goals in her discussion of translation, in the twofold context of Christine de Pizan's reception in England and of twentieth-century critical discourse. When Chance discusses gender tropes in postmodern reflection on translation in Derrida, her goal is to unravel the troping of gender and thus create a theoretical text allowing discussion of the mechanics of gender violence in translation. Postmodern tropes of translation are based on the Freudian and Derridean concept of the maternal as the "vanishing point" of language, the ineffable origin of the text (as in the Lacanian model of the discarded mother). These tropes monopolize the category of gender and dispose of the Other by ascribing it to the virtual realm of "origins," from which theory and literature emerge as purified monoliths. As Chance notes, postmodern translation theory abounds in gendered imagery (vaginal, uteral, and umbilical), producing a theoretical blind spot where the specificity of women as producers of texts, readers, or translators becomes unrecognizable.

Chance overcomes the Derridean refusal to recognize women's presence "theoretically and literally" as she investigates precisely this "doubly excised," blind spot of postmodern translation theory: a situation "when the translated is herself female—when translation involves an author who is, because of gender difference, Other, a passive victim of the translator's desire to return to the mother (tongue)." While in Derridean terms the gender cancels out, Chance shows through her analysis of Christine de Pizan's texts in translation that gender is indeed the essential category. She posits three relationships as the setting of her discussion of the translations of Christine: translation as agon (Johnson); violence as the product of the erosion of power (Arendt); and irony as the kynic weapon of the woman (Lévesque and Derrida). Christine de Pizan, "who wrote ironically and hence subversively in Middle French in the first three decades of the fifteenth century," is for Chance the exemplar of ironic, erosive, and antagonistic writing. Christine's writings are the site of multiple and often hostile translations, which Chance enumerates: Christine's own translation from Italian to French culture; the manuscript copies of her works she authorized, and the ones she did not; printed copies; readership, particularly female; translations (chiefly Middle English and Portuguese); "castrations" by male translators and printers who felt threatened by French literary hegemony as well as by Christine's femaleness.

Chance traces the distribution of Christine's texts through the transmission of the major manuscripts to England and establishes the order of translations. In this rich intertext, she tracks the pattern of scholastic misogyny through various instances of immasculation (Judith Fetterly's label of male appropriation) and excision, or what Chance herself terms linguistic castration. She ascribes the hostile, "diminished reception" of Christine's works to the wars and resulting "politicization of the literary scene"; to the peculiarities of manuscript transmission; and, most significant, to gender violence in translation, "the triumph of a masculinized nationalism over a feminized intertext."

Further, Chance discusses an essential locus of translation, too often ignored by literary critics: the iconography. She shows how the transmission of both the text and the illustrations cancels out "Christine's feminization of history." The focus on illustrations (manuscript illuminations of the original vs. woodcuts in the translated, printed versions) allows us to quantify the loss suffered in cross-gender, hostile translation: the female figures suffer diminution, sex change, omission—they are redrawn in supplicatory positions (kneeling) and contained (literally, boxed); the male figures undergo aggrandizement—they are magnified, shown frontally, regnant, dominating the scene.

Finally, Chance focuses on the positive aspects of Christine's reception, emphasizing that "the male and female aristocrats who patronized Christine in France or England did not feel as threatened by her, it appears, as did the *male* secretaries and scholars who were themselves presumably vying for position, prestige, and patronage." Tracing Christine's sympathetic reception, Chance evokes anonymous poems (most importantly the *Assembly of Gods*) and reveals their dependence on and amplification of Christine's feminine mythography. Borrowing, rather than excision, becomes the trope, as the English texts rewrite the dominant cultural tradition into an ironic mythography similar to Christine's. Thus, the assertive nature of Christine's influence is emphasized by Chance, evidenced *a fortiori* by the excisions and abuses of her texts by male translators toiling to render these feminine bodies of writing fit for consumption within the standards of "mankyndlynes."

In a manner complementary to Chance's discussion of the immasculation of Christine's texts for the use of the dominant culture (assimilation), Deborah Ellis and Jody Enders analyze the functioning of gendered constructs of domestic space and mental space for the purpose of persecution (elimination). Ellis focuses on the persecution of Jewish women by the Spanish Inquisition, arguing that "the violence against suspected women judaizers . . . derives from a long tradition of medieval unease with women's domestic roles, and . . . displaced anxieties about female sabotage in the home." Stating the ambivalent perception of the woman at home, "thought simultaneously to foment domestic discord and to preserve domestic tranquillity," Ellis shows how the domestic space betrays women instead of sheltering them. While she notes the essential domesticity of medieval institutions—monarchy, business, family—Ellis emphasizes the dichotomy of the domestic space as it applied to women (shelter vs. claustration, detention, disenfranchisement) and shows how the inquisitorial violence relied on the complementary aspects of this dichotomy, both on its anxieties and its restrictive power.

One of the foci of anxiety was the issue of privacy (in the form of a locale or a mental space)—"gendered female, not just ideologically but also architecturally," since women occupied the inner, private quarters (solars, chambers, bowers, residential tower) in the culture marked by gender distinction and isolation. Conversely, women's "exteriorized aspects"— house and body, the apertures of which were to be closed—could metonymically designate their gender role (as Stallybrass has shown).

Anxiety over women's possession of private space was the more acute since women's control of the domestic space and housekeeping granted them a measure of social leverage. This leverage was especially suspect in the minority women groups, whose "hold on security was most tenuous," including women who were, or were suspected of being, Jewish. A host of domestic activities is used as evidence in the inquisitorial proceedings. Ellis emphasizes the gendered character of these tasks, pointing out that "women's domesticity became their vulnerability"; the denunciations, accusing women of keeping their houses too clean or not clean enough, testify to the struggle "over the control and even the *idea* of the house."

While Ellis plentifully documents the anxieties, her emphasis on examples of breach of domestic security indicates that these anxieties were founded on a prejudice rather than on the effective security of the domestic space. The hostile testimonies of the Inquisition attest to vulnerability by accessing the domestic space from without. The scrutiny of neighbors and family members politicizes domestic tasks and, in some cases, imposes dissimulation: covertly Jewish women cook two meals (kosher for consumption and unkosher for display), carry work utensils, and retreat into the privacy of their thoughts when the enacting of their religious identity "out" in the domestic space is impossible.

Ellis's groundbreaking work on the architecture and politics of the domestic space highlights the unanticipated complexity of the problem. In her study of the role of the domestic space in inquisitorial violence against minority women, she is able to analyze the domestic space in its extreme (dis)functionality. The series of paradoxes and oppositions that characterize this extreme functioning demonstrate the inconsistencies of the gender system, masked by the seemingly nonconflictual everyday transactions. The gender separation of women creates anxieties, which are relieved by the modification of architectural (and affective) space: the division between public and private and the creation of women's inner, private quarters in the house. This modification, in turn, results in further, contradictory anxieties. The privacy is politicized, the house gendered, and the closing of the house and the body becomes a metonymy of women's gender roles. The ambiguity of the cultural construct of women, feared as sources of domestic discord (too powerful) and inadequate in preserving domestic decorum (not powerful enough), leads to extreme polarization of the domestic space; the house, instead of shelter, becomes the locus of vulnerability for women under the Spanish Inquisition.

A similar, insidious translation, turning the private (mental) space into an instrument of persecution, is described by Jody Enders in her analysis of women's memory under the Inquisition. Linking medieval conceptualization of mental processes to gender violence in Heinrich Kramer's *Malleus maleficarum* (1486), Enders shows how women's memory was transformed into the site of translation between rhetoric and violence. She analyzes the *Malleus* to retrieve the inquisitorial construct of memory and demonstrates how memory becomes both an analytic (prosecutive) and executive device, since it defines both "diabolical acts as well as the legal redress that might be effected to regulate and punish them." Starting from the definition of memory as the locus of corruption, and the male-normative definition of women's memory and speech, Enders shows how the inquisitorial definition turns women from victims to demons, and more specifically into both victims and demons, in the tradition of "simultaneously persuasive and scapegoated Eve." By corollary, violence against women is violence against demons; mutilation and torture become natural, permitted, even sacred.

To build her case, Enders evokes the rhetorical tradition of memory as a "treasure chest of language," the repository of virtual objects and cultural paradigms to be activated in performance (speech). She then notes a series of reversals, which constitute the crucial trope of the persecution of witches. First, memory: "the faculty designed to engender speech was *not* to engender it in women." Second, the inquisitorial representation of witchcraft casting women as persecutors, not victims, a reversal Elaine Scarry identifies as "a premier ideology of torture." From this reconfiguration of the victim as persecutor derives a potentially infinite series of misogynist translations: "Agency becomes passivity, birth becomes death, natural becomes unnatural, desire becomes fear, preservation becomes extermination," notes Enders. The final reversal observed by historians such as Murray constitutes the crucial condition of the persecution of witchcraft—the reconfiguration of superstition into heresy, providing the seemingly paradoxical foundation to *Malleus*—"to *dis*believe in [witches'] magical meetings was heretical," says Enders, quoting Murray.

Enders then traces the persecution of witches from theory to practice, from memory-body of knowledge to bodily sites of memory, where as Scarry points out, "pain is pain, and not a metaphor of pain." The reconfiguration of the rhetoric tradition to exclude women's memory and speech from the male-normative definition is projected out of the metaphorical confines by the instruments of torture built according to the theoretical blueprint to enclose and modify the female organ of memory and speech. Enders discusses the brank, a "gendered torture device" which screws the temples, covers the eyes, and holds (pins, severs) the tongue, torturing the three essential bodily sites of defective, female memory, perception, and speech, as they are conceptualized in the *Malleus*. The result of torture is (as Scarry reminds us) a regression "to prelinguistic cries of pain"; it is also a "hypercorrection" of the female organs by the male-normative torture device, a permanent silencing of victims. Enders then notes that the socialized cruelty of the rites of passage, to which Deleuze and Guattari (following Nietzsche) ascribe the function of "creating a memory for man," is amplified by the Inquisition into a socialized means of recreating/destroying the memory of women. Thus, by emphasizing the dependence of the inquisitorial practice of torture on theory, Enders demonstrates how memory became "for the medieval and early modern woman a literal 'prison house of language'."

The studies collected in this volume do not show that violence against women was inevitable, organic, or natural in medieval society. Indeed, some analyses, including Blacker's and Jeay's, show that certain texts or textual traditions depict violence affecting women and men in similar ways, suggesting that violence, not misogyny, is the focus of these texts or traditions. Rather, these studies focus on strategies through which violence against women was naturalized and sanctified by particular, gendered constructs of heroism, nationalism, domestic space, memory, and so forth. Furthermore, the studies demonstrate a paradox: while these hostile constructs were not the "subject" of their respective texts (although the contrary may be argued in the case of the *Malleus* or inquisitorial depositions), nonetheless the habits of thought "normalizing" violence against women persisted, inscribed in narratives whose popularity withstood the trial of many centuries. To use a genetic metaphor, these normalizing strategies were reproduced much as some nonfunctional features are carried through generations, sometimes becoming functional in a particular environment. Based on the evidence presented in this collection, we discover that the nonfunctional elements of the textual encoding of violence against women—variously identified (for different texts) as "surplus-enjoyment" indicating an interpretive "quilting point" in a text (Finke and Shichtman), automatism (literary game of tag, or "quiting," in Weisl), anachronism (in Dinshaw's deconstruction of the literary-historical myth of rivalry between Chaucer and Gower)—are indeed as significant as the functional elements (for instance, those analyzed by Gravdal). Violence against women was not a distinctive trait of medieval society (distinguishing it from other periods), nor was it limited to overtly misogynistic discourse. It was an insidious flavor detectable in writing, whether an ornament, a trope, a plot, or a premise.

Apart from ethically motivated inquiry (which lies beyond the scope of this collection), there exist many conceptual reasons to inquire into the presence of violence against women in medieval texts. To give but one example: in the case of the narrative equivalence between marriage, rape, and *raptus* (demonstrated by Gravdal and acknowledged by Finke and Shichtman, and Laskaya, among others), the exchange of women between men involves worth being redistributed, indiscriminately, through gifts or rapes of women, and supposes no place for women as subjects. However, we do see women as subjects in medieval texts—whether their presence is episodic (ending in the glorified reinstatement of the patriarchal family at the conclusion of the romance), accessorial (subordinate to transcendental interpretation as in hagiography), or limited to a minority of examples or texts in a predominantly objectifying textual tradition (as shown by Blacker, Jeay, and Chance in this volume). In addition to the textual issues explored at length by the contributors, the presence of women as subjects may also be elucidated via a return to the anthropological "text of origin" that sustains the majority of approaches to the study of marriage, raptus, and rape. In his plea for a discriminating use of the *Elementary Structures of Kinship*, Claude Lévi-Strauss reminds us that feudal society is only reductively described by the elementary model. Women as objects in the exchange represent one model among many, and some of the models do allow female subjectivity. As Lévi-Strauss observes, economic exchange can supplement (and, as Duby suggests, it gradually replaces) the elementary structures, and it is in this and other ways that the elementary structures on the one hand accommodate exceptions and individualism and, on the other hand, allow evolution and adaptation to changed external circumstances.

We may ultimately ask why violence against women outlived the social structures in which women were exclusively objects, exclusively vehicles of exchange. The answer is in the conceptual encoding of sexual violence and violence against women: the necessity of rape in the economy of the Anglo-Norman chronicles; Cinderella-like rewards promised to the "patient wife" by the very structure of the romance narration; immasculation of women's literary presence in text transmission, translation, and literary canonization; demonizing of female body, memory, and domestic space by the Inquisition; and other phenomena analyzed in this collection. If certain habits of thought amount to the institutionalization of violence against women, as is suggested in this volume, then further exploration of the connivance between text and violence against women is warranted.

NOTES

I would like to thank the outside readers, Nancy Jones and Elizabeth Robertson, for their critique of this and other essays in the collection, as well as Gillian Hillis and other editors of the University Press of Florida. I also wish to gratefully acknowledge a Small research grant and a commitment grant from the School of Arts and Sciences of Miami University of Ohio, as well as faculty development grants from Kenyon College.

1. Robert F. Yeager, ed. *Chaucer and Gower: Difference, Mutuality, Exchange.* English Literary Studies Monograph Series 51 (Victoria, B.C.: University of Victoria, 1991).

1

The Violence of Exegesis

Reading the Bodies of Ælfric's Female Saints

Shari Horner

The *Lives of Saints*, written by the homilist Ælfric of Eynsham in the last decade of the tenth century, problematize categories which might otherwise seem stable, specifically the categories of "text," "body," "gender," and "interpretation."[1] Ælfric's *Lives* of virgin martyrs conform to hagiographic conventions: they present stories of young Christian women whose virginity is violently threatened but who maintain their bodily integrity in the face of grave danger. The inevitable emphasis on the saint's body and her potential sexuality points to a key paradox in medieval hagiography: the bodies of female virgin martyrs are of primary importance in texts that purport not to be about the body at all.[2] In this essay I seek to account for that paradox through an analysis of Ælfric's own hermeneutics. As the work of an author who was profoundly interested in issues of interpretation, the *Lives of Saints* offer a valuable opportunity to apply theory to practice: to analyze these narratives within the critical discourse of the author who produced them.[3]

Ælfric's *Lives*, like so many medieval saints' lives, revolve around what Kathryn Gravdal has called a "sexual plot," in which the saint is sexualized through the threat of rape, forced prostitution, the eroticized display of the saint's naked body, and so forth. Gravdal's groundbreaking study of rape in medieval French literature and law demonstrates ways in which medieval literary texts both prescribe and normalize the representation of violence against women's bodies; she writes: "the representation of seduction or assault opens a licit space that permits the audience to enjoy sexual language and contemplate the naked female body" (Gravdal, *Ravishing*

Maidens, 24). Such cultural legitimation, in fact, becomes the "business" of saints' lives, to the extent that violence against women is all but invisible to many readers of these texts, because it is so common.

How can we interpret images of extreme and gruesome corporeality in texts that are meant to offer spiritual "refreshment"?[4] How, in other words, can we read the bodies of female virgin martyrs?[5] In the pages that follow, I argue that in the *Lives* of Saints Agatha, Lucy, and Agnes, the saint's body acts as a text displaying the tensions between the practices of reading literally—as the pagan torturers do—and spiritually—as the saint herself does, along with (ideally) all Christian readers.[6] Thus, the saint's body functions as the hermeneutic tool that enables spiritual signification, to the extent that it is only through the display of literal violence that spiritual meaning is achieved. The bodies of female virgin saints and martyrs are of primary importance in texts which repeatedly deny that the body matters at all; Ælfric's hermeneutics rewrites sexual violence as spiritual exegesis.

Like sacred texts, saints' bodies are beautiful on the outside but contain important spiritual mysteries deep beneath their surfaces. Through the use of corporeal metaphors, Ælfric identifies two ways of reading sacred texts: readers may read *lichamlice* (carnally, in terms of the body), or *gastlice* (spiritually, allegorically). Reading *lichamlice* is, for Ælfric, akin to the literal sense, referring to both the literal understanding we might have upon first viewing (or reading) an object and to bodily behaviors.[7] Ælfric's corporeal hermeneutics also encompasses another body metaphor: *ða nacodon word*, the naked word. Again, the metaphor is based upon the notion of a corporeal text, a text-as-body; like the saint herself, the naked words of scripture must be "clothed" by the homilist with the veil of spiritual meaning.

The key to understanding Ælfric's hermeneutics occurs in his Homily on Midlent Sunday (*Dominica in Media Quadragesima*). In discussing Christ's miracle of the loaves and fishes, Ælfric explicates the very act of interpretation by distinguishing between those who simply admire beautiful letters as they would a painting, and those who know how to decipher the meaning found "deop" within the written characters. He takes a rather lenient attitude toward the former:

Þis wundor is swiðe micel, and deop on getacnungum. Oft gehwa gesihð fægre stafas awritene, þonne hera ð he ðone writere and þa stafas, and nat hwæt hi mænað. Se ðe cann ðæra stafa gescead, he hera ð heora fægernysse, and ræd þa stafas, and understent hwæt he gemænað. On oðre wisan we sceawiað metinge, and on oðre wisan stafas. Ne gæð na mare to metinge buton þæt þu hit geseo and herige:

nis na genoh þæt þu stafas sceawige, buton ðu hi eac ræde, and þæt andgit understande. Swa is eac on ðam wundre þe God worhte mid þam fif hlafum: ne bið na genoh þæt we þæs tacnes wundrian, oþþe þurh þæt God herian, buton we eac þæt gastlice andgit understandon. (Thorpe, *Homilies*, 1:186)

(This miracle is very great, and deep in meanings. Often someone sees beautiful letters written, then praises the writer and the letters, but does not know what they mean. He who understands the art of the letters praises their beauty, and reads the letters, and understands their meaning. In one way we observe a painting, and in another way letters. Nothing more is needed for a painting than that you see and praise it; but it is not enough to look at the letters unless you also read them and understand their meaning. So it is also with the miracle which God worked with the five loaves; it is not enough that we admire the symbol, or praise God for it, unless we also understand its spiritual meaning.)[8]

As Paul Szarmach has suggested, the distinction Ælfric makes here is really between "no understanding at all and its antinomy, understanding. . . . The human element, praise—which both learned and unlearned may give to fair writing, to illustration, or to God—appears to be part of the process of understanding." Further, Szarmach notes that "praise is insufficient by itself without true understanding to complete it. . . . By implication those who praise and do not understand are not on the wrong path so much as not far enough along the way" (Szarmach, "Ælfric as Exegete," 239). Thus Ælfric, in positing such a dichotomy, puts readers on a continuum. By establishing this continuum, this process of exegesis, Ælfric implicitly acknowledges the inevitability of the literal sense: *all* readers first see, admire, and praise beautiful letters, while skilled readers will go on to interpret their spiritual signification.[9]

When Ælfric distinguishes between *lichamlic* and *gastlic* reading, he is usually explaining some aspect of the Old Testament in terms of the New.[10] He uses *lichamlic(e)* to refer not just to bodily practices but also to a kind of literal understanding—that is, a behavior or action based on a literal reading of an Old Testament text. The juxtaposition of *lichamlic* and *gastlic* is found throughout the First and Second Series of Catholic Homilies but is most prevalent in Second Series Homily XV, Sermon on the Sacrifice on Easter Day (*Sermo De Sacrificio in Die Pascae*). In explaining the mysteries (*gerynu*) of the Holy Eucharist, Ælfric explicitly contrasts the spiritual and the bodily or carnal at least seven times—not surprising, of course, in a homily explaining that Christ's body becomes the spirit.[11] The following comment is typical:

> Cristene men ne moton healdan nu ða ealdan .æ. lichamlice. ac him gedafenað þæt hi cunnon hwæt heo gastlice getacnige . . . æfter gastlicum andgite. (Godden, *Ælfric's Catholic Homilies*, 151)

> (Christian men may not now hold the old law bodily, but it is appropriate that they know what it symbolizes spiritually . . . according to the spiritual sense.)

Ælfric's move here between carnal and spiritual understanding is a slippery one, conflating literal behavior with spiritual understanding. The distinction between bodily and spiritual readings of Old Testament laws is clearer in the Homily on the Nativity of Holy Virgins (*In Natale Sanctarum Uirginum*):

> Eal seo gelaðung ðe stent on mædenum. and on cnapum. on ceorlum and on wifum. eal heo is genamod to anum mædene. swa swa se apostol Paulus cwæð. to geleaffullum folce; Disponsaui uos uni uiro virginem castam. exhibere christo; Þæt is on englisc. Ic beweddode eow anum were. þæt ge gearcian an clæne mæden criste; Nis ðis na to understandenne lichamlice. ac gastlice; Crist is se clæna brydguma. and eal seo cristene gelaðung is his bryd. (Godden, *Ælfric's Catholic Homilies*, 329–30)

> (The whole church, which consists of virgins and of young men, of men and of women, is all called one virgin, just as the apostle Paul said to the faithful: Disponsaui uos uni uiro virginem castam exhibere christo; that is, in English: I have betrothed you to one man in order that you prepare a pure virgin for Christ. This is not to be understood bodily, but spiritually. Christ is the pure bridegroom and all the Christian church is his bride.)

To "understand bodily" in the sense that Ælfric uses it here, is to understand literally, which is of course prohibited. The distinction becomes particularly urgent in the Homily on the Octaves and Circumcision of Our Lord, where Ælfric reminds his listeners:

> Nis nu alyfed cristenum mannum þæt he þas ymbsnidennysse lichamlice healdan; ac þeah-hwæðere nan man be bið soðlice cristen, buton he ða ymbsnidennysse on gastlicum ðeawum gehealde. (Thorpe, *Homilies*, 1:94)

(It is not now allowed to christian men to observe circumcision bodily, but, nevertheless, no man is truly a christian, unless he observe circumcision in spiritual conduct.) (Thorpe's trans.; Thorpe, *Homilies*, 1:95)

At the least, *lichamlic(e)* carries a double meaning: "literally" and "with the body." Yet to "understand bodily" is insufficient, even "illicit"; such understanding has not yet progressed beyond carnal literalism to spiritual truth.[12]

Finally, to return to the Homily on the Sacrifice of Easter Day, we see Ælfric's most frequently cited discussion of the literal vs. the spiritual sense, where he distinguishes between the body in which Christ suffered and that found in the Eucharist:

Micel is betwux þam lichaman þe crist on ðrowade. and ðam lichaman þe to husle bið gehalgod; Se lichama soðlice ðe crist on ðrowode wæs geboren of Marian flæsce. mid blode, and mid banum. mid felle. and mid sinum. on menniscum limum. mid gesceadwisre sawle geliffæst, and his gastlica lichama ðe we husel hatað is of manegum cornum gegaderod buton blode. and bane. limleas. and sawulleas. and nis for ði nan ðing þæron to understandenne lichamlice. ac is eall gastlice to understandenne. (Godden, *Ælfric's Catholic Homilies*, 154)

(There is much difference between the body in which Christ suffered and the body which is consecrated for the Eucharist; truly the body in which Christ suffered was born of the flesh of Mary, with blood and with bones, with skin and with sinews in human limbs, brought to life with a rational soul, and his spiritual body which we call the Eucharist is gathered from many grains, without blood or bones, limbless and soulless, and therefore there is nothing in it to be understood bodily but all is to be understood spiritually.)

Again, *lichamlice* carries a dual meaning: "of or pertaining to [Christ's] body" and "literally." Ælfric insists on naming parts of Christ's material body—blood, bones, skin, sinews, limbs—as well as on the literal composition of the communion loaf (it is made of grain), thereby delineating the differences between the literal composition of physical objects and their spiritual symbolism. As with beautiful letters on a manuscript page, both Christ's literal body and the communion loaf become the visible tokens of a deeper spiritual message.

With another body metaphor, *ða nacodon word*, the naked word, Ælfric bridges the gap between literal and spiritual interpretation:

We habbað nu gesæd sceortlice on Englisc
þis halige godspell, swa swa ge gehyrdon nu,
þa nacedan word ana; ac we nu wyllað
mid fægerum andgite hi gefrætewian eow,
þæt hi licweorðe beon to lare eow eallum,
gif ge þæt gastlice andgit mid godum willan underfoð. (Pope, *Homilies,*
359)

(We have now said briefly in English this holy gospel, as you have
just heard, the naked words alone; but now we will adorn them for
you with fair meaning, so that they may be acceptable to you all as
teaching, if you receive that spiritual meaning with good will.)

Here Ælfric refers simply to bare, unexplicated words as they are found on
the page. The homilist "adorns" naked words with spiritual meaning in
order to make their meaning accessible to an unskilled audience. The
metaphor recurs in the *Letter to Sigeweard,* where Ælfric again distinguishes between the words on the page and the meaning with which the
homilist endows them: "Nu miht þu wel witan þæt weorc sprecað swiþor
þonne þa nacodan word, þe nabbað nane fremminge" (Crawford, *Old English Heptateuch,* 74; Now you may well know that the work speaks much
more than the naked word, which has no purpose). A third and related use
of the metaphor is found in the *Preface to Genesis,* in a passage in which
Ælfric warns against the dangers of unlearned priests, unskilled in Latin,
who may fail to interpret properly (that is, *gastlice*) the lessons of the Old
Testament:

We secgað eac foran to þæt seo boc is swiþe deop gastlice to understandenne, 7 we ne writaþ na mare buton þa nacedan gerecednisse.
Þonne þincþ þam ungelæredum þæt eall þæt andgit beo belocen on
þære anfealdan gerecednisse, ac hit ys swiþe feor þam. (Crawford,
Old English Heptateuch, 77)

(We also say beforehand that the book is very deep to understand
spiritually, and we write no more than the naked narrative. Then the
unlearned think that all the meaning is locked in the one-fold narrative, but that is very far from [the case].)

The danger inherent in the "naked" narrative (*naceden gerecednisse*) is that
it may be perceived by unskilled readers as the only narrative (*anfealdan
gerecednisse*). The "naked words" are analogous to the "fair characters"
with which this discussion began, and it takes a skilled interpreter to "un-
lock" the spiritual meaning contained deep within the literal surface.

Ælfric's corporeal hermeneutics can inform our understanding of how the bodies of virgin martyrs in the *Lives of Saints* function as texts that embody literal and spiritual meanings. As we have seen, corporeal metaphors take on powerful hermeneutic values in Ælfric's system of sacred exegesis. Through metaphors of body, spirit, materiality, and space, Ælfric conflates texts and bodies, such that reading the text of a saint's life means interpreting the hermeneutic truths contained within her body, on public display throughout each *vita*. Most important, this hermeneutics exposes the dangers inherent in focusing solely on the *naceden gerecednisse,* the "naked" or "literal" text of each saint, even as it depends upon those "naked texts" to convey a deeper spiritual message.

For modern readers, reading medieval virgin martyr narratives can be a somewhat alienating experience, not least because of the extended descriptions of torture and attempted mutilation done to the saint. How are we to understand such descriptions, concerned as they are with the display, exposure, and attempted rupture of female bodies? What do they say about how medieval readers perceived and were conditioned by these representations of women, Christianity, and (sexual) violence? Elaine Scarry's discussion of pain and torture in her important study *The Body in Pain* can help illuminate the "cultural logic" of torture; that is, the discursive structures and power relations that develop within scenes of torture.[13] Scarry's work investigates pain and torture in circumstances far removed from medieval saints' lives but provides a useful interpretive framework for reading these narratives. The "grammar" of torture that Scarry describes has important implications for the representations of torture in the saints' lives.

Pain, Scarry argues, because it is internal, invisible, "resists verbal objectification" (Scarry, *Body in Pain,* 12). Thus the expression of pain may only be achieved through an external agent, whereby a weapon of torture "convey[s] something of the felt-experience of pain to someone outside the sufferer's body." Because the agent of pain "either exists . . . or can be pictured as existing . . . at the external boundary of the body, it begins to externalize, objectify, and make sharable what is originally an interior and unsharable experience" (Scarry, *Body in Pain,* 15–16). Conveying the felt experience of pain to another is only possible through the perceptions of "inside" and "outside" the body; that is, only when the pain can be imagined at the body's "border," so to speak, can it begin to be felt by another.

Making visible the (potential) pain inflicted on bodies is the business of saints' lives. Of course that potentiality is never realized; but nonetheless the agents of pain—torturers, racks, rods, whips, burning coals—are explicitly described. Saints' lives narrate the *potentiality* of pain that might result from the breakdown of the Christian will. The audiences of these texts can begin to share in these narratives of pain when the pain is made explicit through the vehicle of the saint's body—which in this case itself becomes an agent for expressing that potentiality. The audience can readily identify with the saint's human body, and thus representations of violence "convey something of the felt-experience of pain to someone outside the sufferer's body."

This identification is precisely what Ælfric suggests in the Homily on the Nativity of Holy Martyrs (*In Natale Sanctorum Martirum*). While the martyrs obviously suffered intensely, their suffering pales in comparison to what may lie ahead for nonbelievers. And although his contemporaries may not be able to prove their belief through the kinds of suffering the martyrs faced, Ælfric asserts that his fellow Christians are no less martyrs:

> Twa cynn sind martirdomes. An dearnunge, oðer eawunge; Se ðe on ehtnysse for cristes geleafan his lif alæt. se bið openlice martir; Eft se forberð ðurh geðyld hosp. and teonan. and ðone lufað þe hine hatað. and his agene unlustas. and þæs ungesewenlican deofles tihtinge forsihð. se bið untwylice martyr on digelre dæde. . . . And we magon beon martiras, ðeah ðe we mid isene acwealde ne beon. gif we þæt geðyld on urum mode unleaslice healdað. (Godden, *Ælfric's Catholic Homilies*, 314–15)

> (There are two kinds of martyrdoms. One is secret, the other public. He who loses his life through persecution for belief in Christ is openly a martyr; but he who, in patience, suffers insult and injury, and loves the one who hates him, and rejects his own lusts and the accusations of the unseen devil, he is certainly a martyr in secret deed. And we may be martyrs, although we are not killed with iron, if we truthfully hold that patience in our minds.)

Reading or listening to the *Lives* of Christian martyrs means, for Ælfric, that readers actively imagine and identify with suffering. Readers are not permitted to look away, to ignore or objectify the pain, but rather they become subjectively engaged with it. The experience of imagining felt pain is inherent in the reading lessons taught by the *Lives* of virgin martyrs. Scenes of torture create in readers the desire to suffer (to be a secret martyr) on behalf of—and alongside—Christ. The tortured bodies of the martyrs are essential for the narrative to function; representations of the literal enable spiritual signification.

The *Lives* of Saints Agatha, Lucy, and Agnes exemplify this process. In each case, a young Christian woman is the object of a pagan ruler's desire. When she refuses to submit to him, she is tortured and eventually killed for her faith. In the process, the bodies of the virgins are consistently misread by the torturers, who focus single-mindedly on the saint's literal flesh. As Ælfric's exegesis suggests, however, meaning is not to be found at the level of the "naked" text, and skilled Christian readers will read beyond the literal surface—the object of so much narrative attention—to reach the spiritual meaning.

In the Life of St. Agatha, the virgin is set against two pagan opponents early in the text. Quintianus, the "murderous persecutor" (*se cwealm-bære ehtere*) and suitor wishes to corrupt the virgin; to do so, he sends her to a prostitute, Aphrodosia, so "þæt heo (Agatha) . . . hire (Aphrodosia's) þeawas leornode / and hire (Agatha's) mod awende þurh þæra myltestrena forspennincgæ" (so that [Agatha] might learn [Aphrodosia's] evil ways, / and might be perverted in mind by the enticements of harlots; Skeat, *Lives*, 196–97).[14] When Quintianus learns that despite her best attempts, Aphrodosia has been unable to corrupt the virgin, he orders Agatha brought to him, and a lengthy debate ensues. Quintianus's reaction to Agatha's rhetorical skill perfectly illustrates his literalism. He is so enraged by her eloquence that he commands his men to strike her "mid handum . . . / gelome on þæt hleor . þæt heo hlydan ne sceolde" (with the hands / repeatedly on the face, that she might not declaim; Skeat, *Lives*, 198–99).[15] He recognizes the power of Agatha's rhetoric but "reads" her literally, believing that Agatha's mouth is the source of her words, and he seeks to counteract that power through physical violence.

When, after being thrown in a dark prison, Agatha still refuses to submit to Quintianus's desires, he orders her stretched and twisted on a rack, sure that the torture will persuade her:

Agathes andwyrde on ðære hencgene þus .
Swa ic lust-fullige on þisum laðum witum .
swa swa se ðe gesihð . þone þe he gewilnode .
oððe se þe fint fela gold-hordas .
Ne mæg min sawl beon gebroht mid blysse to heofonum .
butan min lichama beo on þinum bendum genyrwod .
and fram ðinum cwellerum on þinum copsum agrapod .

(Agatha answered on the rack thus,
"So greatly I rejoice in these painful torments
even as he that seeth him whom he hath desired,
or as he that findeth many hoards of gold.

My soul cannot be brought with joy to Heaven
except my body be cramped in thy bonds, and by the
executioners be gripped in thy fetters.") (Skeat, *Lives*, 202–3)

Agatha articulates here how the virgin martyr lives work: the martyrs welcome torture precisely because torture of the body is the vehicle for the soul's salvation. She makes the cause and effect relationship explicit. Only through being tightly bound can the saint gain spiritual release from those earthly bonds.

The most compelling event in the Life of St. Agatha follows immediately on the speech just cited. Quintianus, infuriated by her resolve, orders her breast to be cut off:

Þa gebealh hine se wælhreowa and het hi gewriðan
on ðam breoste mid þære hencgene and het siððan ofaceorfan .
Agathes him cwæð to . Eala ðu arleasosta
ne sceamode þe to ceorfanne þæt þæt ðu sylf suce .
ac ic habbe mine breost on minre sawle . ansunde .
mid þam ðe Ic min andgit eallunga afede .

(Then raged the cruel one, and bade men torture her
on the breast in the rack, and bade it afterward be cut off.
Agatha said to him, "O thou most wicked!
art thou not ashamed to cut off that which thou thyself hast sucked?
but I have my breast sound in my soul,
with which I shall at any rate feed my understanding.")
(Skeat, *Lives*, 202–3)

Agatha's speech transforms the violent mutilation of her literal breast into a spiritual triumph. Her distinction between the literal and spiritual breast confirms that cutting off the exterior flesh will not affect the interior spirit. Like a text, Agatha's literal surface symbolically contains meaning; inability to interpret the sign system correctly denies signification to uninitiated readers. Quintianus, like all pagan torturers, mistakenly believes that literally opening up the saint will give him access to her. But as we know, only an initiated reader can open up that body to reveal its meaning.[16]

Yet what about Agatha's breast? Allen Frantzen has argued that the disfigurement "masculinizes" the saint. When her breast is cut off, he suggests, she is "manlike," and when it is restored, she is "restored to womanhood." Agatha's sexual identity, in his view, is "central to the story, for she has transcended the female body and become, however briefly, like a man" (Frantzen, "When Women Aren't Enough," 160). I would argue, however, that rather than enabling her to "transcend" her gender, the text insists upon Agatha's female body—does not permit us to forget that body as the object of physical violence. Agatha's breast, even as lack, draws attention to itself, and thus although she may be "breastless," Agatha can never be fully masculinized. She is always associated with the female breast (this is likewise true in the iconography) even when—especially when—she does not have one. Her own references to suckling in the speech cited emphasize the lactative and nutritive—that is, the biologically female—functions of the breast.

In fact, these images of suckling and nurturing, which at first seem unexpected in the narrative of a virgin saint, may anticipate the rich tradition of maternal imagery found in religious literature from the twelfth century onward. While we are not to assume that Quintianus has literally sucked from Agatha's breast, her statement aligns her generally with all women, and specifically with both the Virgin Mary and Christ. As the representative of Mary, Agatha's body can nourish souls; and as Caroline Walker Bynum has shown, Christ's body was similarly represented in medieval culture as able to nourish bodies through suckling (see *Holy Feast and Holy Fast*, 270–75). Further, the medieval identification of breast milk with transmuted blood meant "an association of Christ's wounds with woman's body" (271), while late medieval artists depicted the "breast [of the Virgin] as food, parallel to the bleeding (i.e., nurturing) wound [of Christ]" (272). Thus just as the blood of Christ's wound will provide nourishment for Christians, the wounding of Agatha's breast signals its similarly nourishing capabilities. Agatha herself is nourished through the breast (Christ) within her own soul. Yet in a richly ironic twist, as soon as she makes this point Quintianus orders her to be deprived of food and drink; clearly he has not yet learned the difference between literal and spiritual that Agatha has demonstrated.[17]

Agatha's identity thus lies in both the essential materiality of her female body and the spiritual truth veiled by that body. Quintianus believes that the outer breast matters; Agatha asserts that it does not, drawing attention away from the literal body to the spiritual breast. This image was anticipated by Aphrodosia, who reported to Quintianus: "'Stanas magon hnexian . and þæt starce isen / on leades gelicnysse . ærðan þe se geleafa mæge / of agathes breoste . beon æfre adwæsced'" (Stones may soften, and hard iron / become like lead, or ever the faith / in Agatha's breast can be extinguished; Skeat, *Lives*, 196–97). Quintianus evidently took Aphrodosia's words literally when he ordered the mutilation. Agatha reconfirms the idea that the breast to which both she and

Aphrodosia refer is spiritual, not corporeal. The breast emblematizes the hermeneutic function of the virgin martyr narratives: its violent mutilation stirs our horror and pity, yet the saint's denial of the significance of her own flesh reminds us that the truth of this text is not found at the literal level but deep beneath its (her) beautiful surface. Agatha's spiritual reading of her own body depends upon its literal sense, while the torturer's repeated assaults on her flesh demonstrate his inability to read beyond the literal level.

Ælfric's Life of St. Lucy immediately follows the life of Agatha in the manuscript, and like Agatha, Lucy herself provides a lesson in reading bodies as texts. The narrative follows a recurrent structural pattern, in which, first, violence is done to Lucy—she is threatened with forced prostitution, smeared with oil and lit on fire, and then disemboweled by a sword; and second, she interprets the significance of those acts of violence and her own ability to resist them. Like the Life of St. Agatha, the Life of St. Lucy can only achieve its spiritual signification through the representation of literal violence done to a female body.

The spatial dimensions of the virginal female body are of particular concern in this life. In a dream vision at Agatha's tomb, St. Agatha describes Lucy's virginity as a "pleasant habitation," a *wynsume wununge*, in which the virgin dwells with Christ. The image of the virgin as dwelling place resurfaces in Lucy's argument with her pagan suitor Paschasius:

> . . . pascasius orgellice befran .
> wunað se halga gast on þe eornostlice .
> Lucia andwyrde þam arleasan and cwæð .
> Se apostol behet þam ðe healdað clænnysse .
> þæt hi sind godes templ . and þæs halgan gastes wunung .
>
> (. . . Paschasius arrogantly enquired,
> "Dwelleth the Holy Ghost in thee, in good earnest?"
> Lucy answered the impious one, and said,
> "The apostle promised those who preserve chastity,
> that they are God's temple, and the Holy Ghost's habitation.")
> (Skeat, *Lives*, 214–15)

The tension between literal and spiritual interpretation structures this explanation. She has spoken metaphorically of course, but Paschasius understands her literally:

> Þa cwæð se arleasa . Ic hate þe ardlice lædan .
> to þæra myltestrena huse . þæt ðu þinne mægð-had forleose .

þæt se . halga gast þe fram fleo . ðonne þu fullice byst gescynd .

(Then the impious one said, "I shall straightway bid men lead thee
to the house of harlots, that thou mayst lose thy maidenhood,
that the Holy Ghost may flee from thee, when thou art foully
dishonoured.") (Skeat, *Lives*, 214–15)

The sacred space of Lucy's virginal body is juxtaposed with the "house of
harlots" (a space which by its nature implies a penetration of the female
body); Paschasius here reads the "text" of Lucy's body literally, believing
that rupturing her body will open up the dwelling place and release the
Holy Ghost. In a response that seems meant to reassure a Christian audience who might find themselves in similar danger, Lucy asserts that a sub-
stantive difference separates body and will:

Lucia andwyrde þus . ne bið ænig gewemmed .
lichama to plihte . gif hit ne licað þam mode .
. . . .
gif þu me unwilles gewemman nu dest.
me bið twifeald clænnysse . geteald to wuldre .
Ne miht þu gebigan minne willan to þe .
swa hwæt swa þu minum lichaman dest . ne mæg þæt belimpan to me.

(Lucy thus answered, "no one's body is dangerously
polluted, if it pleases not the [possessor's] mind.
. . . .
If now, against my will, thou causest me to be polluted,
a twofold purity shall be gloriously imputed to me.
Thou canst not bend my will to thy purpose;
whatever thou mayest do to my body, that cannot happen to me.")
(Skeat, *Lives*, 214–15)

The subsequent events illustrate Lucy's statement. As Paschasius attempts to drag her toward the brothel, her body becomes rooted to the
spot; although they try pulling her with ropes and even harnessing a team
of oxen to her body, she cannot be moved. When Paschasius covers her
body in oil and lights a fire around her, she remains untouched. Her body
has become an immutable force, solid and impenetrable. Lucy herself, in a
passage which again seems specifically geared toward her "audience(s),"
describes how to understand the torture of a martyr:

Ic abæd æt criste þæt ðis cwealmbæra fyr
me ne gewylde . þæt þu wurðe gescynd .

and hit þam geleaffullum afyrsige þære ðrowunge forhtunge .
and þam unge-leaffullum þa yfelan blysse of-teo.

(I have obtained of Christ in prayer that this deadly fire
may have no power upon me, that thou mayst be put to shame,
and that it may dispel all fear of torture from believers,
and take away from unbelievers their evil joy.) (Skeat, *Lives*, 216–17)

Lucy's words explicate Ælfric's hermeneutics. Witnessing the torture done to the saint's body is fundamental in order to understand her spiritual truth; seeing Lucy unburnt in the fire (and unharmed by all the various tortures) dispels the fear of torture from believers and frustrates nonbelievers. Lucy's words recall as well the two kinds of readers imagined by Ælfric in the Homily on Midlent Sunday: those literal readers who admire only beautiful appearances without understanding, and those spiritual readers who look deep within the letters to comprehend allegorical truths. Most important, Lucy's words point to the paradox inherent in the representation of virgin martyrs: in a text that rejects the body, Lucy's body—and, in particular, the violence done to her body—is in fact the key to both textual and spiritual meaning.

Lucy's imperviousness to torture finally results in the infuriated Paschasius ordering her stabbed with a sword, "so that her bowels fell out" (þæt hire wand se innoð ut; Skeat, *Lives*, 216–17). Death by sword is common in virgin martyr narratives, as is the ability of the saint to live for several days after receiving a mortal wound. This final wounding is a literal rupture, confirming the paradox that the saint's body both does and does not matter. The literal rupture of Lucy's body proves that her body is finally of no significance, but the representation of violence done to that body is of central importance to prove that point.[18]

Ælfric's Life of St. Agnes—not surprisingly—tells of a young Christian virgin who is tortured and finally killed when she refuses to agree to marry her pagan suitor and to worship his gods. Like his source, Ælfric associates St. Agnes with the Song of Songs, giving her a lengthy (38-line) speech in which she identifies Christ as her true bridegroom and herself as a *sponsa Christi*.[19] The metaphor of the virgin as *sponsa Christi* pits the literal suitor (Sempronius) against the spiritual one (Christ). Agnes's speech underscores the mystery through which the literal (her own body) provides access to spiritual truth:

his bryd-bedd me is gearo . nu iu mid dreamum .
. . . .
Of his muðe ic under-feng meoluc . and hunig .

nu iu ic eom beclypt . mid his clænum earmum .
his fægera lichama is minum geferlæht .

. . . .

Þam anum ic healde minne truwan æfre .
ðam ic me befæste mid ealre estfulnysse .
Þonne ic hine lufige . ic beo eallunga clæne .
þonne Ic hine hreppe . ic beo unwemme .
ðonne Ic hine under-fo . ic beo mæden forð .
and þær bærn ne ateoriað . on ðam bryd-lace .
Þær is eacnung buton sare . and singallic wæstmbærnyss.

(His [Christ's] bridal bed hath been now of a long time prepared for me
with joys,

. . . .

From his mouth I have received milk and honey;
now already I am embraced with His pure arms;
His fair body is united to mine

. . . .

To Him alone I ever keep my troth,
to whom I commit myself with all devotion.
When I love Him, I am wholly pure
when I touch Him, I am unstained,
when I receive Him, I am still a virgin,
and there, in the bridal, no child lacketh.
There is conception without sorrow, and perpetual fruitfulness.) (Skeat,
Lives, 172–73)

The metaphor of spiritual marriage to Christ, read through the body of
the virgin—(*ic eom beclypt, ic beo . . . clæne, ic beo unwemme, ic beo mæden,
eacnung, wæstmbærnyss*)—sits in sharp juxtaposition to the literal violence
of subsequent events.

In the narrative's most dramatic moment, Agnes's torturer Sempronius
orders her to be stripped, led naked through the streets, and forced into a
brothel. Miraculously, if not unexpectedly, God subverts this attempted
literal reading in three ways: first, as soon as her clothing is torn off,
Agnes's body is instantly covered by her hair; second, God sends a bright
light, which blinds anyone who tries to look at her nakedness; third, he
clothes her in a beautiful, perfectly fitting garment. Thus Agnes's body is
simultaneously sexualized and desexualized, at once the public spectacle
of the male gaze and the spiritual mystery that is hidden from view. The
image of Agnes naked dominates this section, not least because of the

judge's command that the news of her nakedness be announced throughout the streets. Yet the illicit spectacle of the naked virgin body is immediately subverted by the various coverings—hair, light, clothing—which surround and protect it. Moreover, the corrupt enclosure that threatens the virgin becomes instead a means to her salvation; in this case, "Þa wearð þæra myltestrena hus mannum to gebæd-huse" (that house of harlots [became] a house of prayer for men; Skeat, *Lives*, 178–79). Interestingly, the shining light protects Agnes not only from being seen but also from being physically touched; when her suitor tries to rush at her, intending to assault her sexually, he is struck down as if dead (*swa dæd*), and only Agnes's intervention with God can bring him back to life.

Finally, the torture and martyrdom of Agnes can be seen to conform to previous examples of the genre. The virgin is forced into a great fire, which leaves her unharmed but turns outward and burns up the surrounding crowd before it is miraculously extinguished. Her actual death by sword is typically anticlimactic, followed by a postmortem miracle. The Life of St. Agnes overall provides fewer detailed descriptions of torture than the others we have seen, but it emphasizes instead both the material aspects of a spiritual relationship between the virgin and Christ and the need to conceal the saint's naked body from a pagan gaze, by clothing it with spiritual adornment.

In many ways, of course, the saint's body has always mattered. To cite only the most obvious example, relics (often parts of bodies) have traditionally been an integral feature of the veneration of saints.[20] But the function of the saint's body before death has received little critical attention. The purpose of my analysis here has been to suggest some ways in which the saint's body functions in the narrative while she is still alive. Ælfric's hermeneutics provides us with a crucial framework for reading scenes of torture in medieval hagiography. Reading the *Lives* of virgin martyrs in relation to this corporeal hermeneutics demonstrates how tangibly the body matters in these texts, and confirms the extent to which the *Lives* of female virgin martyrs depend upon the carnal to produce and ensure spiritual truths.

NOTES

1. I wish to thank the National Endowment for the Humanities for funding the research for this essay through a summer stipend. The arguments here were refined during an NEH summer seminar in 1995, and my special thanks go to the seminar director, Professor Paul E. Szarmach, for his generous and perceptive advice, and to the participants in that seminar, for their willingness to talk—at

length—about St. Lucy. Finally, I am grateful to Anna Roberts for her cogent remarks about the earlier version of this article, presented at the 30th International Congress on Medieval Studies, in Kalamazoo, Michigan, in May 1995.

2. Although several recent essay collections study the role of bodies and gender in medieval cultures (see Kay and Rubin, Lees, Lomperis and Stanbury, and Partner, among works cited here), it is rare to find an essay on Anglo-Saxon literature in such a collection. Notable exceptions include Lees, "Men and *Beowulf*"; Frantzen, "When Women Aren't Enough"; Szarmach, "Ælfric's Women Saints"; and Roy, "A Virgin Acts Manfully." Both Kay and Rubin and Lomperis and Stanbury focus specifically on medieval bodies, yet neither pair includes an essay on Anglo-Saxon literature. See, however, the recently published *Holy Men and Holy Women: Old English Prose Saints' Lives and Their Contexts,* ed. Paul E. Szarmach, which will now be the starting point for anyone interested in Anglo-Saxon hagiography. Regrettably this collection was published too late for me to incorporate it fully into the present essay.

3. All citations from the *Lives of Saints* are from Skeat, 1881–88, rpt. 1966. Unless otherwise noted, translations from the saints' lives are Skeat's.

4. In his preface to the *Lives,* Ælfric writes, "But I think those things which I am now going to write will not at all offend the hearers, but will rather refresh by their exhortations such as are slothful in the faith" (Illa uero que scripturus sum suspicor non offendere audientes, sed magis fide torpentes recreare hortationibus; Skeat, *Lives,* 2–3).

5. In addition to Gravdal, a number of feminist scholars have begun to ask this question of Middle English and Old French hagiography. See Cazelles' splendid introduction to *The Lady as Saint,* and, among works cited Innis-Parker; Wogan-Browne; Robertson; and Blumenfeld-Kosinski and Szell. In general, these scholars see a marked emphasis on the pragmatic and the corporeal in female saints' lives. Moreover, Cazelles argues that the "emphasis on the protagonists' body . . . has no equivalent in male Saints' Lives" in Old French (34) and she notes that the focus on removing the saint's clothing is not to be found in male lives (52). In Ælfric's *Lives,* several male saints endure extreme bodily torture, but any emphasis on the sexuality or nakedness of the male saint is rare; yet it is a common feature of female lives.

6. For my understanding of the tensions between "literal" and "spiritual" reading I am indebted to Carolyn Dinshaw's influential discussion of this issue (*Chaucer's Sexual Poetics,* 20–24). See also Horner, "Spiritual Truth and Sexual Violence," 662–70, for a more detailed discussion of the battle between "pagan" literalism and Christian spirituality in the Old English *Juliana.*

7. Peter Clemoes writes that "[a]llegorical exegesis was applied to scripture to extract from it what Ælfric called *þæt gastlice andgit,* the spiritual sense, as against *þæt anfealde andgit,* the literal, specifically historical meaning" (Clemoes, "Ælfric," 188). Yet it is much more common for Ælfric to pair *gastlice* with *lichamlice* in discussions of this type. I have located three instances of the *anfealde* (one-fold)/*gastlice*

pairing, but nearly two dozen instances of *lichamlice/gastlice*. While the phrase *anfealde andgyt*, the one-fold (or literal) understanding, occurs quite frequently in Ælfric's writings, I am more interested in his specific and frequent juxtaposition of *lichamlice* and *gastlice* as they relate to understanding and interpretation.

8. Unless otherwise noted, all translations from Ælfric's homilies are mine.

9. Ælfric's discussion of spiritual understanding is here based on Augustine. See Augustine, *Tractates*, 1988, 231 ff.

In *Early English Devotional Prose and the Female Audience*, Elizabeth Robertson argues that Ælfric "eschews the literal in favor of the allegorical" (160) and that he considers "[t]he literal world [to be] unworthy of contemplation" (161). I would suggest instead that Ælfric's exegesis is more complicated: rather than "unworthy," Ælfric sees the literal as "insufficient"; as I shall demonstrate, in the *Lives of Saints*, as in the homilies, Ælfric sees the literal as the necessary first stage in readers' spiritual progression. Thus I would argue that Ælfric displays the "quotidien realism" that Robertson shows operating both in anonymous Anglo-Saxon homilies and in twelfth- and thirteenth-century English devotional prose written for women. In particular, Ælfric's *Lives* of female saints demonstrate a concern for the corporeal that aligns him quite closely with the English literary traditions Robertson identifies.

10. The juxtaposition of *lichamlic/corporalis* and *gastlic/spiritualis* can likewise be found in Ælfric's *Grammar*, where this particular correlation of terms appears to be his alone; Ælfric's source does not link these terms in this way. I am grateful to David Porter for providing me with this information in a private communication.

11. Lines 36 ff; 119 ff; 126 ff; 135 ff; 140 ff; 156 ff; and 190. There are several other implicit references, as for example ll. 287 ff, where *gastlicum andgite* seems to imply its opposite. See also Szarmach, "Ælfric as Exegete," 243–44, for a discussion of these terms in this homily.

12. It should be noted that Ælfric also uses *lichamlic(e)* in a perfectly straightforward way, to refer to things people do with their bodies; in the Homily on the Nativity of John the Baptist, for example, he explains, "Twa forhæfednysse cynn syndon, an lichamlic, oðer gastlic" (there are two kind of continence, one bodily, the other spiritual; Thorpe, *Homilies*, 1:360); in the Homily on the Octaves and Circumcision of Our Lord, he writes, "Þa wearð he on þam eahtoðan dæge his gebyrd-tide lichamlice ymbsniden" (then on the eighth day from his birth he was bodily circumcised; Thorpe, *Homilies*, 1:94). Thus it is not simply through the juxtaposition of the terms that Ælfric conflates the literal with the bodily, but more precisely the juxtaposition must occur within a discussion of reading, interpretation, and understanding.

13. See also *Torture and Truth*, in which Page duBois argues that, for ancient Greek culture, the body (in particular the slave body) contained and concealed truth; only by means of torture could reliable truths be produced.

14. Aphrodosia here fills a secondary role common to these narratives: the

older, corrupt woman who, especially in her juxtaposition with the saint, represents all the traditional misogynist notions of women—particularly older women—such as their insatiable sexuality, garrulousness, and grotesque corporeality. For a general discussion of medieval misogyny, see Bloch, *Medieval Misogyny*.

Significantly, the verb used here, *awendan*, is commonly used by Ælfric to mean "to translate," thus carrying not only the sense of "to pervert," which Skeat employs here, but also the sense of material—and textual—transformation. See Ann E. Nichols, "*Awendan*: A Note on Ælfric's Vocabulary," for a discussion of Ælfric's use of this verb in terms of translation.

15. It is quite common for the virgin martyrs to have active speaking roles in these narratives. This points to a significant difference between stylized narratives of martyr torture and actual torture; as Scarry has argued, torture deconstructs or inhibits discourse, whereas in saints' lives, torture very frequently incites or enhances the saint's discursive role.

16. Ælfric frequently uses the "opening up" metaphor in his explanations of scripture; for example: "We habbað anfealdlice gesæd eow nu þis godspel and we willað geopnian eow þæt andgit nu" (Now we have told this gospel to you simply, and we will now open up to you its meaning; Pope, *Homilies*, 250).

17. When Agatha's breast is restored, our gaze follows hers: "Æfter ðam gebede . beseah to hyre breoste . / and wæs þæt corfene breost . þurh crist geedstaðelod . / and ealle hire wunda wurdon gehælede ." (After that prayer she looked at her breast, / and the breast that had been cut off was restored through Christ, / and all her wounds were healed; Skeat, *Lives*, 204–5). In describing the act of looking, Ælfric builds a narrative space within which readers can locate themselves. This "sight" of Agatha's breast likewise confirms the breast as the site of her (female) identity.

18. As Jane Chance has suggested, "the description of the [saint's] torture often veils with obvious sexual symbolism the act of intercourse. . . . [W]hen the naked Saint Lucia must be tortured, she is finally wounded in the stomach with an obviously phallic sword. The virgin martyr becomes a type of the feminine soul joined with Christ to become a *miles Christi*. . . . Appropriately, then, the threat of seduction of the virgin martyr symbolically represents the Devil's adulterous assault on the feminine soul" (Chance, *Woman as Hero*, 56).

19. On the image of Christ as bridegroom in Old English literature, see among works cited Morrison; Bugge; and Matter. For the early (and mistaken) view of Ælfric's use of Ambrose as a source, see Ott. Scholars now agree that Ælfric's source was not in fact written by Ambrose. See Zettel; and see Moloney, "Another Look," especially p. 17. See also Robertson's discussion of this motif (and its benefits for the female virgin) in the Middle English prose treatise *Hali Meidenhad* (*Early English Devotional Prose*, 81–93).

20. As Michael Lapidge writes, "We should not imagine that the saints were con-

ceived abstractly as disembodied spirits. Theirs was a physical and palpable presence: that is to say, the saint was physically present in each shrine insofar as that shrine contained a relic of his/her body—a bone, a fingernail, a lock of hair, whatever" (Lapidge, "The Saintly Life," 243). On relics, see also Geary, *Furta Sacra*.

WORKS CITED

Augustine. *Tractates on the Gospel of John 11–27*. Trans. John W. Rettig. The Fathers of the Church. Volume 79. Washington, D.C.: Catholic University of America Press, 1988.

Bloch, R. Howard. *Medieval Misogyny and the Invention of Western Romantic Love*. Chicago: University of Chicago Press, 1989.

Blumenfeld-Kosinski, Renate, and Timea Szell, eds. *Images of Sainthood in Medieval Europe*. Ithaca and London: Cornell University Press, 1991.

Bugge, John. Virginitas: *An Essay in the History of a Medieval Ideal*. The Hague: Martinus Nijhoff, 1975.

Bynum, Caroline Walker. *Holy Feast and Holy Fast: The Religious Significance of Food to Medieval Women*. Berkeley: University of California Press, 1987.

Cazelles, Brigitte. *The Lady as Saint: A Collection of French Hagiographic Romances of the Thirteenth Century*. Philadelphia: University of Pennsylvania Press, 1991.

Chance, Jane. *Woman as Hero in Old English Literature*. Syracuse: Syracuse University Press, 1986.

Clemoes, Peter. "Ælfric." In *Continuations and Beginnings*, ed. E. G. Stanley, 176–209. London: Thomas Nelson and Sons, 1966.

Crawford, S. J., ed. *The Old English Version of the Heptateuch, Ælfric's Treatise on the Old and New Testament and His Preface to Genesis*. Early English Text Society. Original series 160. London: Oxford University Press, 1922.

Dinshaw, Carolyn. *Chaucer's Sexual Poetics*. Madison: University of Wisconsin Press, 1989.

duBois, Page. *Torture and Truth*. New York: Routledge, 1991.

Frantzen, Allen J. "When Women Aren't Enough." In *Studying Medieval Women*, ed. Nancy Partner, 143–69. Cambridge, Mass.: Medieval Academy of America, 1993.

Geary, Patrick. *Furta Sacra: Thefts of Relics in the Central Middle Ages*. Princeton: Princeton University Press, 1978.

Godden, Malcolm, ed. *Ælfric's Catholic Homilies: The Second Series*. Early English Text Society. Supplementary series 5. London: Oxford University Press, 1979.

Gravdal, Kathryn. *Ravishing Maidens: Writing Rape in Medieval French Literature and Law*. Philadelphia: University of Pennsylvania Press, 1991.

Horner, Shari. "Spiritual Truth and Sexual Violence: The Old English *Juliana*, Anglo-Saxon Nuns, and the Discourse of Female Monastic Enclosure." *Signs: Journal of Women in Culture and Society* 19 (1994): 658–75.

Innis-Parker, Catherine. "Sexual Violence and the Female Reader: Symbolic 'Rape' in the Saints' Lives of the Katherine Group." *Women's Studies* 24 (1995): 205–17.

Kay, Sarah, and Miri Rubin, eds. *Framing Medieval Bodies.* Manchester and New York: Manchester University Press, 1994.

Lapidge, Michael. "The Saintly Life in Anglo-Saxon England." In *The Cambridge Companion to Old English Literature,* ed. Malcolm Godden and Michael Lapidge, 243–63. Cambridge: Cambridge University Press, 1991.

Lees, Clare A. "Men and *Beowulf.*" In *Medieval Masculinities,* ed. Clare A. Lees, 129–48. Minneapolis: University of Minnesota Press, 1994.

———, ed. *Medieval Masculinities.* Minneapolis: University of Minnesota Press, 1994.

Lomperis, Linda, and Sarah Stanbury, eds. *Feminist Approaches to the Body in Medieval Literature.* Philadelphia: University of Pennsylvania Press, 1993.

Matter, E. Ann. *The Voice of My Beloved: The Song of Songs in Western Medieval Christianity.* Philadelphia: University of Pennsylvania Press, 1990.

Moloney, Bernadette. "Another Look at Ælfric's Use of Discourse in Some Saints' Lives." *English Studies* 63 (1982): 13–19.

Morrison, Stephen. "The Figure of *Christus Sponsus* in Old English Prose." In *Liebe-Ehe-Ehebruch in der Literatur des Mittelalters,* ed. Xenja von Ertzdorff and Marianne Wynn, 5–15. Beiträge zur deutschen Philologie 58. Giessen: Schmitz, 1984.

Nichols, Ann E. "*Awendan:* A Note on Ælfric's Vocabulary." *Journal of English and Germanic Philology* 63.1 (1964): 7–13.

Ott, J. H. *Über die Quellen der Heiligenleben in Ælfrics Lives of Saints I.* Halle: Inaugural Dissertation, 1892.

Partner, Nancy F., ed. *Studying Medieval Women.* Cambridge, Mass.: Medieval Academy of America, 1993.

Pope, John C., ed. *Homilies of Ælfric: A Supplementary Collection.* Vol. 1. Early English Text Society. Original series 259. London: Oxford University Press, 1967.

Robertson, Elizabeth. *Early English Devotional Prose and the Female Audience.* Knoxville: University of Tennessee Press, 1990.

Roy, Gopa. "A Virgin Acts Manfully: Ælfric's *Life of Saint Eugenia* and the Latin Versions." *Leeds Studies in English* 23 (1992): 2–27.

Scarry, Elaine. *The Body in Pain: The Making and Unmaking of the World.* New York and Oxford: Oxford University Press, 1985.

Skeat, W. W., ed. and trans. *Ælfric's Lives of Saints.* Early English Text Society. Original series 76, 82, 94, 114. London: Oxford University Press, 1881–88. Rpt. in two volumes, 1966.

Szarmach, Paul E. *Holy Men and Holy Women: Old English Prose Saints' Lives and Their Contexts.* Albany: State University of New York Press, 1996.

———. "Ælfric's Women Saints: Eugenia." In *New Readings on Women in Old English Literature,* ed. Helen Damico and Alexandra Hennessey Olsen, 146–57. Bloomington: Indiana University Press, 1990.

———. "Ælfric as Exegete." In *Hermeneutics and Medieval Culture,* ed. Patrick J.

Gallacher and Helen Damico, 237–47. Albany: State University of New York Press, 1989.

Thorpe, Benjamin, ed. *Homilies of the Anglo-Saxon Church [Ælfric]. The First Part Containing the Sermones Catholici or Homilies of Ælfric.* Vol. 1. London: Ælfric Society, 1844.

Wogan-Browne, Jocelyn. "Saints' Lives and the Female Reader." *Forum for Modern Language Studies* 27 (1991): 314–32.

Zettel, Patrick H. "Saints' Lives in Old English: Latin Manuscripts and Vernacular Accounts: Ælfric." *Peritia* 1 (1982): 17–37.

2

Women, Power, and Violence in
Orderic Vitalis's *Historia Ecclesiastica*

Jean Blacker

While it is unadvisable to accept all that he presents as factual, Orderic Vitalis's *Historia Ecclesiastica* (c. 1114–40) is a rich source of historical figures, perceptions, and events.[1] Originally conceived as a history of Saint-Evroult, the Norman Benedictine abbey where the English-born Orderic spent all but ten years of his life, the *Historia Ecclesiastica* gradually grew to encompass Norman history beyond the abbey (including Sicily and the First Crusade) and the lives of the apostles and the popes.[2] Orderic's work is marked both by an acceptance of the conventional social order and by an avid interest in human nature and events, though, like the majority of historians and chroniclers of his era, he did not seek to develop a specific set of theories regarding historical causation or human motivation. Were a study to be done of quantifiable elements of the *Historia Ecclesiastica*, it would likely yield a surprisingly high occurrence of events associated with women, as compared with the works of other contemporary historians, such as Robert of Torigni and William of Malmesbury.

Although in the social order of the *Historia Ecclesiastica* women are limited to two spheres, family and church, on the moral plane Orderic equates women with men, attributing to both groups the ability to exercise power wisely and to decide between good and evil. Aside from the occasional recourse to standard remarks condemning women, such as that of Solomon, from Ecclesiasticus xxv, 26 (19), "Brevis omnis malitia super malitiam mulieris," (VI, xii, 213n.3; "There is nothing so bad as a bad woman," 213), Orderic's text is not misogynistic; negative comments are balanced with praise of women who have achieved worthy goals while avoiding violence. In addition, while gender determines roles, it does not predicate how an individual will exercise his or her free will within those roles. In the *Historia Ecclesiastica,* a text notable not only for its encyclopedic scope but also for its author's fascination for individual personalities, which often transcend socially prescribed models, biology is not necessarily destiny. Orderic's primary motivation in describing violence is not to ascribe it universally to one group as agent and another as victim but to demonstrate how violence results from the perverted use of power, by both women and men, against both women and men. What might be construed as Orderic's temperance toward women, as seen in his remarkably bias-free portraits of female figures, can also be seen as a vilification of violence as a solution to human discord, a solution often excused in misogynistic texts as most merited by women.

In the general introduction to her edition of the *Historia Ecclesiastica,* Marjorie Chibnall notes Orderic's abhorrence of cruelty and his compassion for the innocent harmed through the abuse of power (I, 41). Though it is certainly possible to view Orderic's interest in events concerning women as indicative of an "unshakable romanticism" (I, 41)—his inclusion of the lengthy narrative on Melaz, the "enamoured Saracen princess," who frees Bohemond in Jerusalem and then converts and marries happily Roger of Salerno (V, x, 358–76) falls into this category—it is equally plausible to view his interest in events involving women as central figures as part of his vision of power.[3] Orderic establishes a hierarchy of human behavior, with those who exercise power wisely at the top and those who abuse it at the bottom. What is unusual about this is Orderic's inclusion of women as equal to men in this respect: women are equally capable of making good or bad decisions about how to use power and are often, though not always, in a position to implement those decisions. In the *Historia Ecclesiastica,* gender does not appear to be a primary determining factor in violent behavior.

Though there are exceptions, Orderic's female figures fall into four groups: married women, single women, widows in cloisters, and female children. The married women can be broken down into four subgroups: wives who use their persuasive powers on their husbands for good; wives who use their persuasive powers on their husbands for evil; wives who exercise power wisely in their husbands' absence; and wives who exercise power against their husbands. Thus, although Orderic's women are often seen acting through men, the range of women's activities also extends beyond men, and they are evaluated by Orderic in much the same way as are men—that is, through the filter of their relationship to the Church and monastic institutions in general and to Saint-Evroult in particular.[4]

Young children's activities are rarely discussed in the *Historia Eccle-*

siastica except in the context of inheritance. In a passage on relations between King Henry I and his son-in-law, Eustace of Breteuil, a powerful
Norman noble, Orderic relates how the king sent the son of Ralph Harenc,
the custodian of Ivry castle, to Eustace to guarantee his promise to grant
him Ivry castle (VI, xii, 210, 212). For reasons that remain unclear, Eustace
cruelly mistreated the boy, having his eyes put out; Ralph demanded revenge and Henry handed over Eustace's two daughters (the king's own
granddaughters), who were consequently blinded by Ralph; the tips of
their nostrils were also cut off. Orderic concludes that "innocens itaque
infantia parentum nefas proh dolor miserabiliter luit" (VI, xii, 212; "so innocent childhood, alas! suffered for the sins of the fathers," 213), making
no distinction between the boy and the girls, both equally innocent victims.

Orderic is also sympathetic toward young women forced to marry
against their will, especially when forced to marry one of Orderic's least
favored figures, as in the case of Bertrade of Montfort. Count Fulk of
Anjou, whom Orderic criticizes on other occasions for "scandalous habits"
and "pestilential vices" (IV, viii, 187), sought the hand of Bertrade, daughter of Simon of Montfort, in order to secure the county of Maine for himself. He achieves his ends through the assistance of Duke Robert Curthose
of Normandy, another of Orderic's less favorite leaders, marrying Bertrade
while at least two of his three, possibly four, former wives were still living
(IV, viii, 184, 186, 187n3). Although Orderic does not explicitly describe
Bertrade's views on the marriage, it is clear that he disapproves of marriages contracted for political gain, where women were often pawns between families vying for control of territory.

Orderic also decries the repudiation of wives, as in the case of Fulk of
Anjou. Orderic's narrative supports Hildegarde, countess of Poitou, in her
appeal for papal clemency (VI, xii, 258). Hildegarde's case against her husband, William, duke of Aquitaine, apparently caused widespread scandal;
Pope Calixtus II ordered her husband to return to her (VI, xii, 258 and n2).
Orderic reports that Hildegarde stated her claim herself in a clear, high
voice ("alta et claraque uoce," VI, xii, 258), whereas bishops from Aquitaine made excuses for William's absence on account of illness. Although
the hearing was rescheduled for a time when William could be present,
Hildegarde is seen in control, through the power of her words and the
papal support of the institution of marriage, in this case in the woman's
favor.

In a study of clerical images of wives in the twelfth and thirteenth centuries, Sharon Farmer notes that Orderic includes roughly as many passages on wives whose influence was negative as he does on "pious wives," suggesting a range of interpretive possibilities ("Persuasive Voices," 522). At the positive end of the scale, where wives are shown to exercise economic as well as moral influence through their husbands, fall Adela, daughter of William the Conqueror; Avice of Auffay; Isabel of Tosny; and Adelais, second wife of Roger of Montgomery, among others. Adela, the "mulier sagax et animosa" (V, x, 324; "wise and spirited woman," 325) "used to say" to her husband, Stephen, count of Blois, "between conjugal caresses" (V, x, 325; "inter amicabilis coniugii blandimenta dicebat," 324) that he ought to return to the crusades; Orderic credits Adela as having exercised the most persuasive influence upon her husband among all those who had endeavored to convince him to take up arms again after having fled Antioch in disgrace (V, x, 324). That this influence is framed within an image of conjugal happiness further reinforces Orderic's stand on the power of positive marriage, not exclusively at the institutional but on the personal level as well; resemblances between this passage and Chrétien de Troyes' *Erec et Enide* have not gone unnoticed.[5]

Avice of Auffay is one of the wives whose positive influence protected Saint-Evroult from the vagaries of her husband, Walter, who, Orderic claims, was "handsome but lacking in wisdom" (III, vi, 257; "elegans sed parum sapiens," 256), and had "continually injured and harassed monks and clerks and honest peasants" (III, vi, 257; "monachos ac clericos legitimosque colonos iniuriis crebro illatis perturbauit," 256). Orderic praises Avice for having turned Walter away from his earlier folly, but also, in the epitaph he wrote for her burial in the church at Saint-Evroult, for having been "generous in giving to priests, monks, all of God's needy," and "gentle and well-doing" to "widows, waifs, and the sick" (III, vi, 259; "Presbiteros, monachos, uiduas, aegros et egenos: / Semper honorauit multoque iuuamine fouit," 258). Although Walter spent the last three years of his life as a monk at Saint-Evroult after Avice's death, his epitaph is one-quarter the length of Avice's. Apparently, for Orderic, while there may have been "nothing as bad as a bad woman," there was nothing as good as a good one.

Under the category of wives who exercised power wisely in their husbands' absence are Sibyl, wife of Robert Bordet of Cullei (now Rabodanges), and Isabel of Tosny. In addition to being wives, these two women are characterized as female knights, Sibyl as she protected the Spanish town of Tarragona by standing night watch while Robert Bordet traveled to Rome and on another occasion to Normandy (VI, xiii, 404), and Isabel as she rode into battle as a knight among men to protect her family's claims.[6] In Book VIII, written between 1133 and 1135 (iv, xix), Orderic says of Isabel, another daughter of Simon of Montfort, and wife of Ralph of Tosny:

> Isabel was generous, daring, and gay, and therefore lovable and estimable to those around her. In war she rode armed as a knight among the knights; and she showed no less courage among the knights in hauberks and sergeants at arms than did the maid Camilla, the pride of Italy, among the troops of Turnus. (IV, viii, 213, 215)

> (Isabel uero dapsilis et audax atque iocosa, ideoque coessentibus amabilis et grata. In expeditione inter milites ut miles equitabat armata, et loricatis equitibus ac spiculatis satellitibus non minori prestabat audacia? quam decus Italiae Turni commanipularibus uirgo Camilla.) (212, 214)

The portrayal of Isabel is not wholly flattering, however, for Orderic assigns partial blame for the battle to Isabel, who had made disparaging remarks to Countess Helwise of Evreux, who, in turn, encouraged her husband the count to wage war against the Tosny clan; thus, "the brave hearts of men were moved to anger through the suspicions and quarrels of women" (IV, viii, 213; "sic per suspiciones et litigia feminarum, in furore succensa sunt fortium corda uirorum," 212). Earlier, in Book V, written between 1127 and 1130, Orderic relates that Isabel took the veil after having repented of the mortal sin of luxury, in which she had indulged in her youth (III, v, 128); Orderic provides no details in support of his conclusion on the necessity of Isabel's repentance.

In contrast with the positive comparison of Isabel to Camilla and four Amazon queens, Orderic's portrait of Juliana, daughter of Henry I, and wife of Eustace of Breteuil (mentioned in connection with the blinding of Ralph Harenc's son), is unflattering; in fact, it is in the context of this narrative that Orderic cites Solomon on bad women. Juliana, the "unfortunate warrior" ("infausta bellatrix," VI, xii, 214), sent by her husband to defend their castle at Breteuil against Henry, uses her skills in battle (albeit a private one) to defend her husband against her father. She tries to kill the king but fails and is forced to surrender the castle of Breteuil to Henry, who also forces her to jump from the ramparts into the moat, in mid-February, "nudis natibus" (VI, xii, 214; "with bare buttocks," 215). She slinks back to her husband at Pacy, remarks Orderic, who does not condone her actions but praises her later decision to become a nun at Fontevrault (VI, xii, 278). While Juliana has made some poor decisions, Henry I—who is usually seen in the *Historia Ecclesiastica* in his guise as the "lion of justice," a label typically attached to this king by historians of the period—is seen in the two incidents of the blinding of his granddaughters and his treatment of Juliana to have engaged in what can be construed, even in this violent period, as ill-advised acts of gratuitous violence.

At opposite poles of the continuum of wives, power, and violence are Mabel of Bellême, first wife of Roger of Montgomery, and Adelais, his second wife. Adelais receives much less attention in Orderic's narrative than Mabel does. Orderic comments that Adelais was the opposite of Mabel in character and praises her ability to convince Roger to make up for past ill-treatment of Saint-Evroult (III, v, 138, 140). According to Orderic, Adelais's advice was central in Roger's decision to bequeath the bulk of his properties in England and Normandy to Saint-Evroult, recorded in a charter of 1085 (III, v, 138 and 138–139n2).

Mabel of Bellême is the most nefarious of Orderic's female figures, by virtue of her own activities and by being the mother of Robert of Bellême, considered at the time of Henry I's accession in 1100, as C. Warren Hollister notes, "the wealthiest and most powerful magnate in the Anglo-Norman world" ("Campaign of 1102," 193). Concerning Mabel's son, Hollister adds that "his reputation for savage cruelty must be regarded as a factor contributing to Henry I's success in isolating him from his fellow nobles," and when "Robert was under attack, the only magnates to rally to him were his own brothers" (194). Concerning Mabel, Marjorie Chibnall has concluded that her "excesses must have gone beyond what was acceptable even in a violent age for some of the knights dispossessed by her to have burst into her castle one night and cut off her head as she lay in bed" (*World of Orderic Vitalis*, 24).

Orderic's enmity toward Mabel and Robert stems in part from personal factors, from his favoritism toward monastic institutions, and from his disdain for excessive cruelty, as seen for example in his description of William the Conqueror's subjugation of the English countryside after the Conquest (II, iv, 230, 232; IV, vii, 94) and elsewhere. Orderic's father, Odelerius of Orleans, had served in the household of Roger of Montgomery when the latter was made earl of Shropshire by William after the Conquest (Chibnall, *World of Orderic Vitalis*, 7). In addition, in the second half of the eleventh century, the Montgomery-Bellême family was in conflict with one of the families who cofounded Saint-Evroult, the Giroie (II, iii, 54 and Chibnall, *World of Orderic Vitalis*, 22). While these personal connections might help explain Orderic's interest in the Montgomery-Bellême family, they do not explain his animosity toward Mabel and her firstborn son.[7]

If more material of this kind were found in the *Historia Ecclesiastica*, one

might think that Orderic were proposing a paradigm of matrilineal violence, so great is his insistence on the cruelty of this mother and son. To
illustrate even the poisonous nature of her breast milk, Orderic relates an
anecdote which supposedly transpired as Mabel was fleeing the lands of
Saint-Evroult, having offended Abbot Thierry of Saint-Evroult and fallen
sick; passing by the house of a townsman, Roger Sowsnose, Mabel "compelled his infant child to suck the nipple which was causing her most pain"
(II, iii, 55; "inde quandam infantulam lactantem assumi praecepit, orique
eius mamillam suam in qua maxima pars infirmitatis collecta erat ad
suggendum tradidit," 54); the child died immediately and Mabel recov-
ered and returned home.

Elsewhere in the *Historia Ecclesiastica*, Mabel is associated with poison.
Orderic relates that Mabel twice tried to poison Arnold of Echauffour, son
of William Giroie and nephew of Robert Giroie; the first time she failed and
instead killed Gilbert, Roger of Montgomery's brother (II, iii, 122), but the
second time she succeeded in killing Arnold with poisoned wine (124).
Another wife is associated with poison—Adelaide, kinswoman of Duke
William (the Conqueror) and wife of Robert Giroie, who rebelled against
the duke—but is absolved by Orderic: she held four apples in her hands,
and her husband playfully snatched two of them and ate them against her
protests (II, iii, 78, 80). This incident is noteworthy both for its conventional
association of a wife with poisoned apples and for its lack of direct attribution of the crime to the woman; the crimes in which Orderic implicates
Mabel are notably more sinister due to the attribution of intent.[8]

It is difficult to say whether Robert of Bellême is portrayed as being more
cruel through his association with his mother, Mabel, or otherwise, but what
is clear is the intensity of negative feeling on Orderic's part and the nature of
Robert and Mabel's crimes: insensitivity toward the Church, and use of extreme violence. With respect to insensitivity toward monasteries, Orderic
criticizes Mabel for allegedly having treated Abbot Thierry of Saint-Evroult
with disdain: upon arriving at the monastery with a retinue of more than
one hundred knights, Mabel reportedly flew into a rage at the abbot's suggestion that she might be imposing. Her reply, "Next time I will bring even
more knights with me," apparently prompted Abbot Thierry's scolding and
Orderic's conclusion that her milk became poisoned forthwith (II, iii, 55).
Although Orderic mentions in passing the couple's foundation of the abbey
of Saint-Martin at Séez (II, iii, 66),[9] Orderic blames Mabel for Roger of Montgomery's lack of generosity to Saint-Evroult in particular and to the Church
in general, stating that "as long as his wife Mabel, who had always hated the
sons of Giroie, the founders of Saint-Evroul, lived, he showed himself hostile

to the monks in many ways at her instigation" (III, v, 135; "quamdiu Mabilia uxor eius quae Geroianos Ebrulfiani monasterii fundatores semper exosos habuerat uixit, Vticensibus illa stimulante pluribus modis molestus extitit," 134). Records do attest to a distinct increase in ecclesiastical patronage on Roger's part following Mabel's death.[10] For his part, Robert of Bellême, "one of the best-known and least-liked of the Anglo-Norman magnates" did not distinguish himself in the area of monastic endowment (Hollister, "Campaign of 1102," 193). Orderic states that among other things, Robert had compelled the monks of Saint-Evroult to work on his castles under threat of deprivation of familial property, that he laid waste to lands surrounding Bellême including those belonging to monastic houses, and that Bishop Serlo of Séez, formerly abbot of Saint-Evroult (1089–91) eventually excommunicated him (IV, viii, 296, 298).

Apart from his report of ill-treatment of the monks of Saint-Evroult, Orderic castigates Robert for his general cruelty, comparing him to Pharaoh, Ishmael, Nero, and Domitian, summing up the implications of his activities with the phrase, "Normandy was often disturbed by the foul plots and changes of allegiance of this butcher, while the county of Maine and all the neighbourhood around was mercilessly ravaged by his looting, slaying, and burning" (IV, viii, 301; "Diris conatibus et tergiuersationibus prefati lanionis Neustria sepe turbata est ? et Cenomannica retio uicinitasque circumiacens predis ac cedibus incendiisque feraliter profligata est," 300), an image reminiscent of the excesses of Raoul de Cambrai, fictional hero of the *chanson de geste* that bears his name.[11]

While a less lengthy and repeated treatment is reserved for Mabel, Orderic appears hard-pressed to suppress his joy at her passing: he relates that Hugh Bunel, whom she had undeservedly deprived of his inheritance, accompanied by his three brothers, finding her relaxing in bed after a bath, sliced her head off with a sword. He adds that "when the murder of this terrible lady had been accomplished many rejoiced at her fate" (III, v, 137; "Peracta itaque caede feralis erae, multi de ruina eius exultauere," 136), commenting that her positive epitaph by the monks of Troarn must have been accomplished "more through the partiality of friends than because of any special deserts of hers" (III, v, 137). Though Isabel of Tosny, Sibyl wife of Robert Bordet, and Juliana of Breteuil are three women notably characterized as riding into battle as a knight, guarding a fortress as well as a man, or attempting to assassinate the king as a male warrior might, Mabel of Bellême is the only named female figure in Orderic's text to die by the sword (unnamed women and children were among the slaughtered following the Norman Conquest in the north of England, for example). It is worth noting that Mabel is said to have died in her bedroom after a bath, an image which recalls the epic tradition of the warrior's murder in the bath, dating from the time of Agamemnon (III, v, 137n2); though not depicted as a warrior, Mabel's manner of death may associate her with warriors, principally male.

What conclusions might we draw from Mabel's ignominy in the *Historia Ecclesiastica*? The observation that gender reversals in literary and historical texts, as well as in festivals and daily living, may serve to reinforce gender stereotypes rather than to undermine them can be suggestive here up to a point: Mabel's and Juliana's lack of success as dominatrix might imply an endorsement of traditional "female" behavior within traditional "female" roles.[12] But on the whole, defining and prescribing gender-specific behavior does not seem to have been Orderic's aim. Too many of his outstanding figures cross gender bounds and behavioral bounds: women acting like men with positive outcomes (in Orderic's worldview); women acting like men with negative outcomes; men showing compassion for the less fortunate (is this acting like women?); men abusing their power for evil purposes (men acting like men?).

The denominator here is the use and abuse of power. While Orderic's female figures may be expected to "act like women"—that is, in traditional terms, to show compassion, to guide, to nurture—when they act negatively, their actions are rarely attributed to their gender but instead to having used poor judgment. In Orderic's world, men are as prone to use poor judgment as women, and vice versa; one can transcend one's gender, if not on the social plane then on the moral plane, by using one's own (or someone else's) power wisely and by avoiding violence if at all possible. This ability to transcend gender and rank is central in Orderic's thinking: his response to the *démesure* of the great pillaging robber barons of the *chansons de geste* is the proposed formation of both women and men, of courage, faith, and *mesure*.

NOTES

1. All references to the *Historia Ecclesiastica* are to Marjorie Chibnall's edition, including volume number, book number, and page number.

2. See Orderic Vitalis, *Historia Ecclesiastica*, I, 31–36, for Chibnall's discussion of the chronology of Orderic's writing and revisions.

3. On *chanson de geste* echoes in the *Historia Ecclesiastica*, see Warren, "The Enamoured Moslem Princess." Judith Weiss notes that Orderic's fictitious story is possibly the earliest written version in Western Europe of the legend of a Moslem

princess who befriends a Christian hero and prisoner and marries into his faith ("The Wooing Woman," 152 and n14); see also Bancourt, *Les Musulmans*.

4. On the roles and rights of noblewomen in twelfth- and thirteenth-century France, see Hajdu, "The Position of Noblewomen."

5. See Bezzola, *Les Origines*, II, 369n1.

6. Citing William of Malmesbury and Hildebert of Lavardin, Farmer notes that "the theme that *good* women were often 'man-like' was not unusual in the twelfth century" ("Persuasive Voices," 524n18). On various representations of the woman warrior in the thirteenth century, see Solterer, "Figures of Female Militancy."

7. Chibnall sounds a cautionary note with respect to the historicity of Orderic's work in this context: "Since Orderic spent his life in a monastery almost on the frontiers of the Bellême lands, and had a profound, though hostile, interest in the family who were the bitterest enemies of the founders of St. Evroul, his testimony for this period is important, but not always reliable" (Orderic Vitalis, *Historia Ecclesiastica*, II, appendix I, 362).

8. One of the best-known instances in medieval fiction of a woman (often a wife, though the victim is not always her husband) as the agent of murder via a poisoned apple is that of Guinevere in the thirteenth-century Vulgate prose *La Mort le Roi Artu*. The queen is given a poisoned apple intended for Gauvain by one of his enemies; she unwittingly passes the apple to Gaheris de Karaheu, who promptly dies, much to the dismay of (among others) Guinevere, who is accused of intent although she is just the unknowing intermediary (*La Mort le Roi Artu*, 76–78). On the widespread occurrence of stories of poison, see Douglas, *William the Conqueror*, 408–15 (appendix F, "On Poisoning as a Method of Political Action in Eleventh-Century Normandy"). Douglas comments specifically on Orderic's passages on Adelaide and Mabel (413–15).

9. See Thompson, "Family and Influence."

10. For sources on Roger of Montgomery's activity as a founder and benefactor of monasteries, see Chibnall in Orderic Vitalis, *Historia Ecclesiastica* III, v, 142n1.

11. Other parallels exist between Robert and Raoul: as Joan Ferrante comments, Raoul's mother "was not the retiring sort." Having protected her son's lands for fifteen years, she is incensed by Raoul's refusal to heed her advice about their continued protection and curses him (*Raoul de Cambrai* 1131–33); later, she threatens a knight with an iron bar (*Raoul de Cambrai* 5244–45) ("Public Postures," 214).

12. Natalie Zemon Davis argues in part against the view often posited by anthropologists, that "uses of sexual inversion . . . are ultimately sources of order and stability in a hierarchical society," that "they do not question the basic order of the society itself" ("Women on Top," 130). Davis claims that especially "comic and festive inversion could *undermine* as well as reinforce" traditional hierarchical social structures, proposing that "somewhat in contradistinction to Christine de Pisan and the gallant school of feminists . . . the image of the disorderly woman did not always function to keep women in their place" but rather may have served to "widen behavioral options for women" ("Women on Top," 131).

WORKS CITED

Bancourt, Paul. *Les Musulmans dans les chansons de geste du cycle du roi*. 2 vols. Aix-en-Provence: Université de Provence, 1982.

Bezzola, Reto R. *Les Origines et la formation de la littérature courtoise en Occident*. 3 vols. Paris: Champion, 1944–63; rpt. Geneva: Slatkine, 1968, 1984.

Chibnall, Marjorie. *The World of Orderic Vitalis*. Oxford: Clarendon Press, 1984.

Davis, Natalie Zemon. "Women on Top." In Natalie Zemon Davis, *Society and Culture in Early Modern France*, 124–51. Palo Alto: Stanford University Press, 1965.

Douglas, David C. *William the Conqueror*. Berkeley and Los Angeles: University of California Press, 1964.

Farmer, Sharon. "Persuasive Voices: Clerical Images of Medieval Wives." *Speculum* 61:3 (1986): 517–43.

Ferrante, Joan. "Public Postures and Private Maneuvers: Roles Medieval Women Play." In *Women and Power in the Middle Ages*, ed. Mary Erler and Maryanne Kowaleski, 213–29. Athens: University of Georgia Press, 1988.

Hajdu, Robert. "The Position of Noblewomen in the *pays des coutumes*, 1100–1300." *Journal of Family History* 5 (1980): 122–44.

Hollister, C. Warren. "The Campaign of 1102 against Robert of Bellême." In *Studies in Medieval History Presented to R. Allen Brown*, ed. Christopher Harper-Bill, Christopher J. Holdsworth, Janet L. Nelson, 193–202. Woodbridge, Suffolk: Boydell and Brewer, 1989.

La Mort le Roi Artu. Ed. Jean Frappier. Textes Littéraires Français. Geneva: Droz; Paris: Minard, 1954.

Orderic Vitalis. *The Ecclesiastical History of Orderic Vitalis*. Ed. and trans. Marjorie Chibnall. 6 vols. Oxford Medieval Texts. Oxford: Clarendon Press, 1969–80.

Raoul de Cambrai. Ed. Paul Meyer and August Honoré Longnon. Société des Anciens Textes Français. Paris: Firmin-Didot, 1882; rpt. New York: Johnson Reprints, 1965.

Robert of Torigni. *La Chronique de Robert de Torigni*. Ed. Léopold Delisle. 2 vols. Société de L'Histoire de Normandie. Rouen: A. Le Brument, 1872–73.

Solterer, Helen. "Figures of Female Militancy in Medieval France." *Signs: Journal of Women in Culture and Society* 16:3 (1991): 522–49.

Thompson, Kathleen. "Family and Influence to the South of Normandy in the Eleventh Century: The Lordship of Bellême." *Journal of Medieval History* 11 (1985): 215–26.

Warren, F. M. "The Enamoured Moslem Princess in Ordericus Vitalis and the French Epic." *Publications of the Modern Language Association of America* 29 (1914): 341–58.

Weiss, Judith. "The Wooing Woman in Anglo-Norman Romance." In *Romance in Medieval England*, ed. Maldwyn Mills, Jennifer Fellows, and Carol M. Meale, 149–62. Woodbridge, Suffolk: Boydell and Brewer, 1991.

William of Malmesbury. *Willelmi Malmesbiriensis Monachi de Gestis Pontificum Anglorum Libri Quinque.* Ed. N.E.S.A. Hamilton. Rolls Series. London: Longman, 1870.

———. *Willelmi Malmesbiriensis Monachi de Gestis Regum Anglorum Libri Quinque; Historia Novellae Libri Tres.* Ed. W. Stubbs. 2 vols. Rolls Series. London: Eyre and Spottiswoode, 1887–89.

3

The Mont St. Michel Giant

Sexual Violence and Imperialism in
the Chronicles of Wace and Laȝamon

Laurie Finke and Martin Shichtman

We could find no better means to illustrate in popular culture the ways in which sexual violence—especially rape—is generically encoded in our cultural narratives than that incredibly bad "B" science fiction film of 1968, *Mars Needs Women*. In this film, which Leonard Maltin calls "strangely sincere but extremely silly and distended," Tommy Kirk plays a Martian sent along with four other Martians to collect five earth women to take back to Mars to repopulate a barren and sterile planet. What is striking about the film is the horror and absolute resistance with which earth authorities greet the Martians' request. The Martians' tactics run the gamut from seduction to out-and-out rape and abduction. They manage to convince at least one woman to return with them voluntarily; however, earth officials—particularly the military—are willing to go to any lengths (including, of course, atomic annihilation) to see that the Martians do not get even one earth woman.

When we watched the film we were struck by this extreme fear of alien contamination; why was the preservation of five women more important than the lives of the billions of people on the planet? Why were the men responsible for the defense of the planet willing to go to any lengths—including self-destruction—to save five women from contamination by aliens? It isn't that the Martians are repulsive aliens—Tommy Kirk, as both star and head Martian, provides leading-man good looks that work against the audience's horror at this grotesque violation of the purity of earth women. It is simply not possible to read this film as a narrative about the rescue of damsels in distress. Rather, the extremity of earth's reaction seems to stem from the threat the Martians' superior technology poses to earthlings' sense of control over geographical and hence political and ideological space. The fear that earth's territorial boundaries could be violated by technologically superior aliens gets displaced into fantasies about the violation of women's bodies.

We do not intend to sort out all the contradictions in this truly dreadful movie, but it does raise questions that we want to pursue in this essay. What are the circumstances under which the sexual exchange of women between strangers (exogamy) is seen as an acceptable means of establishing political alliances, and what are the conditions under which such exchanges are constituted as involuntary and hence as rape? If all margins are a threat to the integrity of the social body, how does the social body manage anxieties about what lies beyond its borders? The physical body, as Mary Douglas has argued, can be a model for any bounded system, and we must be prepared to see in the body a symbol of society, "to see the powers and dangers credited to social structure reproduced in small on the human body" (Douglas, *Purity and Danger*, 115). We are particularly interested in how rape—the violation of the intact physical body—can figure the violation of political boundaries by an other that is represented as grotesque and monstrous. Like Kathryn Gravdal, we attempt to understand rape as a generic device of narrative (Gravdal, *Ravishing Maidens*, 1–20). What is at stake in our analysis of Wace's and Laȝamon's accounts of the Mont St. Michel giant's rape of Arthur's kinswoman Eleine is not simply the representation of coercive sexual intercourse in historical narratives, as one of many stock episodes that might be used to fill out the contents of a story, but rather the structural function of rape in constituting historical writing as a genre. Following Slavoj Žižek's analysis of ideology, we want to understand rape as a symptom, "a particular, 'pathological' feature, signifying formation, a binding of enjoyment, an inert stain resisting communication and interpretation, a stain which cannot be included in the circuit of discourse, of social bond network, but is at the same time a positive condition of it, . . . a terrifying bodily mark which is merely a mute attestation bearing witness to a disgusting enjoyment" (*Sublime Object*, 75–76). We are less concerned, then, with the specific history of rape in twelfth-century England—the laws, trials, and punishments of actual rapists— than with its imaginative construction in the writing of history as a symptom or trope that functions as a "quilting point" (*point de capiton*), binding together the floating elements that make up ideological space, thereby creating and sustaining a particular ideological formation (Žižek, *Sublime*

Object, 87). What anxieties about boundaries—political as well as bodily— about exogamy and purity are being enacted in such narratives? What is the generic function of rape narratives in historical writing?

While twelfth- and thirteenth-century vernacular histories of King Arthur, such as those produced by Wace and Laȝamon, are generally understood by twentieth-century literary critics as fiction, not history, and are reassigned to the genre of romance, we have to consider the possibility that their medieval aristocratic audiences understood and used these narratives primarily as histories, drawing upon the distant past to shape their understanding of the world around them and thereby to legitimate their political control (see Blacker, *Faces of Time*, 1–52, and Spiegel, *Romancing the Past*, 1–10). Stephen Greenblatt has reminded us that genres are not timeless categories but always "received collected practice[s]," which are shaped by the social conditions that make the genre possible and which create the objects it represents (*Learning to Curse*, 101). The earliest accounts of Arthur encoded as history are written in Latin. This means that the Norman patrons of Geoffrey of Monmouth's *Historia regum britanniæ* would almost certainly not have been able to read it. However learned someone like Robert of Gloucester (to whom several of the manuscripts are dedicated) may have been, his education probably would not have included much Latin. For these patrons, Geoffrey's book was an artifact, a symbol of prestige (for an account of Geoffrey's patrons see Shichtman and Finke, "Profiting from the Past," 18–21). It could, if necessary, be used as documentation of political legitimacy, but such a use would require the mediation of a third party, of a cleric who was capable of reading and interpreting the Latin.

Within one generation, the consumers of such works—the Norman aristocracy—demanded histories written in their own vernaculars, in languages they could read for themselves or at the very least have read to them. Though Geoffrey of Monmouth was the first to record the narrative of the Mont St. Michel giant, Wace and Laȝamon were the first to produce accounts that could actually be understood by the Norman patrons for whom they were written. Since we are primarily interested in understanding the social function of this episode (rather than, say, its literary function) within the genre of historical writing, we must explore the social conditions under which vernacular "Bruts" were produced at the end of the twelfth century and the beginning of the thirteenth by looking at the interests of their patrons and potential patrons.

The aristocrats who could have commissioned vernacular histories, from the English King Henry II (who may have patronized Wace) down to the minor nobility on the western "marches" of the kingdom (who may have been Laȝamon's patrons), were responding during this period to a series of disturbing political and economic developments that threatened many of the ideological boundaries by which the medieval aristocracy defined itself. Twelfth-century Europe experienced what Robert Bartlett has called an "aristocratic diaspora," a period of military expansion during which the aristocracy of Western Europe, especially those who occupied the old Carolingean empire, spread out from their homelands into new areas, where they settled and augmented their fortunes (Bartlett, *Making of Europe*, 24–56). This acquisitive expansionism coincided with—but was not limited to—the age of the crusades. It included the "conquest" of such far-flung and exotic places as Sicily, Spain, Syria, Palestine, Castile, Poland, and Prussia as well as places like England, Scotland, Wales, and Ireland, which to us seem much less exotic and alien but which to their Norman conquerors must have seemed like the borderland between culture and utter chaos. It was during this period, almost simultaneously, that both genres—vernacular history and romance—first emerged (or reemerged). Both genres manage the anxieties—of both conqueror and conquered, the powerful and the exploited—about the chaos that lies beyond what is known, during a period of expansion; during an era in which geographical, political, and social boundaries, both in England and abroad, are forming and reforming.

In *The Sacred and the Profane,* Mircea Eliade attempts to encode anthropologically the construction of territorial boundaries in what he refers to as "traditional"—or preindustrial—societies, such as that of twelfth-century Europe. He argues that traditional societies create rigid boundaries between what he calls sacred territory—territory consecrated, inhabited, and known—and that territory which lies beyond, in which lurks danger, demons, turmoil (*Sacred and Profane,* 20–65). Sacred territory is "our" territory. "We" have claimed it from the chaos, from the monsters who ruled before our coming. We have cleansed this territory, killing its previous evil inhabitants, often decapitating them and displaying their hideous heads as reminders of both our victory over disorder and the possibility that disorder may once again reign if we become overly complacent. New churches are erected on the former sacred sites.

Vernacular histories, like those of Wace and Laȝamon, which represent the antique history of England, illustrate just this process of marking geographical spaces with the signs of the political body. Both Wace and Laȝamon, for instance (like Geoffrey of Monmouth, whose *Historia regum britanniæ* serves as a source text for all British histories well into the seven-

teenth century), describe Brutus landing at Totnes on the Cornish coast
and discovering the land inhabited by giants. The giants are horrific; they
are described as demons and fiends. Their leader, Gogmagog, is the worst
of all—Laȝamon calls him "Godes wiðer-saka" (God's adversary; *Laȝamon's Brut*, line 906). Wace and Laȝamon both stress his huge size; in Wace,
he is leader of the giants "Pur sa force e pur sa grandur" (Because of his
power and his greatness; *Le Roman de Brut de Wace*, lines 1071–72).[1] To establish their claim to this new land, Brutus and his men must immediately
banish these creatures to the geographical margins of the land, to the
mountains.

Banishment to the periphery, however, is not enough to secure the new
boundaries. The giants return and violate the Trojans' religious observations, their sacred space. The Trojans kill nineteen of the giants and force
Gogmagog to wrestle Corineus in front of Brutus. Corineus dispatches the
last threat to the Trojan conquest of the island by throwing him over a cliff,
"& mid swilce ræde. þas eotentes weoren deade. / Nu wes al Þis lond. i-
ahned a Brutus hond" ("And so by this policy those giants were destroyed.
/ Now to Brutus's hand was allocated all this land"; 966–67).

Eliade's model, however, neglects the political, economic, and ideological implications of the differentiations he identifies between sacred space
(secured and ordered space) and what lies beyond. He neglects to recognize, for instance, how such differentiations provide the ideological justification for imperialistic ventures in traditional societies. In Laȝamon,
Brutus's defeat of the giants is quickly followed by a scene in which Brutus
surveys his recently conquered territory:

> Brutus hine bi-þohte . & þis folc bi-heold.
> bi-heold he þa muntes. feire & muchele.
> bi-heold he þa medewan. þat weoren swiðe mære.
> bi-heold he þa wateres. & þa wilde deor.
> bi-heold he þa fisches. bi-heold he þa fuȝeles.
> bi-heold he þa leswa. & þene leofliche wode.
> bi-heold he þene wode hu he bleou. bi-heold he þat corn hu hit greu.
> al he iseih on leoden. þat him leof was on heorten. (1002–7)

> (Brutus began reflecting, beholding all those people,
> He beheld the mountains, beautiful and mighty,
> He beheld the meadows which were most magnificent,
> He beheld the waters and the wild creatures,
> He beheld the fishes and all the birds and fowl,
> He beheld the grasslands and the lovely groves,

He beheld the woodland flowering and beheld the cornfields growing;
All this he saw in the country and his heart was light and happy.)

What is significant in his survey is not its contents but its form. The echo of
the biblical creation story—and the story of God's victory over the giants
(Gen. 6.4)—imparts ideological authority to Brutus's appropriation of Britain. He sees that it is good and founds the city of Troynovant. Creation
follows thought.

The migrations of Bartlett's aristocratic diaspora were primarily the result of pressures created by the medieval dependence on land as a source
of economic wealth. Land by its nature is a finite resource, so that landless
aristocrats, disinherited because they were younger sons in a system of
primogeniture favoring eldest sons or because they were not legitimate
sons, needed to go elsewhere to make their fortunes. Control of the land as
an economic resource, however, also depended on control of women as
economic resources. Strategic intermarriage with conquered people
forged necessary political alliances and ensured orderly succession and
inheritance of property through the production of legitimate heirs. Aristocratic women could also be called upon to mediate between the men of
different cultures—between different languages and different cultural
identities.

The portrait of Queen Matilda in the *Chronicle of the Kings of England,*
written by the twelfth-century monk William of Malmesbury, attests to the
ideological significance of such strategic marriages. Matilda became the
wife of the Norman king, Henry I, last son of William the Conqueror and
grandfather of Henry II, who may have been Wace's patron. According to
William of Malmesbury, Matilda was "descended from an ancient and il-
lustrious race of kings, daughter of the king of Scotland" (*Chronicle,* 452).
Her subsequent marriage to Henry symbolically united the native aristocracy and the dukes of Normandy. During the conquest she had taken refuge in a nunnery, as had many other aristocratic women, to protect herself
from rape by invading soldiers. One of the great controversies of the post-
Conquest period concerned which of those ladies should be allowed to
escape their vows and marry Normans once the Normans had secured the
English throne (Elkins, *Holy Women,* 2–5). Matilda "wore the garb indicative of the holy profession. . . . This, when the king was about to advance
her to his bed, became matter of controversy; nor could the archbishop
[Anselm of Canterbury] be induced to consent to her marriage, but by the
production of lawful witnesses, who swore that she had worn the veil on
account of her suitors, but had never made her vow" (William of Malmesbury, *Chronicle,* 493–94). William, who counted himself of both Norman

and Saxon descent, simultaneously praises and covertly criticizes her role as cultural mediator between Saxons and Normans: "Her generosity becoming universally known, crowds of scholars, equally famed for verse and for singing, came over. . . . Nor on these only did she lavish money, but on all sorts of men, especially foreigners, that through her presents they might proclaim her celebrity abroad. . . . Hence, it was justly observed, the disposition crept upon the queen to reward all the foreigners she could, while the others were kept in suspense, sometimes with effectual, but oftener with empty promises" (453). The passage begins as praise for Matilda's patronage but ends up sharply criticizing her for favoring foreign clients (presumably Normans) over her own countrymen. By the late twelfth century, the collective social practices of the aristocracy that sustained conquest and intermarriage spawned a host of new genres—genealogy, romance, vernacular history—that preserved and reproduced this metonymic link between land and women. The aristocracy's search for land, ladies, and legitimacy fueled the popularity of both romance and vernacular history.

If marriage, like warfare, could be used to expand wealth and political influence, then, failing that, rape and abduction might accomplish the same thing (Duby, *Knight, Lady, and Priest,* 38–40, 237–38). The view of women as resources in dynastic expansion no doubt explains the extent to which abduction and rape tend to collapse into each other in medieval law. The term *rape* derives in antiquity from the word *raptus,* literally "to carry off by force." Gratian defined rape as involving the abduction of a woman in addition to unlawful intercourse with her (Brundage, "Rape and Seduction," 141–42). The offense of rape was as much about stealing a woman away from those under whose authority she lived as it was about sexual intercourse. These legal distinctions find their way into Wace's description of the Mont St. Michel giant's rape of Eleine. When Eleine's nurse describes the events, she distinguishes between the actual abduction, for which she uses the term *ravie:*

> Lasse, pur quei l'ai tant nurrie
> Quant uns diables l'ad ravie;
> Uns gaianz mei e li ravi
> E mei e li aporta ci. (11403–6)

> (Alas, why did I nurse her so much
> If some devil ravished her away;
> A giant ravished me and her
> And me and her he brought here.)

and sexual coitus, for which she uses the verbs *purgesir* and *desforcier.*

La pucele volt purgesir,
Mais tendre fu, nel pout suffrir.
. . . .
Par force m'ad ci retenue
E par force m'ad purgeüe.
Sa force m'estuet otreier,
Ne li puis mie defforcier. (11407–27)

([The giant] wanted to couple with the maiden,
But she was tender, she could not endure him.
By force he detained me here
And by force he coupled with me.
I had to yield to his strength,
I could never thwart him.)

Since Eleine dies before she can be raped, the horror of the giant's crime is transferred to his violent abduction of Eleine, while forced sexual intercourse is displaced onto the ancient and lower-class nurse.

If we understand the story of Arthur, as it is related in the vernacular chronicles, to be an ideological legitimation of monarchy and ultimately of the imperialistic ambition that marked the late twelfth-century aristocratic diaspora, then we should be struck by the centrality of rape to the legend, by its obsessive and symptomatic repetitiveness. Arthur's history is structured by rape. Uther Pendragon's rape of Igerna, which leads to Arthur's conception, begins the story. Mordred's rape of Guinevere ends Arthur's career and life. (Medieval historians portray Mordred's abduction of Guinevere variously as consensual or forced, depending on their political loyalties, but the distinction is beside the point; if rape is defined by abduction it cannot be obviated by the woman's consent. The crime lies in stealing a woman from the man under whose authority she lives.)

The Mont St. Michel giant's rape of Eleine and Arthur's vengeance for that act occupy a pivotal moment in Arthurian history. Having previously received an embassy from the Roman emperor demanding tribute, Arthur refuses to pay or to recognize the emperor's authority over him. He assembles an army and travels to Brittany, which will serve as a staging point for his conquest of the continent. With this move, Arthur's dynastic ambitions become imperial ones. No longer content to be merely king of England, he lays claim to the imperial crown, establishing the legitimacy of his claim through a genealogical link with his predecessors Belinus, Constantine, and Maximian.

While in Brittany Arthur hears of a giant, called Dinabunc by Wace, who has abducted his kinswoman Eleine, niece (or, according to Laȝamon, daughter) of King Hoel. The giant has taken her to the remote and inaccessible Mont St. Michel. How does the narration of this incident function generically to transform Arthur from local to world historical hero? How does it legitimate imperial ambition? In *Ravishing Maidens,* Gravdal argues that in the genre of romance, rape narratives can have five principal meanings (44). Three of these, it seems to us, are relevant to Wace's and Laȝamon's accounts of the Mont St. Michel giant and may be significant for our understanding of rape as a generic component of vernacular history, as a "nodal point (*point de capiton* is the term Lacan uses) that 'quilts' an ideological formation" (Žižek, *Sublime Object,* 72). First, rape can function as a trope for military prowess. Arthur proves his worthiness to contest with the Roman emperor for control of all Europe by defeating the giant/rapist. Through this strategic display of violence, he accrues the symbolic capital of military reputation. Wace, like Geoffrey, further emphasizes the significance of the killing of the Mont St. Michel giant by linking this incident to Arthur's encounter with another giant, Riun. In this encounter Arthur earns his reputation as a warrior by defeating a giant who demands his defeated opponents' beards—the symbol of their masculinity—as a tribute. Out of these beards he has fashioned a coat, which serves as a visual symbol of his appropriation of their reputation. Arthur's victory over this giant earns him the coat, which then becomes the sign of his military prowess—of his ability to use violence to achieve tactical aims. By knitting together Arthur's defeat of the giant Riun with his defeat of the Mont St. Michel giant, the narrative unmistakably associates the masculinity represented by the beards and that represented by the possession—even the forcible possession—of women.

The second meaning carried by the rape scene is as a social marker that distinguishes the nobility from all other classes. Insofar as either historian aestheticizes rape in this episode—that is, uses it as a sign of female beauty (Gravdal, *Ravishing Maidens,* 44)—it is in the service of marking class distinctions. Eleine must be characterized as an innocent yet nubile aristocratic woman, which is about all we learn of her. The narrative accomplishes this end in several ways. Both accounts report Eleine's death through the narrative of her wet nurse and foster mother. The effect is to infantilize Eleine, preserving her innocence—her asexuality—while recognizing her sexual value as Hoel's niece and an aristocratic lady. Our attention is focused not on the relations between Eleine and her uncle, between Eleine and the king, between Eleine and a potential suitor, or even between Eleine and her abductor, but on the relation between the young girl and her surrogate mother.

A nurrir m'esteit commandee;
Lasse, pur quei l'ai tant nurrie (11403–4)

(I was ordered to nurse her;
Alas, why did I nurse her so much?)

bewails the nurse mother in Wace. Laȝamon's translation of Wace drama-
tizes the intimacy of their relationship:

Wale Eleine. wale deore maide.
Wale þat iche þe uedde. þat iche þe vuostredde. (12904–5)

(Alas! Helen; alas! dear maid,
Alas! that I thee fed, that I thee fostered.)

Embroidering on Geoffrey's disembodied portrayal of the nurse-child
bond, the vernacular historians embody a material relationship based on
the exchange of milk between mother and infant.

Wace deliberately contrasts the two women's rapes as a pointed reminder of the class difference between them:

La pucele volt purgesir,
Mais tendre fu, nel pout suffrir;
Trop fu ahueges, trop fu granz,
Trop laiz, trop gros e trop pesanz;
L'aume li fist del cors partir,
Nel pout Eleine sustenir. (11407–12)

([The giant] wanted to couple with the maiden,
But she was tender, she could not endure him.
He was too huge, he was too big,
Too ugly, too large and too heavy;
He made her soul depart from her body,
Eleine could not bear him.)

Eleine is so delicate, so refined and "tender" that she cannot endure the
crude advances of the gross and horrifying giant. She simply perishes on
the spot. When the giant turns to slake his lust on the old woman, she is
more able to endure.

Par force m'ad ci retenue
E par force m'ad purgeüe.
Sa force m'estuet otreier,
Ne li puis mie defforcier.
Mais plus sui vielle e plus sui forte

E plus sui granz e plus sui dure
E plus hardie e plus seüre
Que ne fu damisele Eleine. (11424–31)

(By force he detained me here
And by force he coupled with me.
I had to yield to his strength,
I could never thwart him.
But I am older and I am stronger
And I am bigger and I am tougher
And bolder and more solid
Than ever was my young lady Eleine.)

The narrative stresses her difference from Eleine—her otherness. Her age and lower status sexualize her, mark her as someone already possessing sexual knowledge. This sexualization connects her with the giant in a grotesque and coercive parody of lower-class domesticity. The scene is sketchy in Wace but receives Pantagruelian treatment in Laʒamon, where the giant returns with twelve swine, sets six of them on the fire, has sex with the old woman, gets up and eats the six swine, and finally, with a stretch and a roar, goes to sleep (12960 ff). Certainly it is possible to see the old woman as more dispensable, her rape less horrific and hence more representable because she is old—past childbearing—but also, we think, because her presence serves by contrast to call attention to Eleine's social and sexual status.

The third function of rape in this scene, and the most significant for our purposes, is as a spectacle of political hegemony, of Arthur's imperial and dynastic ambition. In both vernacular histories, Arthur defeats the giant/rapist not simply as an individual knight errant out for personal glory—a marker of the romance as a genre—but as the established king of England and potential emperor of Rome. His act of vengeance against the giant provides a fitting transition for Arthur from king to emperor (or potential emperor). Arthur has a prophetic dream prior to his encounter with the giant. When asked to explain this dream of a dragon's battle with and ultimate victory over a gigantic, flying bear, Arthur's wise men claim, according to Wace:

Que li draguns qu'ils out veü
Esteit de lui senefiance,
E li granz urs ert demunstrance
D'alcun gaiant qu'il occirreit,
Ki d'estrange terre vedreit;
Li altre d'altre guise espunent,

Nequedent tuit a bien le turnent. (11267–74)

(That of the dragon which he has seen
He [Arthur] himself was the meaning
And the big bear was a foreshadowing
Of some giant whom he would kill,
Who would come from a foreign land;
Others explain in other manners,
Nonetheless all turn it to good.)

Arthur rejects the explication of his sages and offers another, in which his conquest of the giant serves as a metonymy for his conquest of the Roman empire: "Ainz est, dist il, ço m'est viaire, / La guerre que nus devum faire/ Entre mei e li empereür" (Instead, [the meaning] is truly to me / The war which we must wage / Between myself and the emperor; 11275–77). Laȝamon similarly incorporates the prophetic dream to demonstrate Arthur's power and potential for violence, but his discussion of the dream's analysis is, we think, indicative of his anxieties—far greater anxieties than those of Wace—concerning his marginalization from Norman patronage networks. Laȝamon offers no commentary on the dream:

Biscopes þis iherden. & boc-ilærede men,
þis iheorden eorles. þis iherden beornes;
ælc, bi his witte. wisdom sæiden,
þis sweuen aræhten.
Ne durste þer na cniht. to ufele ræcchen na wiht.
leoste he sculden leosen. his leomen þat weoren him deore. (12788–93)

(The bishops listened to this, and men who'd learned from books;
Earls listened to it; barons listened to it;
Each from his understanding spoke intelligently:
They interpreted this dream [as they thought appropriate];
No knight there had the courage to interpret it unfavourably
Lest he would be made to lose those parts he especially loved.)

Throughout his translation, Laȝamon shows interpretation—either unhappy interpretation or misinterpretation—to be a dangerous activity, one which can carry severe penalties for those who draw power from the business of giving advice. This as much as anything sets Laȝamon's account apart from Geoffrey's and Wace's, suggesting, perhaps, his uncomfortable position as a Saxon priest negotiating indifferent or even hostile Norman patronage networks.

The period of the aristocratic diaspora, not surprisingly since it was a period in which political boundaries were being constantly redrawn, was also marked, as R. I. Moore and John Boswell have both noted, by a growing intolerance and even persecution of those who lay outside the dominant hegemony. Whereas Boswell documents growing state and Church persecution of same sex love, Moore explores the creation of the "persecuting society" in the treatment during the high Middle Ages of heretics, lepers, and Jews. The events that the episode of the Mont St. Michel giant displaces as fantasy were certainly more mundane, though hardly less horrific. They included the persecution and massacre of heretics, lepers, Jews, homosexuals or sodomites (depending on your perspective), and anyone else who for whatever reason threatened the political security of the ruling classes (Moore, *Persecuting Society*). Arthur, however, could hardly achieve world historical stature by riding around the countryside dispatching bands of peasants, lepers, and Jews. As the representative of the forces of order and religion, Arthur must triumph over more menacing and hence more prestigious foes.

The Mont St. Michel giant's rape of Eleine, then, serves as a nodal point (point de capiton) that "quilts" together networks of ideological relations these histories were designed to reproduce, while itself producing a certain excess (Žižek calls this "surplus-enjoyment") that exceeds the rape's ideological and structural function. The event coalesces several anxieties about the maintenance of boundaries during times when they are being redrawn in potentially disturbing ways. The particular ideological field being quilted by the rape is attempting to shore up the boundaries between those born to wealth and those born to poverty, between those trained to fight and those who are not, and, most significantly, between familiar and foreign.

Both Wace and Laȝamon represent the giant not as a homegrown threat but, following Geoffrey of Monmouth, as an exotic outsider; he is said to be from Spain. The giant's origin strikes us as significant, speaking to the aristocratic anxieties represented in the scene on Mont St. Michel. The second half of the eleventh century witnessed extraordinary upheaval in Moslem Spain, ripples of which could be felt at least as far north as Burgundy. During the eleventh century, the Burgundian abbey of Cluny, perhaps the most renowned and influential religious house in the West, was lavishly patronized by Spanish kings, who funneled to the monastery tributes received from the taifa rulers of al-Andalus, the petty kings who ruled Muslim Spain after the eleventh-century dissolution of the Umayyad caliphate of Cordoba. As Richard Fletcher has argued, the Clunaic economy was utterly dependent on the continued flow of gold from al-Andalus; a portion of this annual tribute of two thousand gold pieces was being used to finance the rebuilding of the abbey church. In the last decades of the eleventh century, however, the Moslem rulers of al-Andalus came under considerable criticism from Islamic fundamentalists for embracing increasingly secular lifestyles and forging alliances with Christian Europe. For example, in 1064, shortly before his death, the scholar Ibn Hazm condemned Spain's taifa rulers: "by God, I swear that if the tyrants were to learn that they could attain their ends more easily by adopting the religion of the Cross, they would certainly hasten to profess it! Indeed, we see that they ask Christians for help and allow them to take away Muslim men, women, and children as captives to their lands. Frequently they protect them in their attacks against the most inviolable lands and ally themselves with them in order to gain security" (Fletcher, *Moorish Spain*, 109). The Moslem strategy of appeasement described in this passage, along with its concomitant cultural assimilation, was not enough, however, to satisfy the increasing pressures of the Christian world's expansionism. Spanish kings were forced to acquire more and more resources to meet the escalating demands of their vassals, which included not just gold but also slaves, horses, and land. The increasingly aggressive posture of the Christian lords toward Islamic Spain drove the taifa rulers into the arms of the fundamentalist Almoravid factions. Finally, like Hengest and Horsa of Britain's early history, the Almoravids ultimately displaced the very leaders they had come to protect from an immediate external threat.

The ascendancy of the Almoravids in Islamic Spain dramatically altered the relationship between the Christian and Islamic worlds. Compared with their cultivated predecessors, the Almoravids must have seemed grotesque to European Christians. Fletcher describes them as "outsiders, . . . unsophisticated tribesmen, materially and culturally impoverished." Their leader Yusuf "dressed in skins, reeked of camels, and spoke Arabic only with difficulty. It is impossible to imagine him at the elegant soirées of the Abbadid court of Seville" (Fletcher, *Moorish Spain*, 108). During the early twelfth century, the relationship between Christians and the Almoravids was marked by escalating belligerency. Christian rulers abandoned all pretenses of benign exploitation in favor of a policy of outright conquest. Within a generation, Almoravid rule was being torn apart by Christian incursions from the north, internal strife, and the threat of even more radically fundamentalist Moslems—the Almohads—from the south. Reports about conflicts between Christian chivalry and what to Europeans must have seemed like an alien, even demonic mass, however exaggerated by propaganda, would likely have reached as far as England, where they may have found their way into Geoffrey's characterization of the Mont St. Michel giant and later into the vernacular accounts produced by Wace and Laʒamon.

The giant figures foreignness represented as monstrosity. His defeat carries world historical import in the context of the larger conflict between Arthur and the emperor Lucius, which is portrayed as a conflict between Christian Europe and the rest of the non-European, and largely Moslem, world. While from our geographical and historical perspective, Arthur might seem, at best, to be king of a marginal outpost of the Roman Empire who is invading a wealthier, more powerful, and hegemonic neighbor, both Wace and Laʒamon—following Geoffrey of Monmouth—reconfigure the sides. Arthur's army is composed of knights from England, Scotland, and Ireland but also Jutland, Iceland, Norway, Denmark, Orkney, Man, Normandy, Anjou, Poitou, Flanders, Boulogne, and Lorraine. Together these principalities, coupled with Arthur's claim to the lineage of former emperors Belinus, Constantine, and Maximian, define much of what we usually think of as the Northern European hegemony. The emperor's army, on the other hand, seems composed almost exclusively of foreigners from alien, exotic, and primarily Middle Eastern and Mediterranean lands. They include the king of Greece and the duke of Boeotia as well as the kings of Turkey, Egypt, Crete, Syria, Phrygia, Babylon, Media, Libia, Bitunia, Ituria, Africa, and Ethiopia. The last, according to Laʒamon, "of Ethiope he brohte þa bleomen" (12666); Wace writes: "Africans amena e Mors/ E porter fist ses granz tresors" ([He] led Africans and Moors / And had his great treasure brought along; 11109–12). Like the giant of Mont St. Michel, these potential invaders from the south represent the threat of cultural, political, and sexual violence. Destroying them ensures not only domestic tranquillity but expansion of European hegemony.

Curiously absent from the ranks of both sides are the Spanish, who are represented only by the giant, though, as we suggest above, Spain was at the heart of Christian-Moslem conflict for much of the eleventh and twelfth centuries. In the form of the giant, the actual threat is dehumanized, literally made monstrous, in the interests of creating a credible opponent—a giant—with whom Arthur can exchange violence and, by doing so, win the right to lay claim to empire. Far from calling readers' attention to the legal and social consequences of rape, then, the fantasy renders them invisible. Justification for political, economic, and ideological expansionism is frequently found in the demonization of those "others" who populate contested territories, and this demonization almost always includes a sexual component (Moore, *Persecuting Society*, 100–101). The other is invariably seen as sexually menacing. As Moore writes, "Pollution fear . . . is fear that the privileged feel of those at whose expense their privilege is enjoyed. Marked sensitivity to the possibilities of sexual pollution may therefore suggest that the boundaries which the prohibitions in question protect are threatened, or thought to be. Conversely (what may in practice amount to the same thing) if new social boundaries are being established it will be appropriate to consider whether heightened vigilance over sexual matters may be one means of securing them" (101). As boundaries are extended, those at the margins must be assimilated, pushed to more distant margins, or destroyed. These sometimes contradictory impulses—assimilation, marginalization, and destruction—allow for contradictory mythologies of the other—the leper, the heretic, the Jew, the Moslem—as sexually attractive, perhaps even endowed with extraordinary sexual prowess, sexually dangerous, and sexually hideous. These mythologies allow for such various kinds of domination as rape, dispersion, and murder.

The vernacular historians demonstrate Mary Douglas's argument that violations of physical bodies can be metonymies for violations of the political body by representing the giant as aggressively disruptive of the social order; he threatens not only the intactness of Eleine's female body but that of the social body as well. In Wace's account, the giant not only abducts and rapes a high-born virgin; he also lays waste the countryside:

Mult veïssiez les païsanz
Maisuns vuider, porter enfanz,
Femes mener, bestes chacier,
Es munz munter, es bois mucier.
Par bois e par deserz fueient
E encor la murir cremeient.
Tute esteit la terre guerpie,
Tute s'en est la gent fuïe. (11309–16)

(You could see many peasants
Leave their houses, carry their children,
Lead their wives, herd their cattle,
Climb the hills, hide in the woods.
They fled by woods and deserts
And even there feared death.
The whole land was forsaken,
All the people have fled from it.)

In Laȝamon's account, the threat to the political hegemony is figured by the giant's violent breaching of the walls designed to keep out such chaotic threats to order—a parallel rape of the social body.

þa ȝaten alle he to brac. and binnen he gon wende,
He nom þare halle wah. and helden hine to grunde;
þaes bures dure he warp adun. þat heo tobarst a uiuen. (12919–21)

(He smashed all the gates and squeezed himself inside,
He grabbed the curtain wall and hurled it to the ground,
He tossed down the chamber door and it shattered in five pieces.)

Wace—who throughout most of his career profited from the largesse of Norman imperialism—suggests that Arthur's destruction of the giant comes as a boon to the peasantry, which has been especially harassed by the creature. His narrative thus indicates that the aristocracy must keep the peasantry in check not only to maintain its own privilege but for the sake of the peasantry as well. On the other hand, by mentioning the giant's gestures of geopolitical transgression, Laȝamon—who writes from a much more marginalized cultural position as a Saxon priest from Arley, who would have witnessed, and perhaps even suffered, imperialism's oppressions—strengthens the association between the monstrous "other" and the behavior of an invading army.

Simultaneous to expansionism, and coincidental to the demonization of foreigners, lurks an anxiety that those at the margins, like the Almoravids, not only may succeed in reclaiming their previously held properties (including the women taken from them by invading forces) but also may embark upon imperialistic ventures of their own. Just as imperialistic forces make claim to the women and land they capture, causing their forced assimilation, these same forces anxiously eye the situation of their own property should those on the margins attempt an incursion. Their anxiety hardens defenses against incursions while at the same time fueling further imperialistic enthusiasms—there can be no rest until "difference" is obliterated. The genre of historical narrative necessarily reflects these anxieties and their antidotes, and we find them manifest in the story of the Mont St. Michel giant.

After the giant's defeat, Arthur has the creature beheaded and authorizes expenditures to establish a church honoring the Virgin Mary. Eliade addresses such a consecration as a victory of the sacred over the profane, but we are struck by the ideological ramifications of this gesture. In the place where the giant performed his grotesqueries, in the place where carnivalesque gestures of uncontrolled eating, drinking, and sex were acted out, is now a religious institution. The church functions to restore a specifically Christian order, to restore the purity that was temporarily lost with the giant's rape of Eleine. It also serves to justify Arthur's expansion of his borders, to further acts of imperialism, and to legitimate ambitions of world conquest.

Notes

1. Translations of *Laȝamon's Brut* are from Rosamund Allen. Translations of *Le Roman de Brut de Wace* are our own. We thank Anna Roberts for her help with the translations.

Works Cited

Bartlett, Robert. *The Making of Europe: Conquest, Colonization, and Cultural Change.* Princeton: Princeton University Press, 1993.

Blacker, Jean. *The Faces of Time: Portrayal of the Past in Old French and Latin Historical Narrative of the Anglo-Norman* Regnum. Austin: University of Texas Press, 1994.

Boswell, John. *Christianity, Social Tolerance, and Homosexuality: Gay People in Western Europe from the Beginning of the Christian Era to the Fourteenth Century.* Chicago: University of Chicago Press, 1980.

Brundage, James A. "Rape and Seduction in Medieval Canon Law." In *Sexual Practices and the Medieval Church,* ed. Vern L. Bullough and James A. Brundage, 141–48. Buffalo: Prometheus, 1982.

Douglas, Mary. *Purity and Danger: An Analysis of Concepts of Pollution and Taboo.* New York: Praeger, 1966.

Duby, Georges. *The Knight, the Lady, and the Priest: The Making of Modern Marriage in Medieval France.* Trans. Barbara Bray. New York: Pantheon, 1983.

Eliade, Mircea. *The Sacred and the Profane: The Nature of Religion.* Trans. Willard R. Trask. New York: Harcourt Brace Jovanovich, 1959.

Elkins, Sharon K. *Holy Women of Twelfth Century England.* Chapel Hill: University of North Carolina Press, 1988.

Fletcher, Richard. *Moorish Spain.* Berkeley: University of California Press, 1992.

Gravdal, Kathryn. *Ravishing Maidens: Writing Rape in Medieval French Literature and Law.* Philadelphia: University of Pennsylvania Press, 1991.

Greenblatt, Stephen. *Learning to Curse: Essays in Early Modern Culture.* London: Routledge, 1990.

Laȝamon. *Laȝamon's Brut.* Ed. G. L. Brook and R. F. Leslie. Oxford: Oxford University Press, 1963.

Lawman. *Brut.* Trans. Rosamund Allen. New York: St. Martin's Press, 1992.

Moore, R. I. *The Formation of a Persecuting Society.* Oxford: Blackwell, 1987.

Shichtman, Martin B., and Laurie A. Finke. "Profiting from the Past: History as Symbolic Capital in the *Historia regum britanniæ.*" *Arthurian Literature* 12 (1993): 1–35.

Spiegel, Gabrielle M. *Romancing the Past: The Rise of Vernacular Prose Historiography in Thirteenth-Century France.* Berkeley: University of California Press, 1993.

Wace, *Le Roman de Brut de Wace.* Ed. Ivor Arnold. 2 vols. Société des Anciens Textes Français. Paris: Société des Anciens Textes Français, 1938–40.

William of Malmesbury. *Chronicle of the Kings of England.* Trans. J. A. Giles. London: Bell and Daldy, 1866.

Žižek, Slavoj. *The Sublime Object of Ideology.* London: Verson, 1989.

4

Consuming Passions

Variations on the Eaten Heart Theme

Madeleine Jeay

The *translatio* by Chrétien de Troyes, in his *Philomena*, of Ovid's tale of horror and cruelty in the sixth story of the *Metamorphoses* stands alone like a *hapax* in medieval French literature. The contrast between the open savagery of the Ovidian myth and Chrétien's usual *mesure* is so striking that doubts have been raised about its attribution to the author of *Erec and Enide* (Schulze-Busacker, "*Philomena*"). This story, which relates the sequence of the most horrible and taboo transgressions in human society—rape, incest, murder, mutilation, infanticide, and cannibalism—is not rewritten again until the fourteenth-century version in the *Ovide moralisé*. Thus, there is no direct legacy during the French Middle Ages of the classical myth of Philomela, who was raped and then mutilated, her tongue being severed, by her brother-in-law Tereus. After the rape, she embroiders the details of her misfortune on a cloth sent to her sister and Tereus's wife, Procne, who, wanting to take revenge on her husband, kills their son, Ithis.[1] The two sisters then cook the child and serve him to Tereus. The tale ends with their metamorphosis: Tereus becomes a hoopoe, Procne a swallow, and Philomela a nightingale.[2]

Quite evidently, such an open expression of violence and ferocity does not correspond to the literary manifestations of medieval sensibility. If the story of the crimes told by Ovid, and Chrétien after him, has a posterity in medieval poetry and narratives, it will certainly be as a result of the process of aestheticization theorized by Gravdal in her work on the literary representation of the rape and abduction of women.[3] One of the factors underlying that process is the normalizing effect that accompanies the transfer from the narrative still marked by a mythical dimension—Philomela's metamorphosis—to literary artifacts, narratives related to the legend of the eaten heart.

I argue that the series of texts recounting the theme of the eaten heart should be read in the light of the story of Philomela. If not directly related, these texts nevertheless represent branches of the same tree. My reasons for drawing this link are not primarily of a narrative nature, despite clear analogies in the sequence of events leading to the act of cannibalism: murder by revenge, mutilation of a dead body, cannibalism by revenge and its revelation to the person who just committed it. The triad involved in Ovid's tale—mother, father, and son—belong to a territory distinct from the courtly triad of a lady, lover, and husband. Following that path would amount to the investigation of yet another layer of meaning connected to the motif, a layer still closer to its mythical roots.[4] Instead, I propose to investigate the connection—the node—between the Philomela narratives and the set of stories connected to the so-called "eaten heart motif": the metaphorical figure of the nightingale. That metaphor functions in medieval love poetry and narratives beyond the narrower context of the eaten heart texts. Therefore, the very connection between the texts leads beyond the limited focus of narrative sequencing and allows us to posit a link between the courtly love tradition, on one hand, and the mythical equation between sexual transgressions, blurred identities, and cannibalism, on the other hand.

What interests me most in this essay is showing how the process of metaphorization, because it is an oblique way of expression, contributes to the depiction of sexual violence in the literature of courtly love. We shall see how the image of the nightingale, among other birds, allows expression of the violence inherent in love and how it posits violence as a consequence of sexual transgression—the transgression which in turn results from the confusion of distinctions brought about by desire. However, in that analysis we must acknowledge that the metaphor, because of its polysemy, calls for a theoretically complex interpretation. As we shall see, it cannot be reduced to the cultural habit of conceptualizing male violence against women as a positive expression of love (the model proposed by Gravdal in *Ravishing Maidens*, 20). My purpose is to make explicit the complexity of relationships subsumed in the metaphor of the nightingale. The question we must ask is: does the language of birds contribute to the normalization of male violence or does it allow breaches in the univocity of the expression of male culture?

The scenario of the eaten heart narratives is as follows: a jealous husband has the heart of his wife's lover cooked and eaten by the lady who, when told the truth, chooses death. In the first example of this story (if we omit the mention of the *lai* of *Guiron* in Thomas's *Tristan*), the *vida* of the troubadour Guillem of Cabestaing, the wife of Raimon de Castel Roussillon vows what will become a topos in subsequent texts: she has eaten so good a meal that she will never eat anything else.[5] Threatened by the sword of her furious husband, she throws herself through the window. In a longer version, after the news of and reasons for the lady's death have been brought to the attention of the king of Aragon, he punishes the count of Castel Rousillon and has the lovers buried in the same tomb.

The *Lai d'Ignauré,* attributed to Renaut de Beaujeu, presents a parodic version of this scenario, linking it to the genre of the *fabliau,* and to a certain extent diluting its violence. When the twelve ladies loved by Ignauré discover the truth of their common fate, their first thought is to take revenge, threatening him with knives. However, the knight's *biau parlers* (sweet talk) convinces them to resort to the less radical solution of choosing one of the ladies for his exclusive love. In an ironic turn of events, it is precisely his new loyalty that leads the lovers to tragedy. As the text explicitly states, had Ignauré maintained his habit of visiting several ladies, his too frequent visits to his beloved would not have been discovered nor the truth of their misfortune revealed by an infamous *losengier* to the twelve husbands.[6] In a striking variant to the topos, the husbands have not only the heart but also the penis of the dismembered Ignauré cooked and presented to the ladies, who starve themselves to death after the revelation of the nature of such a delicate meal.

The third text, in the French tradition of the eaten heart, openly plays with the stereotypes of courtly literature in an obvious exercise of literalization of its clichés—among them, the exchange of hearts between lovers. The plot of the *Roman du Castelain de Couci et de la Dame de Fayel* by Jakemes nicely develops the most common topoi of lyric poetry, from the lover imploring the lady to heal his love sickness to the secret trysts and the inevitable denunciation by a slanderer, in this case a lady secretly in love with the Châtelain. Against his rival, the husband does not use direct violence but cunning. The husband binds the rival to a promise: the lover is to take the cross made by himself, in order to follow the Lady of Fayel and her husband. Once the rival is committed, the husband renounces his promise. Injured, the Châtelain asks his servant to restore to the Lady of Fayel, after his death, what belongs to her, namely his heart and a plait of the hair she had given him when they had parted. The husband intercepts the casket.

His suspicions confirmed by reading the Châtelain's last message to the lady, he takes revenge in the way we know. She starves herself to death after consuming the Châtelain's heart; her relatives avenge her.

The common sequence of anthropophagy does not in itself account for the connection between these three texts and the classical tradition of Philomela's tragedy. In a recent study, Jean-Jacques Vincensini strictly defines the eaten heart motif as the combination of three components: adultery, murder, and the unintentional ingestion of an eroticized body part. According to him, the specificity of the motif does not lie in its most striking feature—cannibalism—but rather in allowing the transfer of a sexual union to an identification based on food. The denomination proposed by Vincensini for the motif of the eaten heart—the cannibalistic revenge for a matrimonial disruption—presents a double advantage (Vincensini, "Figure de l'imaginaire," 452–54). First, it provides grounds for the distinction between the eaten heart story and other tales of anthropophagy. Second, as a basic structure of meaning at the deep semantic level, it establishes links with narratives possessing a similar structure of content. The level of generalization justifies the hypothesis that two different sorts of matrimonial disruption, incest and adultery, induce the same consequence.

However, the relationship I propose between the story of Philomela and the eaten heart narratives is certainly not one of filiation. Rather, the analogy revealed by comparison of their content structure is of a mythical nature. Studies of cannibalism (a recurring feature of many fairy tales and legends) confirm the link it has with sexuality.[7] In classical mythology, the story of Oedipus presents the association of patricide, incest, and anthropophagy, providing the emblematic example of the parallel established by anthropologists between sexual transgression and cannibalism (Moreau, "A propos d'Oedipe," 101). Both transgressions consist in the consumption of the same—an erasing of differences which ends in violence (113).

At first sight, the notion of sameness does not apply to the narratives of the eaten heart based on the stereotypical love triangle of husband, lover, and lady. However, a basis for their relation to the story of Philomela lies in their common treatment of sexual transgression. Beyond the variants on figures involved in the act of cannibalism, we may identify the same equation: cannibalism revolves around a disruption of matrimonial and sexual rules. These tales of duplicity and revenge have a distinctly mythical dimension.[8] Taking this dimension into account leads to an interpretative approach that addresses the whole network of texts connected to a given motif, in our case the nightingale.[9]

The motif of the nightingale provides a link among the texts, leading to a multilayered reading. Each text will have to be read in itself and in the intertext of the whole network, the two perspectives interacting with each other. This kind of double approach applies generally to medieval literature, the rhetorical character of which has to be taken into account but not at the expense of its cultural significance.

Thanks to its polysemy, the metaphor operates at both these levels. The analysis of the metaphor will therefore show that the notion of sameness, brought to the fore by an anthropological interpretation of narratives of cannibalism, applies to the medieval stories of the eaten heart. As a result, I argue that the language of the metaphor conveys in its cryptic way a conception of the courtly relationship much closer to these recent interpretations, which stress its ambiguity and potential violence, than to the conventional view of an idealized lady.

A series of comparisons helps explain the functioning of the metaphorization of courtly love through the image of the nightingale. Let us set down the analogies first before detailing them. Beyond the obvious analogy between the nightingale and the singing subject—the courtly lover—our texts equate the lover and the husband and place the lady in a problematic position. The rivalry between the two men implies their potential identification.

In order to illustrate the possible distribution of roles in the nightingale metaphor in the context of the courtly love triangle, two texts are added to the three examples of the eaten heart theme. In the *Laostic* by Marie de France, the nightingale has in some ways the same function as the heart in these stories. The bird is strangled and violently thrown by the husband on the lady's dress; she then sends its corpse to her lover with an embroidery telling him what happened. In the *Escoufle* by Jean Renart, the rival and possible alter ego of the hero, savagely dismembered by him, is represented by the bird—a vulgar kite, which gives the romance its title. Naturally, the substitution of one bird for another reorients the interpretation of the episode.

The representations of the nightingale stem from its dominant presence in lyric (especially troubadour) poetry.[10] Associated with spring and the joy of love, the nightingale is a figure of the lover-poet. Furthermore, it supports the whole spectrum of the expressions of love, from sexual pleasure (since it functions as one of the euphemistic designations of the penis as a bird; Planche, "*Est vrais,*" 255) to mystical symbolism. The presence of the nightingale in mystic poetry, where it is related to Christ's Passion, is coherent with the metaphor's tragic dimension in classical literature.[11]

Even if medieval texts using the image of the nightingale turned away from the brutal cruelty of the classical myth, they retained its heritage of sadness and violence. In particular, one motif present in mystic and profane poetry attests to the fact that violence remained part of the bird's semantism. It manifests itself as a play on the two syllables meant to transcribe the song of the nightingale: "*Oci! Oci!*"—the Latin equivalent of "Kill! Kill!" Its first occurrence is at the very end of Chrétien's *Philomena,* in the narrator's last comments about the song of the nightingale. He reproduces the melody of the bird in an oxymoronic expression that synthesizes eloquently the contradictory range of significations it embodies. The two syllables, summarizing so adequately the ferocity of the story just told, are said by Chrétien to evoke the sweetness of the song of the nightingale heard at the end of winter, when spring comes, a song of hatred against treacherous lovers who are disloyal to their ladies.[12] The coda openly draws a link between the tragedy of Philomela and the ambiguity of emotions suggested by lyric love poetry. In other examples, as in the *Philomena praevia* by John Peacham, the bird's homicidal cry translates the sadness of the Passion; the nightingale represents the soul. In some profane poems, it openly manifests an element of violence and terror, as in two poems by Guillaume le Vinier, in which the violence can be certainly linked to Chrétien's *Philomena* (Pfeffer, *Change of Philomel,* 134–36).

A few observations can be drawn in conclusion to this enumeration of meanings carried by the nightingale. The crude violence of the Ovidian tale, incompatible with the tradition of love poetry, had to be euphemized. However, it could not be completely obliterated, and both sides of the bird's image were considered jointly in spite of their contradictory nature. Most lyric poetry presents sweetened versions of the torments of love, where the voice of the nightingale appropriately tempers elation with melancholy. However, its appearance in some other texts suggests that spring is not the season of pure joy.

A study by James J. Wilhelm shows that March can be the *Cruelest Month* in classical and medieval lyrics. His enumeration of myths related to spring, especially in Ovid's *Fasti,* ends with the question: why are myths of rape, revenge, and murder associated with flowers, birds, and the most beautiful of seasons? After the rapes of Rhea Silvia, the Sabines, and Proserpina, Ovid tells of the rape of Flora, who becomes the goddess of flowers—she has created them from blood—enjoying the perpetual spring of the Golden Age. Two spring flowers, the narcissus and the hyacinth, are also rooted in myths of violence (Wilhelm, *Cruelest Month,* 37–39).

With this range of potential significations attached to the nightingale and its associations with courtly love in mind, let us now see how they may contribute to the deciphering of the texts related to the eaten heart. In the earliest occurrences of the motif, the different versions of the vida of the troubadour Guillem of Cabestaing, the respective dispositions of the two rival males are clearly stated (Boutière, *Biographies*, 530–55; Egan, *Vies*, 102–9). Guillem epitomizes courtesy and chivalry, and Raimon of Castel Roussillon, described as cruel and arrogant, represents excessive jealousy. Not only is he characterized as the villain but the lady's attitude annihilates his revenge, reducing it to an uncontrolled outburst of madness. She uses food—her refusal to absorb any food after she consumes her ideal of delicacy, the lover's heart—as a provocation aimed at her husband. Raimon's response to her statement—assaulting her with his sword—indicates that her intention has been understood. Her death is not presented as the fatal destiny of a victim but as the last decision of a woman who retains her capacity to determine her fate until the last minute: she throws herself through the window.

It is worth mentioning that additions to or modifications of the basic plot of the vida introduce a patriarchal bias. They attenuate the impact of the woman's act, now presented as the involuntary consequence of her flight in panic. Her character in the *razo* (a commentary that introduced the songs) is also more assertive and therefore more questionable. Here, she is the one who initiates the affair with Guillem and finally provokes its disclosure through a song she has requested of her lover, which has been understood all too well by her husband. The count appears here to conform to the persona of the courtly knight, whose concern for his wife's conduct is motivated more by his responsibility toward her reputation than by sheer jealousy.

On the other hand, the final episode added by three manuscripts of the vida upholds the portrayal of the three characters in the original vida. News of the tragedy having reached him, the king of Aragon, suzerain of both lords, passes an unequivocal judgment. Raimon's territories are confiscated, he is jailed, and the lovers are reunited in the same grave. A last detail indicates that Guillem's vida should be understood as an exemplum, a lesson of proper behavior given to courtly lovers. The king orders that each year, knights and ladies of the county of Roussillon celebrate the anniversary of the two lovers' deaths. The longer version of the vida literalizes the topos of love martyrdom in such a way that the lover-poet and the lady experience a triumphant re-membering through ritual celebration and the narration of their story. The troubadour's dismembering and the lady's violent death act as preludes to their final and definitive reunion.

In Boccaccio's adaptation of the vida of Guillem of Cabestaing, the lady plays a major role. She claims full responsibility for her unfaithfulness. We are told that she has fallen in love first and waited for her lover's solicitations. In her final confrontation with her husband, she insists that her disloyalty to him was an act of free will on her part. Publicly assuming her own choices and decisions, she denies having been the object of her lover's violence and, as a consequence, wants to be considered as the only one to be blamed and to deserve punishment.

Coming after these statements, the lady's death is presented by Boccaccio as pure provocation on her part. Her refusal to eat functions, as in the vida, as a way to deprive the husband of his revenge—all the more since, again as in the vida, she throws herself through the window in a deliberate decision to match her actions and her words, and not to escape her husband's sword. In contrast to the situation in the razo, there is in Boccaccio no suggestion that her self-assertive attitude went too far, beyond the boundaries of decency. Boccaccio also transforms the epilogue of the story. While maintaining the essence of the vida's perspective, he omits the husband's chastisement and the ritual celebration of the lovers' destiny. Instead, the lesson to be drawn from their adventure, the lesson that was originally given by the recounting of their story, is now engraved in writing on their tomb.

This silencing of the voice is coherent with another major transposition concerning the lover's identity. Boccaccio has entirely left aside the principal element of the vida, the fact that its main character is a troubadour whose songs induced the lady's love and her husband's suspicions. In the *Decameron,* the lover is introduced as a fellow knight and turns out to be the husband's alter ego. Boccaccio stresses the similarity between them. They are close to each other, filled with mutual affection, to the point of participating in tournaments together and wearing identical clothes. Their sameness extends to their identical first name—Guiglielmo—and to the confusion of their surnames. All names refer to a "singing subject" (poet-nightingale). Both men inherited the troubadour's first name. The lover's surname, Guardastagno, is a manifest adaptation of Cabestaing, while the transposition of the husband's name—Rossiglione for Castel-Roussillon—suggests a word play on the Italian equivalent of nightingale (Stone, "The Eaten Heart," 105–7). The lesson presented by Boccaccio links sexual transgression to the blurring of differences. As in the Oedipal association between incest and anthropophagy, here the sexual confusion and lack of differentiation result in cannibalism, the consumption of the same. However, the lady's decision to follow the lover in his death restores the distance between the two men, which should have been maintained but has been abolished by the husband (as suggested by his adoption of the troubadour's name).

The two versions of the eaten heart theme considered so far propose variations on the consequences of sexual transgression in terms of the blurring of necessary distinctions. But at the same time, they point out the mimetic nature of desire as the longing for something one person lacks and another seems to possess. They also stress the interchangeability of the antagonists, whose similarity can only be resolved through violence, thereby installing violence at the very core of desire and its medieval representation, courtly love. The vida, while identifying the husband as the villain, suggests a questioning of the figure of the troubadour-lover. The oxymoronic association of these functions (poet and lover) translates the instability of courtly love—the poet's song publicizing what by definition should be kept secret. The losengier figure, at least in the vida of Guillem de Cabestaing, is another realization of that inherent instability.

Boccaccio shifts the emphasis on the respective status of the partners in a marital relationship in which husband and wife should play their roles as self-determining individuals. The sensitive issue for the husband is to keep the right distance and distinction between himself and other men. Read in that perspective, both renditions of the vida, on the other hand, point to the troubadour's figure as responsible for a dangerous blurring of the necessary distance that should be kept, for a reversal of status that should be avoided.

Through the play on the name Rossiglione, Boccaccio defines the husband as the troubadour's counterpart and implies a connection between the eaten heart theme and the nightingale. For a more emphatic articulation of this link, we turn to Marie de France's *Laostic* and the parodic *Lai d'Ignauré*. Openly parodying the courtly love situation with a fabliau-type lover, seducer of twelve wives, *Ignauré* has also been interpreted as a parody of the Last Supper (Doueihi, "Lure of the Heart," 58). The text parodies, reveals, and synthesizes the characteristic features of the eaten heart theme as identified in the vida and in Boccaccio's adaptation.

Ignauré's transgressions take place at different levels. The most obvious, his lack of restraint in being simultaneously the paramour of twelve ladies, surely deserves vengeance of an exceptional kind. But it does not in itself explain why, in addition to his heart, his penis has also been severed from his body and cooked to be eaten by the ladies.[13] In an interesting, subversive twist of events, it is Ignauré's return to orthodox behavior, that of loyal lover of the lady of his choice, that induces suspicions and the husband's intervention. However, underlying this superficial and subversive causality, a more traditional explanation can be found in the respective positions of husbands, wives, and lover. In contrast to Guillem de Cabestaing's vida and Boccaccio's adaptation, the guilty parties are now the lover and the wives, accomplices in a plot intended to satisfy their lust at the expense of the husbands' honor.

The decision to kill and dismember their lover and offer the cooked body parts to the ladies is not taken in the fury of an outburst of jealous rage but in a cool-blooded act of legitimate revenge. The association between the sexual satisfaction of the ladies and the pleasure taken in the meal about to be prepared for them is clearly articulated by the husbands in their justification of Ignauré's castration. What was, in the two previous versions of the eaten heart, an affirmation of the lady's sense of her self-determination and an intentional provocation on her part—the refusal to eat—obtains here an entirely different meaning. The motif is introduced before Ignauré's death, as a pledge by the ladies to undertake a sort of hunger strike as long as they do not know whether their captured lover is dead or alive.[14] This narrative device succeeds in removing any trace of provocation from the ladies' decision. Added to that, the narrator's qualifying comment eliminates any doubt about their motives and his narrative choices. Calling them *ordes gloutes* (dirty gluttons), he evidently presents their fasting as a logical consequence of their previous lust and greed.

At least, this is one of the implications of this fundamentally ironic text, open to contradictory interpretations. The long evocation of the ladies' starvation becomes an excuse for their nostalgic remembering, part by part, of Ignauré's dismembered body. The episode cannot be interpreted simply as a manifestation of their lack of shame, since their lament is said to be at the origin of a twelve-line lai made about them after their death.[15] The lamenting women are therefore the origin of the poem, providing a clear link between poetry and sexual desire. As Howard Bloch has already recognized, the lai excites the very desire that its moral lesson appears to repress, inviting us to go further and transcend the contradiction ("The Lay and the Law," 197).

In order to reconcile that contradiction, let us look closely at the issues at stake between Ignauré and the twelve husbands. Our reading begins with two details of his portrait. The first is Ignauré's social status. He does not have the attributes usual in the stereotypical praise of the hero; his lineage is twice characterized as lower than the husbands'.[16] Coming from a knight of lower descent, his offense cannot be forgiven. According to the principles of a society of honor, the dishonored husbands' revenge is a duty they must accomplish; yet, the nature of their revenge depends on the social status of the rival. Their first reaction, when informed of their misfortune, is indeed to ask if their rival is a bourgeois or a knight. Bourdieu's analysis of social rules applied to societies of honor provides a rationale for that question. A man dishonors himself if he challenges someone unworthy of taking up the challenge—in this case a bourgeois. Ignauré's inexcusable transgression lies in having challenged the hierarchy, in having dared to behave as a rival when his lower knightly status does not authorize that prerogative.[17] In this tale of hubris, as in Boccaccio's version of Guillem de Cabestaing's vida, violence originates in the blurring of social differences. The mythical equivalent of this blurring is the ingestion of the same, as in the Oedipal archetype equating incest with cannibalism.

The second detail, previously never fully taken into account in the interpretation of the lai, provides another key element for our demonstration. Ignauré is known among women as Lousignol—Nightingale.[18] This *senhal* (a secret code name between lovers for the lady) confirms an identification between the poet and the protagonist of the lai, and even leads to the attribution of a historical identity to Ignauré.[19] According to the vida of Raimbaut d'Aurenga, the name of the minstrel who sings for the troubadour is Rossignol, Nightingale. The transcription from Occitan to *langue d'oïl* of Raimbaut's *senhal* (Linhaura) and the fact that Raimbaut presents himself in a song as a eunuch both confirm the equivalence between the poet and the hero of the lai.[20] The image of the nightingale points to a parallelism with the fate of Guillem de Cabestaing, who, as a lyric poet, could also be given the senhal of "Nightingale."

It is now time to look at the possibilities of expression allowed by the metaphor of the nightingale, by summarizing what emerges from the texts considered so far. From its mythical origin in Ovid's *Metamorphoses*, one of the effects of the metaphor is to inscribe violence as a consequence of sexual transgression, specifically of violations that consist in the blurring of necessary distinctions. Simultaneously, the implication is that this blurring is inherent in the logic of desire. The narratives of the eaten heart posit the dangerous blurring of differences in the relation of rivalry between two men in the context of a courtly love relationship, again identifying violence as its intrinsic component. In courtly love, the desire of one man for a woman bound to another man of higher status is channeled through the songs of a lyric poet. In that primary model, the poet is the designated target of violence not only because of the rivalry between the two men but also because he appears as the usurper of a desire that should remain the prerogative of the knights. The texts analyzed here only slightly reshape the distinctions between the two men: the lover-poet is also a knight—a rival worthy of revenge—but in each case a knight of lower station than the husband, in agreement with the primary model.

If the dismembered poet-nightingale is the primary victim of the husband's aggression, the wife represents the stake of rivalry between men. In the three narratives analyzed so far, she manages to subvert the violence aimed at her so that she does not become its passive and powerless victim. However, she is still the object and playground of that violence. In very specific terms, her body constitutes the battlefield of her husband's vengeful anger either through a cannibalistic ingestion or, as in Marie de France's *Laostic*, as the target of the dead nightingale representing her love, thrown at her by her husband and spoiling her white dress with a red spot of blood.[21]

But in none of these stories does the husband's violence constitute the final word. All of them end with the poet's revenge on his rival's vengeance, thereby dispossessing the husband of the benefits of his act. In spite of the ambiguities and contradictions they manifest, the songs will perpetuate the lovers' memory, reuniting and remembering them.

The last (chronologically) and perhaps the best-known narrative of the eaten heart theme, the *Roman du Castelain de Couci et de la Dame de Fayel,* does not contradict these conclusions. The fact that the lover is not slain under the husband's orders but dies in the crusades constitutes a significant variant to the topos of the eaten heart, not a radical difference. Indeed, as we know, the Châtelain's journey has been indirectly instigated by the count of Fayel. The purpose of this variation is most certainly to dilute the brutal atrocity of the topos in its canonical version and to normalize its violence at the expense of verisimilitude. It is an embalmed heart that is eaten by the Lady of Fayel, after it has been brought from the Holy Land. The detail helps to literalize the courtly love motif of the exchange of hearts between lovers. The Châtelain's intention in having his heart removed, embalmed, and sent back to his lady is to restore what belongs to her.

In *Couci,* the husband's brutal aggression against his rival is still manifest but is metaphorically transferred onto the casket containing the Châtelain's heart. He does not use a key, says the text, but he opens it *a force,* he forces it.[22] A similar dilution of direct confrontation can be observed in the lady's death. She is presented not in an attitude of provocation in response to her husband's cruelty but rather as eager to be reunited with her lover, as in the *Tristan et Iseut* model pervasive throughout *Couci.* Like the motif of the husband's violence toward the lover, the idea of revenge against him is still present here, albeit transferred to the lady's lineage. In *Couci,* her relatives carry out the revenge which in prior versions was her own doing.

In both instances, the displacement of open violence away from the direct confrontation of the three parties involved in the courtly love relationship results in the socialization of violence through a process of normalization. One of the most obvious objects of that process is the lady's attitude and behavior. The ambiguity of her figure and her role in *Couci* is such that it has led to opposite interpretations of the eaten heart episode. Helen Solterer sees in the introduction of this motif a means whereby the lovers achieve their ultimate communion. She evokes the religious parallel of the Eucharist and the development of the cult of the Sacred Heart in order to justify conferring the dimension of a sacrificial meal on the lady's ingestion of her lover's heart (Solterer, "Dismembering," 116–17). In turn, Roberta Krueger sees in *Couci* a tale of duplicity and vengeance, a gradual entrapment of the heroine. According to this critic, the heroine's autonomy diminishes progressively from her decision to engage in a love that would—she thinks—empower her, to her final demise. In that sense, Jakemes might conform to the ethos of courtly love lyrics and romances in undermining the ideal of true love he purports to expound. For Krueger, the common underlying effect of these texts is to abuse women by seductive and dangerously deceptive models (*Women Readers*, 183–216).

In fact, from the beginning of the romance, the Lady of Fayel is aware of the harmful consequences of engaging in an affair with the Châtelain. Her major concern before any involvement of such a kind is to make sure that her honor will be protected. The notion of a sense of honor specific to women, and the necessity of maintaining it, clearly indicates that she is conscious of the fact that, in the real world where love relationships are less than ideal, women are the ones at risk of losing their respectability.[23] This is why she tests the Châtelain at their first secret meeting, keeping him outside the door in the rain to test the firmness of his affection. As a consequence, she almost loses him because of the sickness that ensues from the successful trial (*Couci*, v. 2362–2893).

Even more indicative of the conflict between her awareness and her feelings is the ambiguity of her attitude during the traditional episode of gift giving to the lover. She gives a ribbon and a ring to the Châtelain while denying that they should be understood—as they normally are—as a preliminary to the ultimate gift of her body.[24] If she has been entrapped by her love, it has not been unknowingly.

Another sign of the ambiguity that characterizes the figures of the lady and the poet is the author's dedication of the narrative to his beloved, both in *Ignauré* and in *Couci*. In spite of different first names, the lover-poet of

Couci can be identified with the *trouvère* Gui de Couci. As in *Ignauré*, or in the troubadour's vida, poets cast themselves in the role of successful but unacceptable lovers whose bodies have to be dismembered to be remembered in the songs and narratives that will be made about their tragic fate. In many ways, they are rightly identified with the nightingale, a powerful messenger of the joys of love, and—through the mythical heritage of the metaphor—the appropriate emblem of its inherent sufferings and violence. Postulated by the myth of *Philomena*, the equation between two major transgressions—sexual and alimentary consumption of the same (incest and anthropophagy)—is transposed into the terms of rivalry and competition between men.

For the lord in possession of a woman, the poet-nightingale represents a permanent threat. As a potential successful rival, his situation is all the more offensive because he is unworthy of such good fortune on account of his lower social status. Women are the natural object of the anxiety created by that threat, at the same time stake and object of their legitimate partner's aggressivity.

Jean-Charles Huchet has convincingly demonstrated how the dissatisfaction inherent in sexuality turns into a misogynistic blame of women.[25] First, he points out the perverse component of sexual *jouissance*, always heading toward fusion but only succeeding in dismembering the partner. The neurotic solution proposed by courtly literature for the failure inherent in sexual intercourse is to suppose a successful rival. It is as if men could not prevent themselves from believing that what fails with them succeeds with a rival. Rivalry is indeed at the center of the courtly love situation. That situation also supposes the existence of two seminal figures who are in the position to reveal to the outside world the secret wound which must be kept hidden: the losengier and the lover-poet.[26]

However, as manipulators of the power of words through dissemination, the losengier and the lover-poet remain beyond control. The woman is the only partner in the love relationship who can be reached. This is why violence toward her is an intrinsic component of love, undermining courtly idealization. To put it in Huchet's words, men want to believe that the woman's body keeps the mark of their embrace in blood drops (Huchet, *Littérature médiévale*, 104). At the core of his demonstration is the pivotal scene of Perceval's ravishment in Chrétien's *Conte du Graal* (v. 4105–4144; transl. 45–46). Here also, the violence of sexual aggression is normalized through a process of metaphorization involving birds. If the goose that is chased by the hawk finally escapes its hold, it is not without losing on the snow the famous three drops of blood that ravish Perceval into the vision of his beloved Blanchefleur.[27]

The aspect of the episode of the *Conte du Graal* relevant in the context of the present argument is the metaphoric representation of sexual possession through the image of birds. Generally speaking, birds are associated with masculinity, the word *bird* itself being in many languages a metaphor for the boy's penis. In traditional cultures, young males are compelled to compete in virility tests involving birds, for instance the capture of nests on top of trees (Fabre, "L'Interprète," 67–76). The most famous literary example of this is the contest of the sparrow hawk won by Erec in Chrétien's *Erec et Enide* (v. 562–603). In the metaphoric language of birds, the falcon becomes an image of Erec, emblematizing knighthood as well as passion. Less known but just as explicit is the episode in *Couci* where the prize in the tournament won by the Châtelain is a hawk (*Couci*, v. 2006–66).

Another series of narratives can be usefully included in the network of texts that use the bird motif as a metaphor of transgression and aggression in courtly love. The most representative, in the context of this essay, is the *Escoufle* by Jean Renart, particularly the episodes of the romance where the hero, Guillaume, is confronted by that despicable bird, a kite. If the hawk represents chivalry, the kite stands for the opposite; the adjectives describing it refer to filthy rubbish. In his two confrontations with the bird, Guillaume traces the jealous husband's itinerary from the loss of his love object, Aelis, through the confrontation with a rival of inferior status to the cannibalistic revenge. In a scene reminiscent of Mark's discovery of Tristan and Iseut sleeping in the forest, the kite steals during Aelis's sleep the ring just given by her to Guillaume and placed in a red purse. Lured by the color of the purse, the kite has taken it for a piece of meat. In the details of the scene, Renart provides the necessary clues for its interpretation. Guillaume's first reaction when the precious object is stolen is to complain about the loss of his personal merit: had he been worthy of his lady, he would have put the ring on his finger and affixed the purse to his belt.[28] The sexual dimension of his inadequacy is easy to decipher. His decision to run after the thief in spite of the danger of leaving Aelis alone in the forest is motivated largely by the vileness of the bird and the fear of being reproached for his lack of courtesy in not being able to keep Aelis's gift safe.

The second encounter between Guillaume and a kite occurs after many adventures following the lovers' separation in the forest as a result of this incident. Under the guise of a servant learning how to hunt, Guillaume follows his master at bird hunting, with a hawk on his fist, filling the hunters with wonder because of his skillfulness. The reader is told, moreover, that Guillaume has learned a lot during his different experiences; the suggestion is that a decisive event is about to occur, a sort of qualifying test. Indeed, thanks to his falcon, Guillaume succeeds in catching a kite. Requesting his companions' forbearance with his strange behavior, he dismembers the bird, pulls out his heart, and eats it raw. Then, in an explicit act of revenge, he burns the rest of the dismembered bird. Renart's mention that Guillaume tears the pelvic part of the kite to pieces removes any doubt about the sexual connotation of the act.[29]

This striking scene suggests an identification between beast and man. On one hand, Guillaume's conduct mimics what a well-trained falcon is supposed to do in a hunting situation—tear up the chest of its prey before bringing the prize to its master, who then rewards it with the heart of the victim. On the other hand, his consumption of the bird's raw heart can be interpreted, in the context of the eaten heart narratives, as the cannibalistic ingestion of a worthless rival's heart. In his case however, the assimilation of the rival is not mediated through the woman's body. During the whole episode, Aelis has been kept out of the confrontation, having successfully gone her way by herself and having become the count of Saint Gilles' protégée. The final reunion of the lovers, a logical consequence of Guillaume's revenge and rehabilitation of his manliness and knighthood, occurs after a verbal remembering of their ordeal. Word of his apparently insane conduct having reached the count's court, his telling of the story is a prelude to the lovers' mutual recognition. As in the other narratives related to the eaten heart theme, the last word is given to the storyteller—the one who succeeds in uniting the dismembered parts. The story told by Jean Renart in the *Escoufle* uses the crudeness of avian symbolism to transform the passionate courtship into an exciting form of chase, the phantasmagoric aim of which is to triumph as the uncontested stag of love.[30]

In that contest of supremacy, the poet is in a position of designated victim in a world where social power belongs to knights. Yet, by his control over the power of words, the poet-narrator is also in a position to reverse the perspective and to gain credit at the symbolic level. Nonetheless, in the triangle of desire, the role conferred on the lady might yet be the most complex. Unlike in the short poems, in the narrative versions of love lyricism, she cannot be the pure—but absent—object of a phantasm; she becomes an acting subject whose attitudes and decisions affect the outcome of the contest between the two rivals. As an autonomous character, with full prerogatives of that position, she might be represented as a questionable figure. In Guillem de Cabestaing's razo or in *Ignauré*, she embodies the threatening (to a man) excesses inherent in the free expression of her desire. In *Couci,* she manifests all the ambiguities of a true romance character. In the episodes of metaphoric cannibalism in the *Escoufle,* she has been put aside, in a variant of the typical scenario that reveals the basic structure of the rivalry plot.[31]

In all these cases, the distancing and ironic character of literary representation has produced its normalizing effect by comparison with the direct expression of violence in the versions of *Philomena* present in the French Middle Ages, namely Ovid's and its adaptation by Chrétien de Troyes, both of which are still close to the myth. The variations on the eaten heart theme normalize violence in both senses of the word: attenuating the unbearable cruelty of the myth but also presenting as acceptable, and unavoidable, the violence of desire.

NOTES

1. We may see a reminiscence of the motif of the embroidered message in Marie de France's *Laostic,* where the lady sends to her lover the corpse of the nightingale killed by her husband, wrapped in a cloth on which she has embroidered the event.

2. On the classical tradition of that myth and its first mention in Homer, see Raby, *"Philomena praevia,"* 435; Baird and Kane, trans., *Rossignol,* 1–12. In the Greek tradition, Procne is changed into a nightingale and Philomela into a swallow. Both birds were considered as psychopomp animals (Angelopoulou, "L'hirondelle," 104–12).

3. The distinction between seduction and aggression is blurred in the process of medieval romanticization (Gravdal, *Ravishing Maidens,* 14).

4. The triad can be found in popular tales (Aarne and Thompson, *Types of Folktale,* 720: "My Mother Slew Me: My Father Ate Me"; Belmont, "L'enfant cuit," 181). A link can be established between mythical representations of the swallow, a bird related to motherly infanticide, and the wild aspect of women who refuse their maternal role (Angelopoulou, "L'hirondelle," 108–11).

5. About the corpus of texts related to the eaten heart theme, see Delbouille, *Le Roman,* xlvi–xlviii, and Vincensini, "Figure," 445–46.

6. *Ignauré,* v. 371–73: "Par le trop aler fu dechus / Et engigniés et percheüs: / Soris ki na c'un trau poi dure" (He succumbed because of going too often / He was trapped and caught / The mouse with but one hole won't last).

7. There exists a significant relationship between male aggression against women and cannibalism (Sagan, *Human Aggression,* 69; Moreau, "A propos d'Oedipe," 124; Sanday *Divine Hunger,* 12–13).

8. By their mythical dimension, these narratives can be considered as manifestations of the universals of the imaginary (Belmont, "L'enfant cuit," 183). The

existence of a legend of the eaten heart in Punjab had led Gaston Paris to propose an oriental origin to the theme, while seven of the references listed in Stith Thompson's *Motif-Index* belong outside the Indo-European domain (Vincensini, "Figure," 449; Thompson, *Motif-Index of Folk-Literature*, Q 241 and Q 478.1).

9. See Belmont, "L'enfant cuit," 183–84, for a theoretical elaboration of that approach.

10. For the different representations of the nightingale, see Baird and Kane, *Rossignol*; Pfeffer, *Change of Philomel*.

11. For the religious connotations of the nightingale, see Baird and Kane, *Rossignol*, 14–17; Napoli, *Le "Livre du Rossignolet,"*; Pfeffer, *Change of Philomel*, 35–41.

12. *Philomena*, v. 1463–67: "Quant il vient au prin d'esté, / Que tot l'iver avons passé, / Por les mauvés qu'ele tant het / Chante au plus doucemant qu'el set / Par le boschage 'Oci! Oci!'" (When the beginning of summer announces / That winter is all behind us / For the evil ones whom she hates so / she sings as sweetly as she can / In the grove: "Kill! Kill!").

13. About the association in medieval medicine between heart, blood, sperm, and sex, see Ribémont, *Le cuer*.

14. *Ignauré*, v. 527–31: "Au message creantet ont / K'eles ja mais ne mangeront / Desci qu'eles [poront] savoir / S'il est u mors u vis, por voir. / Lors commenchierent a juner" (They trust the messenger / That they shall never eat any more / Until they [can] learn / Truly whether he is dead or alive. / Then they started to fast).

15. *Ignauré*, v.617–19: "D'eles douse fu li deus fais, / Et douse vers plains a li lais / C'on doit bien tenir en memoire" (The twelve [douse] women were mourned [deus], / And the lai has twelve [douse] full verses / Which ought to be well kept in memory).

16. *Ignauré*, v. 23: "Ne fu mie de grant hauteche" (He was not at all of great rank). The wives are characterized as: "De haut linage, de grant gent" (v. 43: Of high lineage, from gentlefolk).

17. *Ignauré*, v. 418: "Est chou borgois u chevaliers?" (Is this a commoner or a knight?).

18. *Ignauré*, v. 37: "Femmes l'apielent Lousignol" (Women call him Nightingale).

19. Bloch, "The Lay and the Law," 197, bases this identification on the polysemy of the word *sens:* meaning and semen.

20. Boutière, *Biographies*, 441–44; Egan, *Les vies*, 168–71; Stone, "The Eaten Heart," 112–13, 121.

21. Similar interpretation in Doueihi, "Lure of the Heart," 56.

22. *Couci*, v. 7999–8002: "Le coffre a pris et recheü / . . . Clef ne sierre n'a demandé, / Mais a force l'a deffremé" (He took the chest and dropped it / He did not ask for a key or latch [sierre], / But opened it by force).

23. The striking insistence on the risk of being defamed, expressed so many times by the Lady of Fayel, must be taken into account. See *Couci*, v. 215–16; 784–97; 1957–58; 2172–75; 2186–89; 2356; 3531–34; 3618; 3643–44; 4888–90.

24. *Couci*, v. 642–55: "Car ja ne goÿrés de moi. / Mais se volés avoir dou mien /

Aucun juyel, je le voel bien: / Lach de soie, mance u aniel, / Ce me plaist bien et est moult biel. . . . / Mais ja esperance n'ayiés / Que jour ne heure vous soiiés / Sires ne saisis de men cors" (For you will never have your delight [goÿrés] in me / But if you wish to have something of mine / Some jewel, it suits me fine: / a silk lace, sleeve or ring, / It pleases me well and it is very nice. . . . / But never hope / That one day or one hour you will be / The master or possessor of my body).

25. Huchet, *Littérature médiévale*, 211.

26. There can be no way of speaking of love that does not imply its transgression (Bloch, "The Lay and the Law," 193).

27. That central episode of the *Conte du Graal* has itself fascinated critics, who have linked it with texts such as Béroul's *Tristan* or the *Chevalier à la Charrette* through the image of blood on a white surface. In both cases the lover's access to the loved one is marked that way. Tristan's recent hunt injury reopens when he leaps into Iseut's bed to avoid leaving the print of his feet in the flour spread between the beds to catch him (v. 703–34). Lancelot cuts his hands when removing the bars at Guinevere's bedroom window, staining the sheets, and leaving a piece of evidence which will lead to Kai's false accusation (v. 4598–4837).

28. *Escoufle*, v. 4562–71: "Certes, fait il, c'est male ensaigne / Quant tes puors, tele faiture, / Dont Diex ne li mondes n'a cure, / A devant moi mon anel pris./ Ml't en est abaissiés mes pris / Por ce qu'il ert venus d'amors. / S'il eüst tant de boines mors / En moi com ma dame i cuidoit, / Jou l'eüsse mis en mon doit, / Et l'aumosniere a ma coroie" (Certainly, says he, it is a bad sign / If such stench, such creature, / For which neither God nor the world cares, / Took my ring in my presence. / My worth is greatly diminished by this / Because it was a token of love. / If there were as many good qualities / In me as my lady thought, / I would have put it on my finger, / And attached the purse to my belt).

29. *Escoufle*, v. 6856–61: "Il a lués droit l'escoufle pris / Tout ensement comme ·j. marlart; / Le cuir del penil li depart / Qui ml't estoit et durs et fors, / Les dois li met dedens le cors, / S'en traist le cuer ensanglenté; / Voiant ciaus qui i ont esté / L'a mis en sa bouce et mangié" (He therewith took the kite / Just the same as if [he were holding] a duck; / He pulls the skin off its pelvis (*penil*, from pop. Latin *pectiniculum*, Dauzat) / Which was very tough and strong, / He puts his fingers inside its body, / Pulls out of it the bleeding heart; / On the eyes of those who were there / He put it in his mouth and ate it).

30. I refer here to Thiébaux, *Stag of Love*. See also Planche, "*Est vrais amans*," and Gerli, "Calisto's Hawk," for the explanation of links between hunting, falconry, masculinity, and the expression of desire.

31. René Girard's hypothesis comes to mind, with his stress on the centrality of the mimetic nature of desire, leading to a contest between enemy brothers to determine the supremacy. About the parallelism between the metaphoric language of medieval texts and contemporary theory, we can refer to Huchet's observations concerning psychoanalytic hermeneutic. Psychoanalysis does not provide keys; medieval texts function as examples similar to clinical data for testing the theory.

WORKS CITED

Aarne, Antti, and Stith Thompson. *The Types of Folktale*. Helsinki: Academia Scientiarum Fennica, 1964.

Angelopoulou, Anna. "L'hirondelle et la mort." *Ethnologie Française* 23 (1993): 104–12.

Baird, J. L., and John R. Kane. *Rossignol: An Edition and Translation*. Kent, Ohio: Kent State University Press, 1978.

Belmont, Nicole. "L'enfant cuit." *Ethnologie Française* 25 (1995): 180–85.

Beroul. *Le roman de Tristan*, ed. Daniel Lacroix and Philippe Walter, 24–227. Paris: Livre de Poche, 1989. Transl. Norris Lacy, *The Romance of Tristan*. New York: Garland, 1984.

Bloch, Howard. "The Lay and the Law: Sexual/Textual Transgression in *La Chastelaine de Vergi*, the *Lai d'Ignauré*, and the *Lais* of Marie de France." *Stanford French Review* 14 (1990): 181–210.

Boccaccio, Giovanni. *Decameron*. Ed. Vittore Branca. Firenze: Presso l'Accademia della Crusca, 1976.

———. *Decameron*. Trans. John Payne. Revised and annotated by Charles S. Singleton. Berkeley: University of California Press, 1982.

Bourdieu, Pierre. *Outline of a Theory of Practice*. Cambridge: Cambridge University Press, 1977.

Boutière, Jean. *Biographies des troubadours: Textes provençaux des XIIIe et XIVe siècles*. Paris: Nizet, 1964.

Chrétien de Troyes. *Erec et Enide*. Ed. Michel Rousse. Paris: Garnier-Flammarion, 1994.

———. *Erec et Enide*. Trans. Burton Raffel. New Haven: Yale University Press, 1997.

———. *Lancelot or the Knight of the Cart*. Trans. Ruth Harwood Cline. Athens: University of Georgia Press, 1990.

———. *Le Conte du Graal ou le roman de Perceval*. Ed. Charles Méla. Paris: Livre de Poche, 1990.

———. *Perceval: The Story of the Grail*. Trans. Nigel Bryant. Cambridge: Brewer, Rowman and Littlefield, 1982.

———. *Philomena*. Ed. Cornelius de Boer. Paris, 1909. Rpt. Geneva: Slatkine repr., 1974.

Delbouille, Maurice, ed. *Le Roman du Castelain de Couci et de la Dame de Fayel*. Paris: Société des Anciens Textes Français, 1936.

Doueihi, Milad. "The Lure of the Heart." *Stanford French Review* 14 (1990): 51–68.

Egan, Margarita. *Les vies des troubadours*. Paris: Union générale d'éditions, 1985.

Fabre, Daniel. "L'interprète et les oiseaux." In *Réception et identification du conte depuis le moyen âge*, ed. Michel Zink and Xavier Ravier, 65–90. Toulouse: Université de Toulouse-Le Mirail, 1987.

Gerli, Michael E. "Calisto's Hawk and the Images of a Medieval Tradition." *Romania* 104 (1983): 83–101.

Girard, René. *Violence and the Sacred.* Baltimore and London: John Hopkins University Press, 1977.

Gravdal, Kathryn. *Ravishing Maidens: Writing Rape in Medieval French Literature and Law.* Philadelphia: University of Pennsylvania Press, 1991.

Huchet, Jean-Jacques. *Littérature médiévale et psychanalyse: Pour une clinique littéraire.* Paris: PUF, 1990.

Krueger, Roberta. *Women Readers and the Ideology of Gender in Old French Verse Romance.* Cambridge: Cambridge University Press, 1993.

Marie de France. *Lais.* Trans. Joan Ferrante and Robert W. Hanning. New York: Dutton, 1978.

———. *Lais.* Ed. Karl Warnke. Paris: Livre de Poche, 1990.

Moreau, Alain. "A propos d'Oedipe: la liaison entre trois crimes, parricide, inceste et cannibalisme." In *Etudes de littérature ancienne,* 97–127. Paris: Publications de l'Ecole Normale, 1979.

Napoli, Claudia. *Le "Livre du Rossignolet": Une traduction médiévale de la "Philomena praevia."* Montreal: Ceres, 1979.

Pfeffer, Wendy. *The Change of Philomel: The Nightingale in Medieval Literature.* New York: Peter Lang, 1985.

Planche, Alice. "*Est vrais amans li drois oisiaus de proie . . .* Sur une image de Guillaume de Machaut." In *Etudes de philologie romane et d'histoire littéraire offertes à Jules Horrent,* ed. Jean-Marie d'Heur and Nicoletta Cherubini, 351–60. Liège, 1980.

Raby, F. J. E. "*Philomena praevia temporis amoeni.*" In *Mélanges Joseph de Ghellinck,* vol. 2, 435–48. Gembloux: Duculot, 1951.

Renart, Jean. *L'Escoufle.* Ed. Franklin Sweetser. Geneva: Droz, 1974.

Renaut de Beaujeu. *Le Lai d'Ignauré ou du prisonnier.* Ed. Rita Lejeune. Brussels: Académie royale de langue et de littérature de Belgique, 1938.

Ribémont, Bernard. "*Le cuer del ventre li as trais*—coeur arraché, coeur mangé, coeur envolé: Un regard médico-théologique sur quelques thèmes littéraires." In *Le cuer au moyen âge: Réalité et Senefiance. Senefiance* 30 (1991): 345–61.

Sagan, Eli. *Human Aggression: Cannibalism and Cultural Form.* New York: Harper and Row, 1974.

Sanday, Peggy Reeves. *Divine Hunger: Cannibalism as a Cultural System.* Cambridge: Cambridge University Press, 1986.

Schulze-Busacker, Elisabeth. "*Philomena:* Une révision de l'attribution de l'oeuvre." *Romania* 107 (1986): 459–85.

Solterer, Helen. "Dismembering, Remembering the Châtelain de Couci." *Romance Philology* 46 (1992): 103–24.

Stone, Gregory B. "The Eaten Heart." In *The Death of the Troubadour: The Late Medieval Resistance to the Renaissance,* 101–8. Philadelphia: University of Pennsylvania Press, 1994.

Thiébaux, Marcelle. *The Stag of Love: The Chase in Medieval Literature.* Ithaca and London: Cornell University Press, 1974.

Thompson, Stith. *Motif-Index of Folk-Literature*. Bloomington: Indiana University Press, 1955–58.

Thomas. *Le Roman de Tristan*. Ed. Daniel Lacroix and Philippe Walter, 330–481. Paris: Livre de Poche, 1989.

Vincensini, Jean-Jacques. "Figure de l'imaginaire et figure du discours: Le motif du 'coeur mangé' dans la narration médiévale." In *Le cuer au moyen âge: Réalité et senefiance. Senefiance* 30 (1991): 439–59.

Wilhelm, James J. *The Cruelest Month: Spring, Nature, and Love in Classical and Medieval Lyrics*. New Haven and London: Yale University Press, 1965.

5

The Rhetoric of Incest in the Middle English *Emaré*

Anne Laskaya

> *The silences, the empty spaces, the language itself, with its excision of the female, the methods of discourse tell us as much as the content, once we learn to watch for what is left out, to listen for the unspoken . . .*
>
> —Adrienne Rich

The late fourteenth-century Middle English Breton lay of *Emaré* preserves a version of what is known as the "Constance-saga," a narrative quite popular in late medieval literature.[1] The tale exists in French, Spanish, German, Italian, Arabic, Persian, and Latin renditions and within genres as diverse as chronicle, romance, and drama.[2] It is perhaps best known to English readers and listeners from Chaucer's version in the *Man of Law's Tale* and from Gower's account in Book Two of the *Confessio Amantis*.[3] *Emaré* features a female protagonist who suffers because she refuses her father's incestuous advances. Enraged, her father, the emperor, retaliates by sentencing his daughter to exposure and death in a boat upon the sea. God preserves Emaré and guides her boat to the coast of Galicia, where she eventually marries the king. While the king is away, Emaré gives birth to a son and sends a messenger to inform her husband. Through a series of intercepted and forged letters, Emaré's evil mother-in-law succeeds in exiling her once more out upon the ocean with her little child. Once again she is saved by divine intervention and washes ashore near Rome, where she joins a merchant's household and raises her son. Eventually both her husband (the king of Galicia) and her father (Emperor Artyus) make pilgrimages of repentance to Rome, where, miraculously, across a sea of time, space, and chance, all are restored to one another in a final recognition scene.

The narrative's emphasis on *passio* (suffering and acceptance stemming from faith and its consequences in a fallen world) links it with hagiography. In *Middle English Romances of the Thirteenth and Fourteenth Centuries* Dieter Mehl notes that "the significance of [Emaré's] pitiable fate depends on its being completely unmerited," and, he adds, "she comes very near to being a kind of secularized Saint" (139). As a tale of extreme female sacrifice, *Emaré* shares a common theme not only with women's hagiography but also with tales borrowed from classical sources and preserved in texts like the *Gesta Romanorum*, Chaucer's *Legend of Good Women*, Christine de Pizan's *Cité des Dames*, and in the well-known tales of Ovid and Boccaccio. Legends of long-suffering "good women" obviously function paradoxically in the cultural rhetoric of the late Middle Ages. On the one hand, they offer a defense of women and a glimpse into forms of women's resistance to patriarchy and sexual violence. In this way, they usually indict overt violence directed against women. On the other hand, because they often encode females as vulnerable, helpless, weak, and most heroic when they accept grief and extreme violation with Christlike forbearance, these narratives further the naturalization of women's subordination, thereby contributing to the culture's violence toward women.

Emaré does not, by any means, encode the most extreme discursive representation of violence done to women, but it does participate in an entire set of cultural narratives that perpetuate crucial assumptions about reality and gender. While condemning violence, incest, and murder, the text also lends support to a culture that tolerated a high degree of actual violence, specifically, in this case, sexual and physical violence against women. Kathryn Gravdal, in *Ravishing Maidens*, examines the language and dynamics of rape in medieval French legal and literary texts and observes that "sexual assault appears to have been well integrated in the institution of the family in fourteenth-century Normandy and to have been held less shameful than financial debt" (126). Likewise, John Carter, in his study *Rape in Medieval England*, argues that the infrequency of reported sexual assault cases in English court records reveals more about the oppression of women than about the actual condition of women's lives. His work is corroborated by Judith Bennett, whose careful study of fourteenth-century Brigstock uncovers the relationship between women's political, legal, social, and familial disenfranchisement and their absence from historical documents, materials which might have established fuller and more accurate views of their lives.

In contrast to historical records, literary texts of the high and late Middle Ages frequently encode narratives featuring violence against women. Rape, incest, various forms of torture, imprisonment, and abandonment flourish in the imaginary worlds of hagiography and romance. But these literary accounts, like many modern ones, frequently construct interesting paradoxes within their textual representations of violence against women. *Emaré*, for example, while it records the tale of a woman who successfully avoids incest-rape, also records the potentially mortal consequences of such resistance; and although it creates a saintly heroine capable of surviving great suffering, it also affirms the power of violence as a force that limits women's freedom, polices women's behavior, and fosters the patriarchal assumption that women need male protection. In this way it contributes to what Susan Brownmiller calls "rape culture," a culture wherein rape functions as "a sufficient threat to keep all women in a constant state of intimidation" (*Against Our Will*, 209; see also Tomaselli and Porter, *Rape*).

Of course readers and listeners, whether modern or medieval, understand and respond to the narrative, its strategies, and its representations of violence in various ways, because each reading (including this one) emerges from an interplay of particular textual representations and maneuvers, cultural reading conventions, and the assumptions, associations, and experiential resonances of each individual reader. As Laura Tanner notes, "the act of reading a representation of violence is defined by the reader's suspension between the semiotic and the real, between a representation and the material dynamics of violence which it evokes, reflects, or transforms" (*Intimate Violence*, 6). Just as a gap exists between sign and referent, so too a problematic but potent relational space exists between textual representations of violence and what Tanner calls the reader's "empirical subtext" (6). Whereas textual representations of violence deploy strategies which impel readers to respond in particular ways, those who are attuned to disparities between the symbolic and the actual dynamics and consequences of violence are less likely to be implicated by any textual naturalization of violence.

Representations that objectify victims and erase their pain encourage readers to formulate more detached understandings and responses; this is reinforced by the phenomenon of reading, itself, which invites readers to abandon the actual material world and, in a more or less disembodied state, enter an imaginative and fictional realm. Abandoning the body for the imaginary world, readers most easily adopt the interpretations and perspectives carved out for them by the narrative. Textual scenes of violence, like cinematic ones, can locate readers by aligning their perceptions with perpetrators or victims, with "omniscient" narrators or implicated witnesses, or with complex and shifting vantage points which oscillate in a complex combination of some or all of these. Texts that inscribe silent victims and inarticulate human suffering separate the reader from the victims' consciousness and leave a space within which readers create (or ignore) the drama of pain that fictional characters are imaginatively forced to enact and experience. Unlike violent cinematic scenes, reading allows the audience greater detachment and greater manipulation—greater detachment because actual sounds and specific images are lacking, greater manipulation because readers construct the violence imaginatively beyond the starkness of the textual sign. Tanner comments: "Insofar as the reader's [or the writer/narrator's] imagination manipulates the victim's body as a purely textual entity, the reality of pain and vulnerability of that body may be obscured by the participation of a reading subject who perpetuates the dynamics of violation" (10).

If we assume that readers, like texts, are both constructed by and constructing the social, and if we assume that readers import their knowledge of the empirical world into their readings of texts across a gap of potentiality between the symbolic and the real, then we must also grant that readers will bring back ideas and assumptions from the imaginary and symbolic to the actualized material world. The consequences of importing unexamined assumptions about violence into the experiential world from the fictional or symbolic one may be profound. Tanner notes: "The seductive power of representation lies, at least in part, in its ability to naturalize its own conclusions, to obscure its manipulation of the experiential dynamics of violence by veiling the ideological assumptions inherent in its linguistic maneuvers" (10). Likewise, the consequences of reflecting upon the way narrative force naturalizes its representations of violence may also be profound. Recognizing technologies of meanings at work in, between, outside, and around texts allows a reader conscious choices and, hence, more opportunities to resist problematic textual strategies which recreate the dynamics of violence. Cultivating oppositional and self-reflective reading responses invites us, as Tanner suggests, "to empower ourselves as readers with the ability to resist the pull of a textual representation of violation, to read ourselves out of models of spectatorship or positions of aesthetic distance that themselves imply a form of victimization" (16).

If we attempt to resist those textual maneuvers in the narrative of *Emaré* which veil the victim's body with conventional descriptions, with magical, moral and religious abstractions as well as with silence, we discover a rhetoric in both plot and language that sets up a "norming" of violence against women. In fact, the narrator's reluctance to articulate Emaré's suffering within a plot that features her suffering is notable; his tendency (here I am assuming a male narrator, though the text is anonymous) to generalize, erase, and evade the particulars of a woman's experience is reminiscent of the rhetoric Guido Ruggiero found prevalent in legal records of actual rape cases from early modern Venice. Observing that the penalties for raping a male were much more severe than for even the most violent or egregious rape of a female *and* that the descriptions of male rape were much more detailed than those concerning female rape, Ruggiero posits a correlation between the specificity of the suffering in the court record and the seriousness attributed to both the crime and the penalty. He writes that "the rape of males was reported with much more physical detail, [and] this suggests that the lack of detail in cases involving women was less a matter of prudery or protecting the woman's reputation than a reflection of the lesser importance of women and their victimization" (*Boundaries of Eros*, 125). Of course, this rhetoric also reflects the realities of Europe's legal codes, which, by and large, considered violence against women to constitute crimes against the men who had legal custody of them—fathers, brothers, sons, and husbands.

In *Emaré*, a rhetorical strategy of muting and evading women's suffering does a kind of violence both to a familiar tale and to women's experience. Where some versions of the Constance-saga elaborate more fully on the protagonist's suffering and where they represent her perceptions and perspective empathetically (even if still using third-person narration), the Breton lay of *Emaré* shifts the emphasis away from the woman's suffering toward a moralizing framework and toward the perceptions, losses, and transformations of the male characters surrounding the heroine. In the opening stanzas of his tale, the narrator promises his audience that the mourning and grief in the poem will be intermingled with "much mirth" (19–21).[4] It is an oddly jarring promise, given the plot's dependence on Emaré's years of exile and sacrifice, but a promise consistent with a detached reading of her suffering. The muting of her suffering is also accomplished as the narrator, replicating his culture's emphasis on the afterlife and following narrative convention, frames his tale with short prayers, which encourage readers and listeners to interpret the text within a Christian moral framework. Both beginning and ending, holding narratological and rhetorical power, posit that great suffering on earth (if endured with great faith) brings its own reward. Both conventional reading strategies and the text itself encourage us to grant definitive meaning to beginning and ending and to find the protagonist's years of suffering and exile relatively less significant. Her sorrow has been, we learn several times, ordained from long ago: "Such sorow was here yarked yore" (Such sorrow was destined for her long ago; 329) as "hyt was Goddys wylle" (327). This rationalizing of Emaré's suffering is echoed rhetorically throughout the text, as betrayal and agony are punctuated by, or captured in between, moral reassurances. Lines 675, 677, and 680–81 illustrate this principle of moral punctuation, as they interrupt and frame the description of Emaré's second ordeal on the sea:

Now thys lady dwelled thore   *there*
A full sevene nyght and more,
    As hyt was Goddys wylle;
Wyth karefull herte and sykyng sore,   *sighing*
Such sorow was her yarked yore,   *destined for her long ago*
    And she lay full stylle.
She was dryven toward Rome,
Thorow the grace of God yn trone,   *Through; on throne*
    That all thyng may fulfylle.
On the see she was so harde bestadde,   *beset*
For hungur and thurste allmost madde,
Wo worth chawnses ylle!   *Cursed be such bad luck*
(673–84; my emphasis)

Kathryn Gravdal notes that rape is often "troped" in romances and hagiography in such a way that "it heightens figurative elements and manipulates the reader's ordinary response by suspending or interrupting that response in order to displace the reader's focus onto other formal or thematic elements. The mimesis of rape is made tolerable when the poet tropes it as moral, comic, heroic, spiritual, or erotic" (*Ravishing Maidens*, 13). In the case of *Emaré*, threats of incest and death, along with exposure and prolonged exile, are primarily troped as moral. The narrative's moral framework veils a reality of sexual and physical violence in the same way that Emaré's body is hidden beneath the brilliant robe given to her by her father.

The narrator's interpretation of the story within a specific moral code explains, perhaps, the problem of his failure to articulate her suffering more explicitly. He escapes responsibility by setting the ultimate cause for Emaré's grief at the foot of the divine. When Syr Artyus puts his daughter out to sea for her refusal to bend to his will, the narrator comments that God knew of it (269); he later notes that her exposure on the open sea lasted "seven nyghth and more, / As hyt was Goddys wylle" (326–27)—this comment is repeated in lines 674–75 during Emaré's second sea journey. Responsibility for the textual representation (or suppression) of violence belongs, the narrator says, with tradition: the material is *not* his own creation. The text has a genealogy he works to preserve: "Thys ys on [one] of Brytayne layes / That was used by olde dayes, / Men callys 'Playn d'Egarye'" (1030–32). The narrator seems concerned to establish his own reliable recitation of a received story; he makes no claims for his own imaginative manipulation or revision of source material. He constructs his text "as the story telles in honde [at hand]" (115) and several times asserts his truthfulness in storytelling, his faithfulness to his sources (see lines 96, 115, 144, 162, 216, 319, 381, 405, 465, 544, 880, 1029). In a move found throughout medieval literature, allegiance is given primarily to the source, not to the title character or innovations; consequently, both God and the source are given prior responsibility for the shape of events and characters in the narrative.

Not surprisingly, then, the construction of subjectivity within this Breton lay is reminiscent of early modern sex crime records, which detailed men's suffering and downplayed women's, and is congruent with medieval legal codes, which usually considered men the legally injured parties when women were assaulted. The scenes leading up to Syr Artyus's threat of incest also suggest that although Emaré is appointed heroine within the title, she will rarely occupy the narrative's subject position. In fact, she functions, most often, as an object for the narrator to describe in third person or from the point of view of a male character. When Syr Artyus condemns Emaré to die, the textual representation of the violence distances us from the daughter, suppresses her experience, and directs us to see and understand the father's anger, his actions, and, belatedly, his regret:

The Emperour was ryght wrothe,	*angry*
And swore many a gret othe,	*oath*
That deed shulde she be.	*dead*
He lette make a nobull boot,	*boat*
And dede her theryn, God wote,	*put her; knows*
In the robe of nobull ble.	*bright color*
She moste have wyth her no spendyng,	*might; money*
Nothur mete ne drynke,	*Neither food*
But shate her ynto the se.	*shoved*
Now the lady dwelled thore,	*there*

Wythowte anker or ore,
    And that was gret pyté!

Ther come a wynd, y unthurstonde,
And blewe the boot fro the londe,
    Of her they lost the syght.
The Emperour hym bethowght
That he hadde all myswrowht,   *done amiss*
    And was a sory knyghte.
And as he stode yn studyynge,   *meditating*
He fell down in sowenynge,   *swooning*
    To erthe was he dyght.   *fallen*
Grete lordes stode therby,
And toke yn the Emperour hastyly,
    And comforted hym fayr and ryght. (265–88)

Having heard Emaré speak forcefully to her father, having heard her refuse his incestuous desires and articulate her own obedience to God's law in lines 250–64, a critical reader may notice the narrative's curious suppression of her words at the moment she would have experienced overwhelming emotion: namely, when she is cast out of the human community. Any cries she may have made are carried away on the wind that blows her boat out to sea. We do not see the perpetrator standing on the shore fading from her sight; instead, we see her fading away from his vantage point. His loss is emphasized, not hers.

As the scene unfolds, Emaré floats alone—her thoughts, actions, feelings, and prayers sparsely relayed to us in the third person. Furthermore, the narrator's voice is the only one allowed emotional expression. Outraged by his character's suffering, he says, "Woo worth wederus yll!" (336; Woe come to all evil storms!). When Emaré finally lands on the sands of Gaul, the narrator again aligns both himself and his readers with a male character's viewpoint, by choosing to relate the scene through her rescuer's eyes. Syr Kadore, taking some air on the beach with his squires, espies her boat, is amazed by the brilliance of the gem-studded robe she wears, and is overcome by pity when he finds her dying of dehydration and starvation in the bottom of the boat:

A boot he fond by the brym,   *boat; shore*
And a glysteryng thyng theryn,   *glittering*
    Therof they hadde ferly.   *were amazed*
They went forth on the sond   *shore*

To the boot, y unthurstond,
   And fond theryn that lady.
She hadde so longe meteles be   *without food been*
That hym thowht gret dele to se;   *(it) a great sorrow to see*
   She was yn poynt to dye.   *at the point of death*
(349–57)

His thoughts, actions, and emotions during the rescue are described in twenty-three lines. Emaré's entire seven-day experience on the open sea is also given twenty-three lines, most of which actually erase her subjective experience. We are told, instead, that her suffering is fated, that her boat is buffeted about by winds and waves for seven nights or more, that God's grace preserves her, and that the narrator tells us the story exactly as he heard minstrels sing it. Narratology urges us to identify who speaks within a text, who sees, who acts, and as Mieke Bal comments, these simple questions, "when applied to a specific text may either provide direct answers, and thus show the structure of meaning in its pragmatic dimension, or else prove to be problematic" (*Lethal Love*, 21). The narrative of *Emaré* certainly qualifies as problematic in this regard, and Bal notes that "[when a] text's subjectivity is problematic, . . . its ideological impact is blurred" (21). Emaré, not speaking directly until line 251 when she refuses her father's incestuous desires, may be the title character, but by far the greatest number of lines in the narrative express male voices, actions, and perspectives. Constructing scenes in this way aligns *Emaré* with what contemporary feminist film theorists call the "scopophilic." Teresa de Lauretis writes: "The apparatus of looks converging on the female figure integrates voyeurism into the conventions of storytelling, combining a direct solicitation of the scopic drive with the demands of plot, conflict, climax, and resolution. The woman is framed by the look of the camera as an icon, an image, the object of the gaze, and thus, precisely, spectacle: that is to say, an image made to be looked at by the spectator(s) as well as the male character(s), whose look most often relays the look of the audience" (*Technologies*, 99). And thus, *Emaré* raises the same questions Fellini's *Juliet of the Spirits* raises for de Lauretis when she asks (102): "Where does the woman spectator stand . . . ? Can this fantasy be safe for us, when it is clearly not safe for Juliet [or Emaré]? Could we possibly see it as men [or at least many men] do, with the same detached enjoyment or the same erotic participation? What happens to us as we watch it?"

Curiously, this narrative—one that will crescendo in its first section to an incestuous confrontation between Emaré and her father—takes its greatest pains to construct a favorable view of the father. This "gret lord,"

Syr Artyus, possessed lands, wealth, and an unparalleled reputation. He "was the best manne / In the worlde that lyvede thanne" (37–38) and was "curtays [courteous] in all thyng / Bothe to olde and to yynge" (40–41), chaste in his marriage (43–44), and very generous. After a brief account of Emaré's birth and her mother's death, the narrator sends his protagonist offstage to be raised by a nurse, temporarily banishing her from the narrative. Awkwardly, the narrator leaves Emaré and launches into a relatively long story about a marvelous cloth given to her father, the emperor. Of the 1,035 lines in the text, 98 are given over to a full description of the garment itself (lines 82–180). Consisting of four embroidered and bejeweled panels depicting lovers, the cloth was sewn, the narrator tells us, by the Amerayle's daughter for her beloved, the Sultan's son. It is, then, woven by a woman as a wedding gift to be worn by a man, an interesting and suggestive detail which is paralleled in the narrative itself as Emaré steps into the garment, and thereby simultaneously attempts to step into the protagonist's role. She assumes the man's garment just as her character takes on a more central position within the narrative. But if wearing the robe marks Emaré's move toward the hero's role, it simultaneously marks her subjugation as a beautiful female creature within a patriarchal social order, and it also marks her erasure: the robe's gem-studded brilliance is so intense that it blinds the eye. When the emperor first looks at the cloth, he "myght hyt not se, / For glysteryng of the ryche ston; / Redy syght had he non" (99–101). The cloth, originally given in love, is taken by force from the Sultan by the old king of Sicily who, in an act of love, gives it to his son, who, in turn, in an act of feudal devotion, gives it to the emperor Syr Artyus. The emperor, in an act of love which turns sexually coercive, has a robe made of the cloth for Emaré. Thus, the link between the cloth and Emaré, established throughout the narrative, may also reinforce her status as more of an object exchanged between powerful others than as an active subject. The history of the robe interweaves love and violence, paralleling the plot surrounding Emaré herself.

The ambiguous nature of this fantastic cloth also participates in muting the violence Syr Artyus directs toward Emaré, and it contributes to the narrative's generous treatment of the incestuous father. The dazzling cloth, we are told, is woven by a "heathen" and considered a thing of "fayry," a magical and enchanting object, so that its blinding effect on the emperor suggests a cause for his incestuous desires. In fact, if we try to uncover any textual explanation for the father's sexual desire for his daughter, we find two explanations, both of which can be traced back to an absent woman. First, Emaré's mother has died, leaving her daughter vulnerable. The narrative implies that Artyus becomes "anamoured" of his daughter because of her beauty and because of her resemblance to her mother. The death of the mother also creates the opportunity to remove Emaré from her father's home for many years, and this subtly (or potentially) downplays Artyus's culpability. Second, the text hints that a love charm has been woven into the fabric by the Amerayle's daughter and thus suggests that blame for the father-daughter incest rests with chance, with heathen practices, with exotic Eastern magic rather than with Artyus himself. Shaping Artyus in this way, the tale of *Emaré* participates in a long history of father-daughter rape narratives that rationalize violation as uncontrollable passion or that construct infatuation as a motivation for sexual violence. Thus, it contributes to that "amatory" rhetoric which conflates love and sexual violence, a rhetoric extremely widespread in medieval literature. It also participates in a cultural discourse that inflicts psychological violence on women, as numerous studies of the cultural, rhetorical, and conceptual frameworks surrounding cases of rape and incest attest.[5] The absent or inadequate mother and the seductive daughter (here made seductive by the exotic cloth) are myths commonly encountered in incest narratives, even across centuries of historical difference. Judith Lewis Herman, a psychiatrist and influential scholar on the subject of incest in late twentieth-century American culture, writes:

> If it must be conceded, first, that father-daughter incest occurs commonly, and secondly, that it is not . . . harmless . . . , then apologists for the incestuous father are thrown back upon their third . . . excuse: he is not responsible for his actions. Most commonly, they blame his daughter, his wife, [his mother, or all three]. Thus we make the acquaintance of the two major culprits in the incest romance, the Seductive Daughter and the Collusive Mother. Ensnared by the charms of a small temptress, or driven into her arms by a frigid, unloving [or dead] wife, Poor Father can hardly help himself. (*Father-Daughter Incest*, 36)

The narrative of *Emaré* takes yet another rhetorical tack that mutes the realities of incestuous sexual violation by reading Artyus's sexual threats toward his daughter as a marriage proposal. Artyus gives Emaré a wedding gift (the robe), asks his father (the pope) to give him Emaré as a wife, and receives the Vatican's approval. Emaré's isolation is extreme; she can only appeal for protection to a father of the third power: God, the father *of* the father (the pope) *of* the father (Artyus). That Emaré successfully avoids rape against all odds as king, pope, social code, gender codes, and sheer physical power all align against her has an interesting effect. In fact, the circumvention of rape, given such prominence in the narrative, suggests to the audience that Emaré is not, ultimately, a victim, and her heroic defense of her own virginity has the odd effect of reducing the seriousness of her abandonment at sea without water, food, protection, or direction. If she can overcome her father's sexual threat (a threat which spans at least 75 lines), the problem of overcoming a death sentence on the open sea seems to shrink, especially when it is represented in far fewer lines.

Another structural element that attempts to seduce us into forgiving the father's assault on his daughter is the contrast between the "loving" but inappropriate desire the father has for his daughter and the sheer hating and loathing the mother-in-law in Galicia has for Emaré. The text minimizes the father's crimes against his daughter in part by contrasting them with the motives and actions of the demonized mother-in-law. Emaré's second abandonment at sea results not from a fit of desire but from the mother-in-law's fit of jealousy. Additionally, the mother-in-law places two lives at risk, including the most precious and valued life of the son, heir to the kingdom of Gaul. Her jealousy accomplishes its aims by deception and disguise, while Artyus's "love" for his daughter is direct, "honest," and because of the papal dispensation, legitimate in comparison. These parallel scenes and gestures seem to construct incestuous desire on the part of the father for his daughter as a lesser crime within the text.[6] Furthermore, as soon as Emaré's rudderless boat disappears over the horizon in her first ocean ordeal, Artyus collapses on the seashore, overcome by shame and remorse. He sends men by ship to attempt a recovery, but this proves unsuccessful. His grief—paralleling the subsequent grief of the husband-king and Syr Kadore—receives much fuller treatment than does Emaré's suffering on the open sea. By way of contrast, the mother-in-law enacts no remorse scene, nor does she attempt to overcome her murderous jealousy. She is dispossessed of all wealth and exiled "over the sea foam" and out of the narrative. As the only woman who dares to initiate action in the narrative rather than to accept the actions of others, the figure of the evil mother-in-law confirms the oppressive strategies of the narrative. Even as a relatively "active" female character, she is constrained. She cannot condemn Emaré herself but must fabricate a letter of condemnation from her son. Her aggression toward her son is not realized by direct means (that is, exiling him on the sea) but by indirection (that is, exiling Emaré and Segramour). She is both more evil than Syr Artyus and less powerful.

If *Emaré* reinscribes some features of the "incest romance," it comes close and then shies away from sexual violation. Emaré "worthy under wede" (worthy under her clothing)—a phrase constantly repeated throughout the narrative and marking the unseen, reminding us of the presence of a veiled, bodily experience—is able to refuse her father's advances successfully.[7] Thus, *Emaré* offers a reading of women's heroism which is dependent, like many narrative renditions of female heroism, on the threat of rape and/or murder. Anne Middleton finds, for example, that "incestuous rape, threatened if not performed, activates the plot" in Chaucer's *Legend of Hypermnestra* ("The *Physician's Tale*," 29), and Kathryn Gravdal has commented, in reference to medieval hagiography, that "the threat of rape . . . opens a space for female heroism" (*Ravishing Maidens*, 23). Sexual violence and/or a seduction plot is, of course, a staple of hagiography, but *Emaré* veers away from the typical denouement of saintly martyrdom, preferring to corral the narrative back into the domestic marriage plot instead. Where a saint often prefers death to the loss of her virginity, Emaré prefers death to incest. Instead of acquiring sainthood, Emaré acquires marriage and motherhood. She saves her body for those legitimate social, sexual, and political roles prescribed for women under patriarchy—namely the chaste and forgiving daughter, mother, and wife.

Although resistance to patriarchy occurs in *Emaré*—in the daughter's refusal of her father and in her own unfathered negotiation of a marriage with the king of Gaul later in the narrative—these choices also reconfirm patriarchy. Emaré refuses illicit male desire and preserves her own option of assenting to legitimate marriage and motherhood. She attains heroic status not only because she obeys God's law above her father's command but also because she refuses her father's assault on patriarchy's system of exchanging women. The jewel-studded robe echoes these contradictions and tensions: it is war booty and wedding gift; an incestuous gift and a sign marking and protecting Emaré in exile; a depiction of passionate (even adulterous) lovers and a lapidary of virtuous stones.[8] When Emaré wears the garment, she puts on the gift of the father. The robe—its history, its imagery, and its status as the father's inappropriate gift—creates both dissonance and harmony within the moralizing framework. The robe functions, perhaps, like patriarchy does, by blinding men to Emaré's real body "worthy under wede" and covering over the realities of women's suffering; it weighs heavily on Emaré herself, as patriarchy also does, by handing her a conceptual structure that prefers death to sexual violation. The many gems on the garment both acclaim value and precariously weigh Emaré down as she floats alone on the open sea. Although most often interpreted as a sign of virtue, the marvelous cloak, like Philomela's tapestry, may weave other meanings as well.

Notably, the robe makes its way into the narrative at particular moments, moments of emotional intensity and physical distress. Its journey from person to person occurs in a web of love and violence, this dynamic continuing even after it comes into Emaré's possession. It appears at precisely those moments when Emaré is threatened with violation, with starvation, with drowning, *and* at precisely those points in the narrative when she is represented as safe and secure: when she marries the king and when she recovers husband and father at the end. Here, in the image of the robe, then, lies a potential disruption of the text's moralizing framework, a disruption created by structural repetition and a subtle equation of violence with social system. The qualities of the robe as both protection and heavy burden form a contradiction that works against the narrative's strategy of containment and resolution. The appearance of the cloth opens up possibilities for the resisting reader to read the rule of patriarchy in the text as a violation of women, to equate women's subordination and objectification with drowning, dehydration, starvation, and madness, and to see in the narrative a continuum of violence that stretches from threats of violation and death to absorption into the culturally endorsed roles of daughter, mother, wife. This reading is not, apparently, what the narrator works to have us see; rather, it lies potential, like another meaning "under wede," beneath the surface rhetoric of the text.

In her essay "The Violence of Rhetoric: Considerations on Representation and Gender" (in *Technologies,* 31–50), Teresa de Lauretis draws attention to the way language speaks a kind of violence—ways it names or identifies some things as violent but not others, ways it constructs objects and subjects of violence—and she examines the phrase *family violence* in this light. Obviously the term *family violence* most often indicates violence that occurs within the family: incest, wife battering, and child abuse. But, de Lauretis points out, the phrase can also indicate the violence of the family as institution (33–38). As Judith Herman notes, overt incest is "only the most extreme form of a traditional family pattern. . . . [It] represents only the furthest point on a continuum—an exaggeration of patriarchal family norms, but not a departure from them" (*Father-Daughter Incest,* 109–10). Phyllis Chesler, observing the ways in which cultural codes instruct women (figuratively) to marry their fathers, notes that women are taught to seek out men who are usually older, wealthier, taller, and more powerful than themselves. Women, she says, "are encouraged to commit incest as a way of life" ("Rape and Psychotherapy," 76). Whether one is considering the fictional entertainments of the Middle Ages or the popular media of our own times, women are taught to imagine themselves rescued by a man who will raise them up out of the "degradation" of womanhood (often symbolized as poverty, exile, imprisonment, slavery, pain, or isolation). In

Emaré, the title character lives out just such a Cinderella plot.

If Emaré is restored to social standing from obscurity through her connections with powerful men, the *pater familias* is also purified and restored through the sacrifice and suffering of women: Emaré and the mother-in-law. Males in the family are redeemed as they transform themselves into properly traditional relationships with the sacrificial: the king of Gaul as he asserts power over his mother, the emperor Artyus as he relinquishes his daughter to patriarchy's system of exchanging women among men. Emaré's role in the narrative's conclusion is consistent, then, with Lévi-Strauss's well-known observation that the transfer of women between men as objects or gifts provides "the means of binding men together" (*Elementary Structures,* 480). And the rule of the gift is inextricably intertwined with the incest taboo, a prohibition Lévi-Strauss and others have considered foundational to the social contract.[9]

The narrator works to persuade readers that Emaré's position within a family of men at the end of the narrative is redemptive: "Ther was a joyfull metynge / Of the emperour and of the kynge, / And also of Emare; / And so ther was of Syr Segramour" (1021–24). But Emaré's location is, itself, a form of "family violence," for she is isolated from any other female figure—her mother is killed off, the nurse left far behind, and the mother-in-law vilified and banished from the narrative. As soon as Syr Artyus recognizes Emaré as a sexual being, she is cut off from a world of women to be circulated and identified in relation to men. The purification of the men is accomplished through Emaré's exile from other women, through her restoration to men, and through her subjugation as object rather than subject within the narrative. Overt incest may be resisted, but the more subtle dynamic of oppression and objectification remains. The narrative of *Emaré* disciplines the father's sexuality and simultaneously affirms a form of family violence in which women's subjugation is naturalized. The tale works to create a kind of narratological blinding covered with a rhetorical flourish, as Emaré is woven into a design of relations with father, husband, son. In an eerie repetition of events and words, the narrator echoes, in the final recognition scene, the initial encounter between the adolescent Emaré and her father: "And the emperour alyghte tho, / And toke her yn hys armes two, / And clypte and kyssed her sote" (1018–20).[10] What the narrative works to define as a restoration is, in fact, a return to her father's arms.

Notes

1. An early version of this article was presented at the International Congress of Medieval Studies in Kalamazoo, Michigan, in May 1995. I am grateful to Anna

Roberts for inviting me to present the paper there and for organizing the panels on women and violence. I also thank Eve Salisbury, who collaborated with me on our edition of *The Middle English Breton Lays*, and Russell Peck, general editor of the Middle English Text Series, a series sponsored by the Consortium for the Teaching of the Middle Ages.

2. For the relationship between *Emaré* and analogues, see Suchier, *Beaumanoir*, vol. 1, xxiii–xcvi; clix–clx; Gough, *The Constance Saga*; and most especially, Schlauch, *Chaucer's Constance*, 62–114.

3. Two other English documents that contain the tale are noteworthy: the twelfth-century *Vitae Offae Primi*, available in translation within Furnivall's *Originals and Analogues of Some of Chaucer's Canterbury Tales*, 73–84; and the fourteenth-century *Anglo-Norman Chronicle* by Nicholas Trivet, also available in Furnivall, 2–70.

4. All citations taken from *Emaré* indicate line numbers and are from the text as it appears in Laskaya and Salisbury, *Middle English Breton Lays*, 145–99.

5. See Jacobs, *Victimized Daughters*; Herman, *Father-Daughter Incest*, and her more recent book, *Trauma and Recovery*; and see among works cited Benjamin; Dominelli; James and Mackinnon; McIntyre; and Miller. For articles addressing incest in medieval literature relevant to *Emaré*, see Elizabeth Scala, "Canacee and the Chaucer Canon: Incest and Other Unnarratables," *Chaucer Review* 30.1 (1955): 15–39; Maria Bullon-Fernandez, "Confining the Daughter: Gower's 'Tale of Canace and Machaire' and the Politics of the Body," *Essays in Medieval Studies* 11 (1994): 75–85; Anna Walecka, "The Concept of Incest: Medieval French and Normative Writings in Latin," *Romance Languages Annual* 5 (1993): 117–23, and her "Incest and Death as Indices of the Female Hero in Romance," *Romance Languages Annual* 4 (1992): 159–65; Georgiana Donavin, *Incest Narratives and the Structure of Gower's Confessio Amantis* (Victoria, B.C.: University of Victoria Press, 1993); R. A. Shoaf, "'Unwemmed Custance': Circulation, Property, and Incest in the Man of Law's Tale," *Exemplaria* 2.1 (1990): 287–302; Carolyn Dinshaw, "The Man of Law and Its 'Abhomynacions,'" *Exemplaria* 1.1 (1989): 117–48; Elizabeth Archibald, "Incest in Medieval Literature and Society," *Forum for Modern Language Studies* 25.1 (1989): 1–15; C. David Benson, "Incest and Moral Poetry in Gower's *Confessio Amantis*," *Chaucer Review* 19.2 (1984): 100–109; and Thelma Fenster, "Beaumanoir's *La Manekine*: Kin D(r)ead: Incest, Doubling, and Death," *American Imago* 39.1 (1982): 41–58.

6. Judith L. Herman begins her study of father-daughter incest by examining two narratives: the Cinderella tale and the tragic narrative of Saint Dympna. *Emaré*, like the Cinderella tale, grounds its perspective of gender on a narrative that stresses the abuses women dole out upon each other and minimizes the abuse women experience at the hands of men, choosing instead to imagine men as the source for women's salvation.

7. While Emaré's refusal is encoded as heroic, the text's encoding of her refusal still also makes clear that the final decision to violate or not rests with the father.

8. For references and some discussion of the robe's symbolism, see the notes in Laskaya and Salisbury, 185–92.

9. Cf. Gayle Rubin, "The Traffic of Women: Notes on the Political Economy of Sex," in *Toward an Anthropology of Women*, ed. Rayna R. Reiter (New York: Monthly Review Press, 1975), 157–210; and Carolyn Dinshaw, *Chaucer's Sexual Poetics* (Madison: University of Wisconsin Press, 1989).

10. In the lines cited here, as well as in lines 208–14, Emaré and Syr Artyus meet on foot. Line 212 reads, "He klypped her and kyssed here swete."

WORKS CITED

Bal, Mieke. *Lethal Love: Feminist Literary Readings of Biblical Love Stories.* Bloomington: Indiana University Press, 1987.

Benjamin, Jessica. *The Bonds of Love: Psychoanalysis, Feminism, and the Problem of Domination.* New York: Pantheon, 1988.

Bennett, Judith. *Women in the Medieval English Countryside: Gender and Household in Brigstock before the Plague.* New York and Oxford: Oxford University Press, 1987.

Brownmiller, Susan. *Against Our Will: Men, Women and Rape.* New York: Simon & Schuster, 1975.

Carter, John M. *Rape in Medieval England, An Historical and Sociological Study.* Lanham, Md.: University Press of America, 1985.

Chesler, Phyllis. "Rape and Psychotherapy." In *Rape: The First Sourcebook for Women*, ed. Noreen Connell and Cassandra Wilson. New York: New American Library, 1974.

Dominelli, Lena. "Father-Daughter Incest: Patriarchy's Shameful Secret." *Critical Social Policy* 6.16 (1986): 8–22.

Furnivall, F. J., Edmund Brock, and W. A. Clouston, eds. *Originals and Analogues of Some of Chaucer's Canterbury Tales.* London: N. Trubner, 1872–87.

Gough, A. B. *The Constance Saga.* Palaestra 23. Berlin: Mayer and Muller, 1902.

Gravdal, Kathryn. *Ravishing Maidens: Writing Rape in Medieval French Literature and Law.* Philadelphia: University of Pennsylvania Press, 1991.

Herman, Judith L. *Father-Daughter Incest.* Cambridge: Harvard University Press, 1981.

———. *Trauma and Recovery: The Aftermath of Violence—From Domestic Abuse to Political Terror.* New York: Basic Books, 1992.

Jacobs, Janet Liebman. *Victimized Daughters: Incest and the Development of the Female Self.* New York: Routledge, 1994.

James, Kerri, and Lauri Mackinnon. "The 'Incestuous Family' Revisited: A Critical Analysis of Family Therapy Myths." *Journal of Marital and Family Therapy* 16.1 (1990): 71–88.

Laskaya, Anne, and Eve Salisbury, eds. *The Middle English Breton Lays.* Kalamazoo: Western Michigan University Press, 1995.

de Lauretis, Teresa. *Technologies of Gender: Essays on Theory, Film, and Fiction.* Bloomington: Indiana University Press, 1987.

Lévi-Strauss, Claude. *Elementary Structures of Kinship.* Trans. J. H. Bell, J. R. von Sturmer, and R. Needham. Ed. R. Needham. Rev. ed. Boston: Beacon, 1969.

McIntyre, Kevin. "Role of Mothers in Father-Daughter Incest: A Feminist Analysis." *Social Work* 26 (1981): 462–66.

Mehl, Dieter. *The Middle English Romances of the Thirteenth and Fourteenth Centuries.* New York: Barnes and Noble, 1969.

Middleton, Anne. "The *Physician's Tale* and Love's Martyrs: 'Ensamples Mo Than Ten' as a Method in the *Canterbury Tales.*" *Chaucer Review* 8 (1973): 9–32.

Miller, Alice. *Thou Shalt Not Be Aware: Society's Betrayal of the Child.* Trans. Hildegarde Hannum and Hunter Hannum. New York: Farrar, Straus & Giroux, 1984.

Ruggiero, Guido. *The Boundaries of Eros: Sex Crime and Sexuality in Renaissance Venice.* Oxford: Oxford University Press, 1985.

Schlauch, Margaret. *Chaucer's Constance and Accused Queens.* New York: New York University Press, 1927.

Suchier, Hermann, ed. *Oeuvres Poétiques de Philippe de Remi, Sire de Beaumanoir.* Société des Anciens Textes Français. Paris: Firmin Didot, 1884–85; rpt. New York: Johnson Reprint, 1966.

Tanner, Laura E. *Intimate Violence: Reading Rape and Torture in Twentieth-Century Fiction.* Bloomington: Indiana University Press, 1994.

Tomaselli, Sylvana, and Roy Porter, eds. *Rape: An Historical and Social Inquiry.* Oxford: Basil Blackwell, 1986.

"Quiting" Eve: Violence against Women in the *Canterbury Tales*

Angela Jane Weisl

Due to the events in the Garden of Eden, at which Satan, as Chaucer notes, "madest Eva brynge us in servage" (2.368), medieval women were perceived as the offspring of evil, always ready to return to their dangerous nature.[1] Because Eve ate the apple, she was the prototype for female disobedience; because she gave it to Adam, she became the paradigmatic temptress ready to snare innocent men and lead them into folly; because she and Adam were then banished from the Garden, she became the cause of all destruction and sin in the world. Made in her image, women were thus considered perpetually on the verge of repeating—in various and sundry ways—Eve's walk down the primrose path to hell, usually bringing men with them in the process. Because Eve's curse was painful childbirth (and childbirth in general), women were then associated with "all that is vile, lowly, corruptible, and material"; in the "curse" of menstruation, she lay closer to the beasts; the lure of her beauty was nothing but an aspect of the death brought about by her seduction of Adam in the garden (Warner, *Alone*, 58). Adam was charged by God to rule over her, authorizing the subjection of woman. All that was bad was her fault, and she was to be treated accordingly.[2]

As a result of the prevalence of this conception, medieval women inhabited a violent world that often sought to maintain their subjugation by physical attacks on their bodies. In the secular world, women were at the mercy of laws which permitted them to be battered, the most notable of which was widely enough known to become a proverbial expression, the "rule of thumb" being the width of stick a man was permitted to use to beat his wife ("thumb," *OED*). The ability to punish women became a kind of duty for leaders of households, as Georges Duby notes: "the cornerstone of the system of values that governed behavior in the noble household was a precept derived from scripture: women being the weaker sex and more prone to sin, had to be held in check. The first duty of the head of household was to watch over, punish, and if necessary kill his wife, sisters, and daughters, as well as the widows and orphans of his brothers, cousins, and vassals. Since females were dangerous, patriarchal power over them was reinforced" ("Aristocratic Households," 77). Woman, then, was there to be abused, both to keep her under the subservience of men and as retribution for the sins of the first mother, Eve.

Literature, too, served to "quite" Eve by showing woman the dangers she faced.[3] Much of this danger was focused on the physical body; while religious literature offered rewards for the gory martyrdoms female saints endured, courtly literature, both lyric and narrative, used rape as a stock device. Kathryn Gravdal shows examples of literary rapes ranging from the pastourelle to Chrétien's romances and the rape plots of the saints' lives. Rape becomes a test of masculinity, as Gravdal shows through the discussion of the French term for rape, *esforcement*, which "denote[s] effort, power, military force, bravura, and rape. From the notion of strength, manliness, and bravery, we move to the knight's striving after heroism, and then to the idea of forced coitus" (Gravdal, *Ravishing Maidens*, 3). As a result, rape is "built into the military culture in which force is applauded in most forms" (4). These power relations find their literary forms in epic and romance in particular, with the latter genre, because it is more focused on male-female relations, a particular site of rape, virtual rape, metaphoric rape, and abduction. Through these narratives, the "quiting" of woman is enforced and spread; the normalization of violence against her in life is echoed and strengthened. As Annette Kolodny notes, "the power relations inscribed in the form of conventions within our literary inheritance . . . reify the encodings of those same power relations in the culture at large. And the critical examination of rhetorical codes becomes . . . the pursuit of ideological codes" ("Dancing," 147). Art does not just reflect life, it has a "normative effect" on it (147). The power structures of medieval life, then, are embodied in the literature, just as the literature seeks to enforce the power conventions of life. While rape is by no means the only secular violence done to women in medieval life and literature, it is the most documented. However, more domestic examples of violence inhabit both the *fabliau* and the romance, as all medieval genres embody the sense that "to control and punish women, particularly their bodies and their dangerous disruptive sexuality was . . . man's work," since "women, through whom death, suffering, and toil came into the world, were creatures dominated by their sex" (Klapisch-Zuber, "Including Women," 13).[4] Man's need to control women through violence, doubly revealed in literature and life, becomes a kind of quiting of them for the sins of Eve, a continuous justified abuse that goes primarily unquestioned through a long and varied tradition.

This is the history of normalized violence against women that Chaucer inherits and reflects in the *Canterbury Tales*. Recent critical works have shown Chaucer to be sympathetic to gender concerns, and indeed, the *Tales* pay great attention to the position of women, both allowing them greater opportunities than the literary tradition he follows has done and considering carefully the disservice done to them.[5] While Chaucer's women act and negotiate in a world ready to give them consideration and a voice, they still do so against a background of violence that is sometimes questioned or rectified but is more often ignored or mitigated. The patterns of this violence divide into categories along genre lines; the fabliaux, romances, and holy tales each show particular qualities in their definitions of women's roles and the ways those are impinged upon, both overtly and covertly, by threats, images, and acts of violence against women. Each group of tales functions in its own milieu, colored by the shades of violence embodied in it. The fabliaux turn violence against women—particularly sexual violation—into a slapstick comedy that distracts from its severity through humor; the romance works before a background of the physical danger that threatens women who do not conform to its rules and regulations; holy tales valorize violence by giving it a transcendent result, while reveling in its detail, rather like a contemporary horror film.

The tales told by Chaucer's three female tellers represent this generic breakdown no less than those told by male tellers; they show, however unintentionally, how profoundly women become what is said about them. Rather than presenting worlds without violence against women, or even redressing this violence, these three tellers tell some of the most overtly violent tales in the collection.[6] These tales demonstrate just how pervasive the narrative necessity of violence against women really is in medieval literature. Although these tellers are not real women and cannot be treated as such, they reflect the narratives that real medieval women tell and incorporate accordingly the threats women face.

The *Canterbury Tales* are framed by a story-telling competition that becomes increasingly heated as tellers (particularly the male tellers) attempt to "quite" one another's stories. As the decorum of the *Knight's Tale* moves into the more chaotic world of the Miller, Reeve, and Cook, hostilities between tellers become both more personal and more vicious. The Miller tells a tale about a carpenter; the Reeve, a carpenter, tells a nastier story about a Miller. The Friar and Summoner deride each other's professions in dramatic tales involving pacts with the devil and the distribution of a fart in a debased image of Pentecost. Beneath this male conflict, however, is another kind of quiting: the quiting of women, of Eve, through a continuous pattern of violent acts against her.

Mentions of Eve's sin occur throughout the *Canterbury Tales*. In the *Man of Law's Tale*, she is linked to the evil Sultaness and Donegild (both of whom work to destroy the Christian Custance) through Satan, who "Thyn instrument so—weylawey the while!—/ Makestow of wommen, whan thou wolt bigile" (2.370–71). The Wife of Bath's husband Jankyn reads to her from his *Bokke of Wikked Wyves*, beginning with the story "Of Eva first, that for hir wikkednesse / Was al mankynde broght to wrecchednesse, / For which that Jhesu Crist hymself was slayn" (3.715–17), which leads to the physical battle between the Wife and her Husband that results in her deafness. Even the Second Nun, who is more closely allied with Mary because of her virginity and piety, says to the Virgin: "And thogh that I, unworthy sone of Eve / Be synful, yet accepte my bileve" (8.62–63). Because even she, a holy woman, is a sinner because of her descent from Eve, her tale of violence against a female saint shows the prevailing opprobrium all women—even those who model themselves on the sinless Mary—receive because of their sex. Even as St. Cecelia (and the Second Nun) deny their fleshly natures through the preservation of their virginity, they are still punished. Finally, the Parson, the *Tales'* most uncompromisingly good pilgrim, who receives no criticism at all in the *General Prologue* and refuses to tell "fables and swich wrecchednesse" (10.34), includes the story of the Eve in his sermon in order to remind his audience that "There may ye seen that deedly synne hath, first, suggestion of the feend, as sheweth here by the naddre; and afterward, the delit of the flessh, as sheweth here by Eve; and after that, the consentynge of resoun, as sheweth heere by Adam" (10.331). Again, Eve is shown to be the cause of sin, close to the devil, and responsible for the sins of the world through her lustful body.

The need to repress women as a result of their dangerous power that leads to sin is raised at the beginning of the first of the *Canterbury Tales*, when the Knight describes Theseus's conquering of "al the regne of Femenye" (1.866), his destruction of the Amazons. The triple reminder of this event, how "wonnen was the regne of Femenye / By Theseus and his chivalrye" (1.877–78) and "the grete bataille for the nones / Bitwixen Atthenes and

Amazones: / And how asseged was Ypolita" (1.879–81) demonstrates both its literal and symbolic importance. While Chaucer does not include any details of the battle or describe the Amazons' mutilated bodies, the opening of the tale—and perhaps the whole tale-telling enterprise—provides the suggestions and the necessity of the destruction of unruly women, in body as well as in spirit. Hippolyta and Emelye are not dead, but they have been turned into conventional figures of romance. By the end of the tale, the "regne of Femenye" of the romance, which leads to broken alliances and violent, animalistic behavior, has been conquered by the rational, masculine world of the epic and has taken Emelye along with it.

While Emelye is conquered by narrative necessity rather than physical violence, women in the tales that follow are threatened and often overborne by more corporeal means. And when they are not, masculine desire to quite them still inhabits the tales. This quiting of women parallels the quiting between tellers, just as the prototype for fabliau violence appears in the *Miller's Tale*, with which the Miller promises "I wol now quite the Knyghtes tale" (1.3127). Alison may finally triumph over the men who seek to possess her, but it is impossible to forget that Absolon intends to commit his violent act against Alison, not Nicholas.[7] The Miller makes this act part of a consummate (pun intended) joke, which mitigates the inherent horror of what Absolon has done—and planned to do; he has committed a rape with a red-hot poker. Were this not a fabliau, whoever was the "butt" of Absolon's joke would be in far too much pain to leap up and help humiliate John the Carpenter—if she or he were not dead. The tale's humor, then, covers up its horror.

This slapstick humor at women's expense continues in the next tale, another male instrument of quiting, in which the Reeve attempts to repay the Miller for his perceived slights against carpenters. Aleyn and John, the two clerks, having been cheated by the Miller, quite him by "swyvyng" his wife and daughter. That a man is quited through the virtual rape of two women shows their objective role in this tale, and in the fabliau in general. Neither woman even has the benefit of the fair words with which Nicholas convinces Alison to go to bed with him. Both discover lusty clerks beside them, and both go along with the joke. However, when "John the clerk up leep, / And on this goode wyf he leith on soore" (1.4228–29), the spectre of rape enters the picture. Although we are told, "So myrie a fit ne hadde she nat ful yoore" (1.4230), the next line, "He priketh harde and depe as he were mad" (1.4231) makes one wonder. As in cartoon violence—in which characters get hit so hard with frying pans that their heads assume the pan's shape, but then merely shake their heads to return to normal and continue with the fight—the fabliau mitigates the violence it enacts by making it funny; this rape is humorous because the wife is supposed to like it better than what she gets (or doesn't get) from her drunken husband. As in the *Miller's Tale*, the humor takes place before a backdrop of violence against women, which it normalizes by turning it into the punch line of a joke. The women are there to be had, to be taken; because they are merely props in a humorous story without any real identity, they are precluded from the sympathy—or even the notice—that women in other genres receive. We are forced to read between the lines to see what is really done to these women—a reading that the tale itself, in its drive to quite the Miller's in the story and on the pilgrimage, does not encourage. In this male game, the women who help the winner are merely chess pieces ready to be captured.

The other fabliaux enhance this pattern, if less overtly. The *Merchant's Tale* makes Eve an ironic example of female behavior through Januarie's alliance of himself with Adam; he has a garden and now desires a helpmate. Once he acquires May, she proves her connection to Eve by playing out the metaphor that Januarie has claimed in ways he never expects. Januarie's ridiculousness in imagining marriage as a perfect Eden is enhanced by May's deception—and her clever escape from blame (which Eve cannot manage); here the sinful woman, ripe for the quiting, is able to beguile Januarie into believing in her innocence. Readers marvel at May's wiliness but, having seen the entire story unfold in Januarie's snake-ridden Eden, remain unduped. Januarie is blind to women's deceit; readers are not. May is appealing, and readers are encouraged to sympathize with her situation when Chaucer says, "But God woot what that May thoughte in hir herte" (4.1851), reminding us of what Januarie must seem like to her, and yet, at the end of the tale, she has been shown to be a true daughter of Eve. In an overdetermined narrative space—the walled spring garden—she has deceived her husband with the help of a pear tree. Subtly enhancing the condemnation of May is the rape imagery in the background of the tale; the presence of Proserpina and Pluto in the garden suggest that women become men's "queenes" by problematic means (Hansen, *Chaucer and Fictions of Gender,* 262). May is not strictly abducted, but Januarie does "chees hire of his owene auctoritee" (4.1597), and she is "feffed in his lond" (4.1698) through "scrit and bond" (4.1697), not through her own consent, which is never mentioned in the tale. The reference to Pluto and Proserpina serves as a reminder of what may happen if May does not acquiesce. Indeed, Januarie imagines their first consummation in pointed terms; "But in his herte he gan hire to manace / That he that nyght in armes wolde hire streyne / Harder than evere Parys dide Eleyne" (4.1752–54). When the time comes, May is "broght abedde as stille as stoon" (4.1818), hardly an enthusiastic agreement.

While the fabliaux often show women like Alison and May triumphing over silly old men, with the violence against them hidden by a smoke screen of physical comedy, the romances, which also appear to uphold female power on the surface, reveal "courtly love to be a game: a masculine game of power, property, and violence" (Gravdal, *Ravishing Maidens*, 208).[8] The drive of romance as a genre toward its fixed conclusion, the "happily ever after" of courtly marriage, coerces woman into compliance that limits her; medieval marriage, as Duby has effectively shown, requires the submission of the woman to her husband's law and will.[9] While less explicit in their violence than the fabliaux, Chaucer's *Canterbury Tales* romances do add to the work's overall normalization of this aspect of medieval life. Each romance places violence into its narrative in a different way; in some it is foregrounded, while in others it informs the background of the tale through images or events; taken together, these different approaches help to create a pattern of violence no less essential than that seen in the fabliaux. The *Franklin's Tale* includes no specific violence against Dorigen, but lurking behind its "gentil" surface are two troubling images. The "blake rokkes" that Dorigen fears are a potent symbol of the dangers of the courtly relationship; both their presence (which might wreck Arveragus's ship and leave Dorigen alone) and their absence (which will require her to give in to Aurelius's desires) put Dorigen in jeopardy. The illusory nature of their disappearance also enhances their symbolic qualities—these dangers can never really disappear. Dorigen, as a heroine in a romance, is subjected to a kind of cleaned-up danger that functions on many levels—the danger of abandonment, the danger that she will be raped by Aurelius if she rejects his advances, the loss of her autonomy in marriage, etc. Nothing violent happens to Dorigen, but we are constantly reminded that it may, that it can. As a tale of *gentilesse*, the *Franklin's Tale* avoids threatening Dorigen overtly with the dangers that the black rocks symbolize, but they remain lurking in the background. The collected wisdom of Chaucer's other *Canterbury Tales* romances and *Troilus and Criseyde* brings these dangers forward in sharper detail. Emelye, the maiden in the *Wife of Bath's Tale*, and Criseyde all reveal the frightening possibilities that Dorigen barely avoids.

The one place danger is explicit in the tale is in Dorigen's meditation on death and dishonor. Once locked into her no-win situation, she "wepeth, waileth, al a day or two, / and swoneth" (5.1348–49), a "sorweful creature" paralyzed by "verray feere," she sees only these two choices. She contemplates her options:

> But natheless, yet have I levere to lese
> My lif than of my body to have a shame,
> Or knowe myselven fals, or lese my name;
> And with my deth I may be quyt, ywis.
> Hath ther nat many a noble wyf er this,
> And many a mayde, yslayn hirself, allas,
> Rather than with hir body doon trespas? (5.1360–66)

Dorigen goes on to cite many examples of "woful maydens, ful of drede," who killed themselves in various ways "Rather than they wolde lese hir maydenhede" (5.1375–76). These examples do not convince Dorigen to kill herself, but they do valorize violence against women who would rather die than be unfaithful. While one might admire these women's concern with morality, their deaths provide a spectrum of slaughter all too easily passed over, which nevertheless remains a crucial example in the background of violence against which these stories are told. Dorigen places herself, by contemplating this literary history of women's destruction, into a tradition of violence against her sex—of the threat of rape (a possibility if Aurelius doesn't get what he wants), death (what may happen to her as a result of her agreements), and dishonor. That Dorigen survives her tale with honor is made possible only by the astonishing kindness of three men, who make the rare choice of selflessness. The Franklin's delight in the gentility with which Arveragus, Aurelius, and the Clerk act, and the question "which was the mooste fre, as thynketh yow?" (5.1622) point to its uniqueness. Dorigen is lucky, but Chaucer has shown, in the black rocks image and the catalogue of dead virgins and wives, how easily she might not have been.

Romance makes sex threatening to women in metaphor as well. In Chaucer's *Tale of Sir Thopas*, the hero's somewhat excessive reaction to his own desire implies the courtly violence that Duby and Gravdal suggest:

> Sire Thopas fil in love-longynge,
> Al whan he herde the thrustel synge,
> And pryked as he were wood.
> His faire steede in his prikynge
> So swatte that men myghte him wrynge;
> His sydes were al blood. (7.772–77)

Perhaps when Thopas found his elf-queen, his vigor would have matched John the clerk's in the *Reeve's Tale*; he certainly drives his horse "harde and depe," and then must rest for his own exhaustion. To be fair, Thopas gives "his steede som solas" (7.782), yet his excesses do suggest the inherent male force in love—or sex. Thopas is a terrible knight and a disastrous lover, yet, like Absolon, his desire, when it becomes powerful and thus violent, makes him masculine, if only for a stanza. And while his horse is not a woman, per se, its position under him (literally and figuratively) in this sexual metaphor puts it in her place. This violent sexuality is the same as that which is overtly expressed by the rape in the *Wife of Bath's Tale*, which helps validate Thopas's metaphor. Figural sex is just as violent in romance as the literal sex of the Reeve's or Miller's tales; that it is not real makes it no less a part of the tale's atmosphere.

Chaucer's religious narratives, the third group of tales that function within a violent context, raise the overtness level significantly, taking the violence from the background, from the worlds of comedy, metaphor, image, and suggestion, into the foreground of the tales. The purpose and role of violence in these tales differs from those in the fabliaux and romances, and as a result, the attention given to it is greater, both in detail and in focus. Martyrdom may get a holy woman into heaven, but the dismemberment of her physical body is still played out on earth.

While religious women were often spared the beating and punishment levied against their secular sisters, they, too, inhabited a world in which violence played a significant role. On the literal level, the preservation of virginity, "the ideal state for women, the perfect life as articulated by the church . . . the single most essential prerequisite for a life of Christian perfection" (Schulenberg, "Heroics of Virginity," 31), often led to self-mutilation, an attack on the body that was assumed to seduce "innocent" men who would rob the virgin of her chastity. The models of literary perfection always chose martyrdom over dishonor (as we noted in Dorigen's catalogue of models); the "innocent" men were divested of value by being merciless pagans intent on having the saint's virginity or having her head. The actual destruction of the female body became the focus of these narratives of martyrdom; "as they defended their virtue, the female martyrs of the Christian calendar are assaulted in any number of ingenious and often sexual ways: in the *Golden Legend*, Agatha's breasts are cut off; Apollonia's teeth are torn out and she is then burned to death; Juliana is shattered on a wheel; . . . then plunged into a lead bath; Euphemia is tormented with all sorts of refinements and then beheaded; Catherine of Alexandria is also broken on a wheel" (Warner, *Alone*, 71). For religious women, then, virginity became most valuable when it was maintained against all odds, resulting in an exchange of sexual violence for sacred violence. Rape violence was degradation and disgrace, but martyrdom violence was glorification and grace. And the difference comes from the result rather than the act. The dwelling on the details of martyrdom, often including quite graphic depictions of torture and dismemberment, shows an enthusiasm for the violation of the female body made palatable by its implicit result—the ascension of the virgin into heaven. The body, a corrupt vessel, was ripe and ready for destruction.

Chaucer's holy stories, patterned on hagiography but which are not primarily saint's lives, fit into the most brutal genre of the Middle Ages. The first of these, the *Man of Law's Tale*, allies Eve, through Satan, with the Sultaness and Donegild, who seek to destroy the pious Custance; Custance then becomes a model saint who quites the evil women by remaining good, Christian, and alive. Because she has a child by her second marriage and thus cannot be gloriously martyred, Custance narrowly escapes violence instead of being brutalized herself. While the Sultan and "the Cristen everichone / Been al tohewe and stiked at the bord" (2.429–20), Custance only has to suffer abandonment and exile in her little ship. When she leaves for Syria the first time, she notes the precariousness of her position: "Wommen are born to thraldom and penance. / And to been under mannes governance" (2.286–87). Custance is sent off to the "Barbre nacioun" by her father's will, exiled again by her first mother-in-law, accused of murder by her second and then exiled a third time, and finally must beg of her father, "Sende me namoore unto noon hethenesse" (2.1112). Certainly, Custance faces mortal danger on the ocean in her little ship, yet the violence done to her by others is more emotional than physical; however, the other women in the story, innocent or guilty, suffer more cruelly. The connection of women to Satan, and as a result to Eve, is made explicit in the Man of Law's description of the Sultaness:

O Sowdanesse, roote of iniquitee!
Virago, thou Semyrame the secounde!
O serpent under femynynytee,
Lik to the serpent depe in helle ybounde!
O feyned womman, al that may confounde
Vertu and innocence, thurgh thy malice,
Is bred in thee, as nest of every vice! (2.358–65)

This evil that the Sultaness and Donegild do makes them worthy of punishment. While the fate of the Sultaness goes unmentioned, Donegild is slain by her son, and Hermengyld is killed by one of Donegild's (male) lackeys ("thurgh Sathanas [here embodied in Donegild herself] temptaciouns" (2.598) in order to frame Custance. Here, the death becomes graphic when the Man of Law tells us that the constable finds "his wyf despitously yslayn" and "in the bed the blody knyf he fond / By Dame Custance" (2.605; 607–8). As a result, violence against women becomes a detailed part of the tale's material, justified by the evil women's connections to Eve through Satan, and by the narrative necessity of getting Custance into the court, where she can begin converting others through her goodness as well as meet Alla the king, whose "gentil herte is fulfild of pitee" (2.660) and who absolves her.

The other holy tales continue to enhance the graphic violence first seen in the *Man of Law's Tale*. The *Physician's Tale* makes the choice for Virginia that Dorigen avoids. A perfect maiden, Virginia (of the allegorical name) is everything the ideal woman can be:

> For in hir lyvyng maydens myghten rede,
> As in a book, every good word or dede
> That longeth to a mayden vertuous,
> She was so prudent and so bountevous.
> For which the fame out sprong on every syde,
> Bothe of hir beautee and her bountee wyde
> That thrugh that land they preised hire echone
> That loved vertu. . . . (6.107–14)

Virginia, like the saints' lives medieval women were encouraged to read, is an exemplum. Ladies are to learn from her and love her. Only Envy, "That sory is of oother mennes wele" (6.115), resents her, and in that comes her downfall. Her beauty causes a Judge to desire her and declare "This mayde shal be myn, for any man!" (6.129). At that point, he joins forces with Satan: "Anon the feend into his herte ran, / And taughte hym sodeynly that he by slyghte / The mayden to his purpos wynne myghte" (6.130–32). Men's violence, here, is mediated; Satan is the actor, bringing evil into Apius's heart and making him act accordingly. Apius, then, may have been moderate left to his own devices; by making Satan the cause of his evil, Chaucer places him in strict contrast to Virginia, who, despite her perfection, cannot help being Eve the temptress, although her Satan does not tempt her first but joins forces with Apius, her Adam, on the road to destruction. Apius builds a false claim against Virginius, claiming Virginia Claudius's "thral by right / Which fro myn hous was stole upon a nyght, / Whil that she was ful yong" (6.183–85); at the end of the trial Apius passes judgment: "I deme anon this cherl his servant have; / Thou shalt no lenger in thyn hous hir save. / Go bryng hire forth, and put hire in oure warde" (6.199–201). Virginius's "fadres pitee" (6.211) presents him with two positions: "Ther been two weyes, outher deeth or shame, / That thou most suffre" (6.214–15). Virginia's suffering is a given in this story; she must be martyred for a sin she did not commit. Because she is a woman, she is a temptress; because she is a woman, men decide her fate. Her choice, to the extent that she has one, is between two acts of violence, rape or dismemberment. For all that she does not "deservedest wherefore / To dyen with a swerd or with a knyf" (6.216–17), even less does she deserve Virginius's accusation that she is the "endere of my lyf" (6.218) since he remains alive, and she dies by his hand. Even Virginia's father thinks this situation is her fault. Still, she must take his sentence over the judge's, since her father's claim on her is more powerful.

Weeping, she asks, "Is ther no grace, is ther no remedye?" (6.236), but Virginius insists that there is not. Virginia is permitted "leyser" . . . / "My deeth for to compleyne a litel space" (6.238–39) and finds small consolation: "Blissed be God that I shal dye a mayde!" (6.248). She has chosen to quite Eve with her own destruction. Her father "with ful sorweful herte and wil, / Hir heed of smoot, and by the top it hente, / And to the juge he gan it to presente" (6.254–56). By having Virginia ask for another option, Chaucer brings Virginius's determination to destroy his daughter rather than give her to another man into sharp relief; Virginia's final choice, her submission to her father's (and God's) greater will, makes this tale an example of affective piety, and provides only undercurrents of questioning to the genre that willingly makes women its victims. Although Apius kills himself in jail, and all his cronies are hanged, the tale gives this revenge little attention. Virginia's murder is the center and apex of this tale. Indeed, the Physician dramatically misunderstands his own tale; at the end he delivers the moral: "Forsaketh synne, er synne yow forsake" (6.286), forgetting that Virginia, whose father forsakes her, is without sin, except the sin of her female body, which locks her into a terrible choice between secular and sacred violence.

The two religious women on the Canterbury pilgrimage seem to have taken to heart the model tales women were urged to read, telling two of the most dramatically violent tales in the collection. Both begin with invocations to Mary, the woman who redeemed the world from Eve's sin through her perfect virginity and conception of Christ, the world's savior. As in the *Physician's Tale*, the perfected bodies—of child and woman respectively—are enough to tempt evil men to sin. In the *Prioress's Tale*, the "litel childe," whose tiny stature and rote piety are constantly mentioned, making him increasingly pathetic as he walks through the "Jewerye" singing *Alma Redemptoris Mater,* is gruesomely murdered: "This cursed Jew hym hente, and heeld hym faste, / And kitte his throte, and in a pit hym caste" (7.569–70). The cutting of the throat and the casting of the child into the "wardrobe . . . Where as thise Jewes purgen hire entraille" (7.572–73) provide a graphic picture of the horror inherent in such a scene, rather than mitigating it or glossing over it. While the child is not a woman, in his virgin innocence he strongly resembles one; he is called, "O martir, sowded to virginitee" (7.579), and like the Prioress, he is aided in his song by Mary, to whom he sings despite his throat wound. Indeed, as the innocent subject at the mercy of violent men, he shares certain attributes of romance womanhood that are often made religious in saints' lives; he occupies the same place in the plot that heroines do, and the destruction of the saint's virgin body is certainly a kind of symbolic rape. At the abbey, we are forced to look at the child's wound again when the abbot asks how he can sing "Sith that thy throte is kut to my semynge?" (7.648). If that reminder is not enough, the child says again, "My throte is kut unto my nekke boon" (7.649). We find that his singing is due directly to Mary's intervention; he lives and speaks because she, the perfect virgin, has sustained his body with a "greyn" on his tongue. When the abbot removes the grain, the child "yaf up the goost ful softely" (7.672), and the abbot and monks, who cannot be converted because they already are Christian, weep and enshrine the "martir" in a marble tomb. As in the *Physician's Tale,* the destruction of the pure body becomes the central and driving image of the narrative. The violence against the "litel clergeoun" is paralleled by the equally strong act of violence against the Jewish community, in which "With torment and with shameful deeth echon, / This provost dooth thise Jewes for to sterve / That of this mordre wiste" (7.628–30). This punishment concludes when "with wilde hors he dide hem drawe, / And after that he heng hem by the lawe" (7.633–34); again it is underplayed because of the focus on the martyred virgin. That Jews and women are often paralleled in medieval literature makes the Prioress's violence against this community another suspect attack on the children of Eve.[10]

While the *Prioress's Tale* does not contain specific violence against women, the recipients of its violence are both substitutes for the female sex, secular and sacred. The Jews, through their dealings with Satan, become cousins of Eve like the Sultaness and Donegild in the *Man of Law's Tale;* as a result, they receive the excessive quiting that women descended from Eve were thought to deserve. Just as women throughout the ages have been abused because of their femininity—an extraordinary punishment for Eve's sin—so, too, are the Jews punished excessively for the murder of the child. Although the Provost alludes to the Jewish law of "an eye for an eye" when he says, "Yvele shal have that yvele wol deserve" (7.632), drawing, quartering, and hanging the entire community is not equal restitution for the murder of one child. Thus these "like women" are subject to the same inordinate violence that real medieval women often suffered.

Yet more striking is the fascination with the destruction of the body as a pietistic tool. Just as the Jews model the secular violence against the women with whom they were allied, the "litel clergeon" receives the same holy violence of martyrdom levied on the female saints. While male saints were certainly martyred, this child's passivity and innocence, and the focus on his virginity and connection to Mary, rather than on his quest for conversion and alliance with Christ, join him with his female counterparts, as the valorization of his wounds also does. Religious women were encouraged to meditate on the virgin martyrs, and as a result, they tell tales that make the horror of dismemberment even greater in an attempt to distance the virgin body from the sinful body of Eve. The punishment of the flawed physical body is the only mode of true spiritual redemption; Eve must be fully rejected for the virgin truly to become Mary. Thus, through two examples of "like women," the Prioress quites Eve, embodying what is done to women on both symbolic and literal levels. In both cases, the violence is glorified, once as a pietistic, and thus exemplary, rejection of the body as a passage into heaven, and once as a justified destruction of the minions of Satan.

The Second Nun follows the Prioress's lead by telling the tale of St. Cecelia, the only true saint's life in the *Canterbury Tales*. Like the "litel childe" of the *Prioress's Tale*, St. Cecelia preaches while being boiled in her bath *and* having her head cut off. With the help of an Angel, Cecelia is able to preserve her virginity in marriage while converting her husband in the process; she goes on to convert several others to Christ and to martyrdom. Indeed, the *Second Nun's Tale* valorizes martyrdom as a part of Christian devotion more than do the other holy tales. Tiburce and Valerian "With humble herte and sad devocioun, / . . . losted bothe hire hevedes in the place. / Hir soules wenten to the Kyng of grace" (8.297–99). Cecelia buries them and then converts the messengers of Alimachius sent to bring her before him to "Doon sacrifice and Juppiter encense" (8.413); she then debates Alimachius into a fury. The next four stanzas top even the Prioress in their violence: Alimachius charges, "'In hire hous'" . . . "'Brenne hire right in a bath of flamves rede.' / And as he bad, right so was doon the dede; /

For in a bath they gonner hire faste shetten, / And nyght and day greet fyr they under betten" (8.514–18). Cecelia "For al the fur and eek the bathes heete / She sat al coold and feelede no wo" (8.520–21); Alimachius "Thre strokes in the nekke he smoot hire tho," furthering her torture (8.526); inexplicably, it is illegal to cut heads off in his country. To make this image even more powerful, the Second Nun tells us that she is "But half deed, with hir nekke ycorven there" (8.533), and that "With sheetes han the blod ful faire yhent" (8.536). For three days she continues to preach and then she dies, commending the souls of her followers to the pope, who buries her "Among his othere seintes honestly" (8.549) and consecrates her house. That most of Cecelia's conversions take place before her martyrdom does not take away from the violent impact of her death scene. In the voice of a female teller, the holy violence against women shown in the Man of Law's and Physician's tales takes on even greater impact and meaning; St. Cecelia becomes an exemplum of the ideal life for women—perfect virginity followed by a violent death.

Saints' narratives abound in medieval literature, and not only were religious women, like the Prioress and Second Nun, asked to meditate on these exempla, but secular women, too, were urged by conduct manuals to avoid romances and read saints' lives.[11] In the *Book of the Three Virtues*, Christine de Pizan urges women to give their daughters "devotional books and others describing virtuous behavior. She will not be allowed to read of vain things, folly or loose living. No such books will be permitted in her presence" (Christine de Pizan, *Mirror*, 104). That a woman writer with great concern for women recommends that women read books which valorize violence against them seems counterintuitive; however, the example of Christine herself, and of other medieval women writers, suggests an education so powerful that it makes its students complicitous in its program.[12] Surely the Prioress and the Second Nun prove themselves to be effectively indoctrinated.

Chaucer's third female teller does not narrate a holy story, but the Wife of Bath, too, places a violent act against women at the center of her tale.[13] The Wife has been a victim of domestic violence herself; in her prologue, she responds to the mental torture of being read Jankyn's *Bokke of Wikked Wives* by tearing out three pages and throwing them into the fire. Jankyn, "up stirte as dooth a wood leoun, / And with his fest he smoot me on the heed / That in the floor I lay as I were deed" (3.794–96). That Alison then tricks him and swats him back, while amusing, does not lessen the impact of his attack—both emotional and physical—on her; we find out in her portrait in the *General Prologue* that she is "somdeel deef" as a result of this battle. The extent to which this attack reflects actual medieval women's domestic lives aside, it sets up her tale, which begins with the sexual violation that the martyrs avoid by dismemberment: the "lusty bachiler" of Arthur's house "saugh a mayde walkynge hym biforn, / Of which mayde anon, maugree hir heed, / By verray force, he rafte hire maydenhed" (3.886–88).

Certainly this real rape reflects a threat with which medieval women lived; as the Middle Ages wore on, laws increasingly favored rapists and made cases against them difficult to prove. The victimization of women was not considered criminal, and its perpetrators received minimal penalties.[14] While the law often suggested death or castration as an appropriate punishment for rapists, the Church, "preaching Christian love, abhorred death and mutilation in principle" (Gravdal, "The Poetics of Rape," 210), reduced the rights of women by leaving the attacker around with minor punishments that often included marrying the victim.

While the *Wife of Bath's Tale* comes the closest to challenging the inherent violence against women by making the Knight spend a year fearing for his life, trying to discover what women most desire, it cannot leave violence out of the tale. The presence of domestic violence in the Wife of Bath's prologue and of rape in her tale is a part of the genres she employs, fabliau and romance respectively. Rape is inherent in romance, as the Franklin's, Knight's, and Thopas's tales (not to mention many other medieval examples) have revealed; here it moves from the margins to the center of the stage. It is uniquely punished, but it remains there. This tension points, in a sense, to the central issue here; it is possible to question or to challenge acts of violence against women, but they still pervade. However one reads the conclusions of the Wife of Bath's prologue and tale, however one understands what happens after the rape, it is still the motivation for the story. Violence against women, it seems, is good copy.

These examples are only a few of the instances of normalized violence against women in the *Canterbury Tales;* Apollo murders his wife in the *Manciple's Tale;* Melibee's wife and daughter are raped and beaten by his "friends" who invade the house, yet Dame Prudence counsels tolerance and forgiveness. But a discussion of violence against women in the *Tales* would be incomplete without a consideration of the *Clerk's Tale.* In this famously disturbing story, the Clerk tells the story of Patient Griselda, who is emotionally tortured by her husband. Walter's savagery against his wife has caused him to take away her children, pretending to murder them, to send her away when he decided to take another wife, and then to call her back to set up the castle for this new woman; at the end of the tale, Griselda tells Walter:

"O thyng biseke I yow, and warne also,
That ye ne prikke with no tormentynge
This tendre mayden, as ye han doon mo;
For she is fostred in hire norissynge
Moore tendrely, and, to my supposynge,
She koude nat adversitee endure
As koude a povre fostred creature." (4.1037–43)

Griselda's acknowledgment of all that has been done to her and her desire not to see it done to anyone else is a poignant moment in the tale, particularly since it brings on the "happy ending" in which Griselda is restored to her position. However, the violence enclosed in the narrative has greater scope. The Clerk then insists on an allegorical reading which allies Griselda with Job, making her punishments, heretofore merely emotional, physical. Her rewards, both literally and metaphorically, come as a result of her forbearance of the violence done to her. Rejecting this violence, or running away from her dangerous husband, is clearly not an option for Griselda; she must accept her lot in life and hope for rewards later. The Clerk "giveth and taketh away" at the end of the tale when he says, "This storie is seyd nat for that wyves sholde / Folwen Grisilde as in humylitee, / For it were inportable, though they wolde" (4.1142–44), but then notes, "For sith a womman was so pacient / Unto a mortal man, wel moore us oghte, / Receyven al in gree that God us sent" (4.1149–51). What women receive, it appears, is violence, to which they should submit in order to live "in vertuous suffraunce" (4.1162). The Clerk urges his readers to take Griselda as a model; his female readers, then, must turn their lives into a metaphor of a saint's, putting up patiently with what they get in exchange for a heavenly reward. The Clerk laments that there are few like Griselda, willing to take what they are given, noting that more women resemble "the Wife of Bath and all her sect," who presumably take their lives into their own hands, rejecting the patience he values. One is reminded of the *Book of the City of Ladies*, which Christine de Pizan concludes with the exhortation:

And you ladies who are married, do not scorn being subject to your husbands, for sometimes it is not the best thing for a creature to be independent. . . . And those women with peaceful, good husbands who are devoted to them, praise God for this boon. . . . And those women who have husbands neither completely good nor completely bad should still praise God for not having the worst. . . . And those women who have husbands who are cruel, mean, and savage should strive to endure them while trying to overcome their vices and lead them back, if they can, to a reasonable and seemly life. And if they are so obstinate that their wives are unable to do anything, at least they will acquire great merit for their souls through the virtue of patience. (Christine de Pizan, *City of Ladies*, 255)

Griselda must take a beating on earth to get her rewards in heaven. Thus, yet another battered woman becomes an exemplum for her own kind; just as the Wife of Bath notes that "it is an impossible / That any clerk wol speke good of wyves, / But if it be of hooly seintes lyves" (3.688–90), so the Clerk, through his tale, shows how secular women can live out their version of the saint's glorious martyrdom. The force of this sentiment returns at the end of the *Canterbury Tales*; a perhaps uncomfortable comment on the persistence of violence against women in literature comes in Chaucer's retraction, when he rejects "the tales of Caunterbury, thilke that sownen into synne" (10.1085) and keeps only "othere bookes of legendes of seintes, and omelies, and moralitee, and devocioun" (10.1087)—the tales that contain the most brutal, and often the most ignored, attacks against women.

This plethora of examples that heap upon each other once one starts looking for violence against women in the *Tales* demonstrate a pattern that puts Chaucer's work into a context in which it is not often considered. Certainly, the major and complex analyses of violence against women in the *Canterbury Tales*, notably those of Elaine Tuttle Hansen and Carolyn Dinshaw, reveal the problematic ways in which individual tales engage the issue of violence against women, overt and covert.[15] But each individual example is important to consider in the context of the *Tales* as a whole, if only to see how extraordinarily "normal" violence against women is in Chaucer's collection. It exists on every level of analysis and observation, from the metaphoric to the marginal to the central; it takes place in almost every example of every genre, to the point that it becomes categorizable. It is present regardless of what any individual tale is saying about women, their roles, and their place in medieval society. Violence lurks in the background of romance and is the foreground of hagiographic stories; it is the source of the slapstick comedy of the fabliaux. It is passed over and displayed in sharp focus. Few readers would automatically think of violence when thinking of the *Canterbury Tales*, and its pervasiveness seems, in this light, almost subversive, as if it were a "magic eye" picture behind the narrative. What this suggests goes beyond Chaucer into narrative itself; it shows how profoundly the spectacle of violence against women informs the medieval text, that it is an essential part of what makes a story. And if art has the normative effect on life that Kolodny suggests ("Dancing," 174), then it takes as part of its normalizing function the violent suppression of women. Chaucer's participation in this quiting of Eve, then, is hardly surprising.

As a "human comedy," the *Canterbury Tales* offer a broad-spectrum analysis of the violent world, literal and literary, that women inhabit, reaching its most striking reflection in the narratives told by its female tellers, who, by becoming literary representations of literal female writers of the medieval period, show forced complicity in a destructive system by telling tales with the most explicit and detailed acts of violence in them.[16] While the tellers quite each other, they also, through a variety of means, quite women for often imaginary offenses. Women, in the medieval eye, are temptresses descended from Eve; their bodies are physical representations of that which brought the world—and continues to bring men—into sin. The Canterbury Pilgrims, fostered like their author in this view, are conjoined to punish Eve through her contemporary representatives. Although the *Canterbury Tales*, and Chaucer himself, often provide support for woman's autonomy and woman's voice, they do not check the secular, religious, and narrative drives to contain, define, and restrain her by force. Whatever goes on in the foreground, the *Canterbury Tales* maintains a backdrop of a world physically antipathetic to the female sex.

NOTES

1. All quotations from Chaucer are from *The Riverside Chaucer*, 1987. Quotations are cited by fragment and line number.

2. See, for example, Geoffrey of Vendôme, who accuses women of poisoning Adam with the apple, killing holy men like Samson and John the Baptist, and finally killing Christ, who was forced to die because of Eve's sin.

3. *Quiting*, in Chaucer, is a form of the Middle English verb *quiten*, meaning "to requite, to repay or reward." Since there is no modern English equivalent, I use the Middle English *quite, quiting*, throughout. This word best defines the rules of competition in the *Canterbury Tales*; I propose that those same rules govern the episodes of violence against women in Chaucer's text. I am grateful to Robert L. Squillace for his help in defining my discussion on that point.

4. For a striking instance, see the scene in *Athelston* (in *Middle English Verse Romances*, 130–53) in which the king kicks his pregnant wife in the stomach until she miscarries and then bemoans the loss of his heir.

5. See, for example, Dinshaw, *Chaucer's Sexual Politics*, most notably chapters 4 and 5, which suggest Chaucer's ability to read women sympathetically to recognize, if only within the fantasy of the *Wife of Bath's Tale*, a world which recognized feminine desire. Other considerations of Chaucer's sympathetic understanding of the women he inscribed in his tales include Mann, *Geoffrey Chaucer*, and Weisl, *Conquering the Reign of Femeny*.

6. The *Wife of Bath's Tale* does, in certain ways, redress the maiden's rape; certainly, it does not leave the rape unpunished. The knight's reeducation is a direct response to it, which seeks to teach him not just *what* women desire but *that* they desire. However, the inadequacies in the tale, and its final reversion to coercive romance modes at its end, prevent it from providing an entirely satisfactory answer to its motivating event. And indeed, the violence in the Wife of Bath's prologue stands unquestioned. The Prioress's and the Second Nun's tales valorize violence both as the vehicle into heaven and as revenge against the martyr's destroyers.

7. Hansen also shows that Absolon's intended violence against Alison "re-masculinizes" him; while he previously appeared more feminine than Alison herself, through his fascination with his looks and clothes and his squeamishness, he gains a power and authority from his revenge.

8. Here Gravdal follows Georges Duby, "Aristocratic Households," which demonstrates how "the ideals of courtly love had little positive effect on the historical experience of women in the Middle Ages" (Gravdal, *Ravishing Maidens,* 208) and indeed helped to restrict their movement and disempower them.

9. On the coercions of romance see Weisl, *Conquering the Reign of Femeny.* On marriage, see Duby, *Medieval Marriage.*

10. On this alliance of female and Jew in the Middle Ages see, for example, Goldberg, "Two Parallel Commonplaces."

11. Christine de Pizan is not the only example; for a later example see Juan Luis Vives, *De Institutione Foeminae Christianae,* which urges women at the beginning of the extensive work not to read romances but to study the Acts of the Apostles, religious philosophy, and saints' lives.

12. In the dramas of Hrostvith of Gandersheim, virgin martyrs, often young children, express so strongly their eagerness to be killed by their pagan oppressors that it becomes almost comic.

13. While violence against women is less common in secular narratives by women, there are certain poignant examples; Marie de France, for instance, provides a striking instance in "Bisclavret," where the woman has her nose ripped off in punishment for her indiscretions—this then becomes a kind of "mark of Eve," as her children are born without noses. But more often, although women are locked in towers and made to suffer emotionally at the hands of old, loathsome husbands, they are not raped and beaten.

14. See, for example, Ruggiero, *Boundaries of Eros,* and Carter, *Rape in Medieval England.*

15. Hansen, *Chaucer and the Fictions of Gender,* and Dinshaw, *Chaucer's Sexual Poetics,* among others, provide extended discussions of violence in specific tales; these studies show the complexity of this issue, which I attempt to supplement here.

16. See Kittredge, *Chaucer and His Poetry,* for a discussion of the *Canterbury Tales* as a human comedy, a formulation still useful but with many more repercussions than Kittredge imagined.

WORKS CITED

Carter, John Marshall. *Rape in Medieval England: An Historical and Sociological Study.* Originally published as dissertation, University of Illinois. Lanham, Md.: University Press of America, 1985.

Chaucer, Geoffrey. *The Riverside Chaucer.* Gen. ed. Larry D. Benson. 3d ed. Boston: Houghton Mifflin, 1987.

Christine de Pizan. *The Book of the City of Ladies.* Ed. and trans. Earl Jeffrey Richards. New York: Persea Books, 1982.

———. *A Medieval Woman's Mirror of Honor: The Treasury of the City of Ladies.* (Le livre des trois vertus) Trans. Charity Cannon Willard, ed. Madeleine Pelner Cosman. Tenafly, N.J.: Bard Hall Press; New York: Persea Books, 1989.

Dinshaw, Carolyn. *Chaucer's Sexual Poetics.* Madison: University of Wisconsin Press, 1989.

Duby, Georges. *Medieval Marriage: Two Models from Twelfth-Century France.* Trans. Elborg Foster. Baltimore: Johns Hopkins University Press, 1978.

———. "The Aristocratic Households of Feudal France." In *Revelations of the Medieval World.* Vol. 2 of *A History of Private Life* (De l'Europe féodale à la Renaissance). Trans. Arthur Goldhammer, 35–156. Cambridge: Belknap Press of Harvard University Press, 1988.

———. *Love and Marriage in the Middle Ages.* Trans. Jane Dunnett. Chicago: University of Chicago Press, 1994. Translation of *Mâle Moyen Age,* Paris: Flammarion, 1967, 1988.

Geoffrey of Vendôme. *Goffridi abbatis vidocinensis opera omnia. . . .* Ed. Jacques-Paul Migne. *Patrologiae cursus completus. Series latina.* Vol. 157. Paris: Garnier, 1844–64.

Goldberg, Harriet. "Two Parallel Medieval Commonplaces: Antifeminism and Antisemitism in the Hispanic Literary Tradition." In *Aspects of Jewish Culture in the Middle Ages: Papers of the Eighth Annual Conference of the Center for Medieval and Early Renaissance Studies. . . ,* ed. Paul Szarmach. Albany: State University of New York Press, 1979.

Gravdal, Kathryn. *Ravishing Maidens: Writing and Rape in Medieval French Literature and Law.* Philadelphia: University of Pennsylvania Press, 1991.

———. "The Poetics of Rape Law in Medieval France." In *Rape and Representation,* ed. Lynn A. Higgins and Brenda R. Silver, 207–26. New York: Columbia University Press, 1991.

Hansen, Elaine Tuttle. *Chaucer and the Fictions of Gender.* Berkeley and Los Angeles: University of California Press, 1992.

Hrotsvitha of Gandersheim. *The Dramas of Hrotsvit of Gandersheim.* Trans. Katharina M. Wilson. Saskatoon: Perigrina Publishing, 1985.

Kittredge, George Lyman. *Chaucer and His Poetry.* Cambridge: Harvard University Press, 1915.

Klapisch-Zuber, Christiane. "Including Women." In *Silences of the Middle Ages* (Il Medioevo), ed. Christiane Klapisch-Zuber. Vol. 2 of *A History of Women in the West* (Storia delle donne in Occidente), ed. Georges Duby and Michelle Perrot, 1–10. Cambridge and London: Belknap Press of Harvard University Press, 1992.

Kolodny, Annette. "Dancing through the Minefield: Some Observations on the Theory, Practice, and Politics of a Feminist Literary Criticism." In *The New Feminist Criticism: Essays on Women, Literature and Theology,* ed. Elaine Showalter, 144–67. New York: Pantheon, 1985.

Mann, Jill. *Geoffrey Chaucer.* Atlantic Highlands, N.J.: Humanities Press International, 1991.

Middle English Verse Romances. Ed. Donald B. Sands. New York: Holt, Rinehart and Winston, 1966; Exeter: University of Exeter Press, 1986.

Ruggiero, Guido. *The Boundaries of Eros: Sex Crime and Sexuality in Renaissance Venice.* Oxford: Oxford University Press, 1985.

Schulenberg, Jane Tibbets. "The Heroics of Virginity: Brides of Christ and Sacrificial Mutilation." In *Women in the Middle Ages and the Renaissance: Literary and Historical Perspectives,* ed. Mary Beth Rose. Syracuse, N.Y.: Syracuse University Press, 1986.

Tannon, Celestin Louis. "Registre Criminel de Saint-Martin-des-Champs." In *Histoire des justices des anciennes églises et communautés monastiques de Paris. . . .* Paris: Larose and Forcel, 1883.

Vives, Juan Luis. *De Institutione Foeminae Christianae.* Madrid, 1523.

Warner, Marina. *Alone of All Her Sex: The Myth and Cult of the Virgin Mary.* New York: Random House, 1976.

Weisl, Angela Jane. *Conquering the Reign of Femeny: Gender and Genre in Chaucer's Romance.* Cambridge: D. S. Brewer, 1995.

7

Rivalry, Rape, and Manhood: Gower and Chaucer

Carolyn Dinshaw

I

I want to go against the grain of current criticism that seeks evidence of interaction between Gower and Chaucer by considering a legend of inter- action for which there is *no* external evidence at all.[1] This is the lingering, if discredited, notion of the "quarrel" between Chaucer and Gower. The leg- end has a strange currency that consists mostly in its negation: scholars even now, over two centuries after Tyrwhitt's initial speculations, find it necessary to dismiss the idea. Thus Patricia Eberle, for example, in the *Riv- erside Chaucer*, whose notes both reflect and produce critical currents, re- ports the quarrel hypothesis, thus perpetuating the notion, while duly re- marking on the lack of external evidence and on the recent scholarship to the contrary.[2] What is the obscure, persistent appeal of this legend? Why was such a feud fabricated in the first place, out of bits and pieces of texts? What purpose does the promotion of such a rivalry serve?

The biography and criticism of Gower are "inextricably intertwined with Chaucer," as John Fisher has observed, and the contrasting arcs of the two poets' critical reputations have been well mapped by Fisher. The two were initially seen as peers, through the sixteenth century; a belief, current through the seventeenth century, was that in fact Gower was Chaucer's mentor.[3] They were both assumed, in 1670, to have been poets laureate; a few years later, Gower, in the words of Edward Phillips, "counted little inferiour, if not equal to *Chaucer* himself."[4] But the reputations diverged soon after; Gower's political alliances were scrutinized anew after the upheavals of the mid–seventeenth century and found to be reprehensible. In contrast, Chaucer's allegiance "to his former master *Richard*," as the Urry Life of Chaucer (1721) put it, kept him from like charges of timidity and "ignominiou[s] flatter[y]," "shamefu[l]" ingratitude and opportunism.[5]

In a climate of burgeoning Gower defamation and Chaucer elevation, then, Tyrwhitt in his edition of 1775–78 initiated the story of a quarrel.[6] Its basis was manifestly speculative, consisting of inference that lines in the Man of Law's introduction about improper tales—of Canacee and of Apollonius of Tyre—are directed deprecatingly at Gower; that Gower subsequently and peevishly omitted verses in praise of Chaucer in the second revision of the *Confessio Amantis;* and that a detail in the Man of Law's narrative archly alludes to Gower and "insinuates" that he has told the tale of Constance "with less propriety."[7] Nineteenth- and early twentieth-century critics had to answer to the issue of the quarrel, and several notable scholars (Godwin, Skeat, Tatlock, and ten Brink among them) hypothesized that there was indeed annoyance, resentment, even "distaste" between the two—the vexation mainly thought to be that of Chaucer, irritated at Gower for the latter's "indecorous" and "provocative" remarks in his verses to Chaucer (Elizabeth Barrett Browning), for his appropriation of Chaucerian materials (Skeat), or perhaps for his criticism of Chaucer for "misogyny and cynicism" (Tatlock).[8] This idea of an active feud was opposed early on by other scholars' careful arguments and certainly now has cooled, in the later twentieth century (with its fresh research into sources and manuscripts), into a suggestion of good-humored but pointed literary differences: thus Donald Howard, in his 1987 biography of Chaucer, explains the lines in the Man of Law's introduction as Chaucer's *aesthetic* swipes at Gower.

> All this is a private joke directed at Gower; evidently Gower was a sententious and avuncular man . . . and he had apparently admonished Chaucer for including the Miller's and Reeve's tales after the Knight's. So the Man of Law . . . condemns Gower for telling dirty stories—the implication is that if Chaucer told of fornication, Gower did worse and told of incest. An audience of their poetical friends must have found this funny, and it is funny enough still; whether Gower thought it was funny is another question. He and Chaucer had a real disagreement, and it may have caused some tension between them, but the old notion that they quarreled is clearly not true.[9]

The "old notion" of quarreling poets is here dismissed, but its "ghost," as Fisher (over twenty years earlier) had put it, "has hardly yet been laid."[10] It seems indeed to make relatively little difference in Howard's account (not unique in its implications) whether the poets had a "real disagreement" with attendant "tension" or an out-and-out row. An atmosphere of rivalry—of "professional jealousy," such as W. J. Courthope imagined in detail in 1895—is still cultivated here.[11] Howard is not merely accounting for or responding to critical tradition in the interest of scholarly completeness; the awkward logic of the last two sentences, with their final preemptive strike, suggests that there is more at stake here than bibliographical assiduity.

What, then, might this promotion of a feud accomplish? What critical need does it serve? What desire might it fantastically fulfill? The particular accusations serve to create a Chaucer who was free of base, ingratiating attitudes toward his sovereign and who was the source of pure poeticality, language and aesthetics unpolluted by self-interest (preparing the way for the twentieth-century poetic idol who still hovers above ideology among some Chaucerians).[12] They create, in opposition, a Gower who was an "ingrate" and "sycophant" (Joseph Ritson, 1802) at court, content to "follow" and imitate (T. Arnold, 1881) in his moralizing, unequivocally second-rate poetical endeavors.[13] This Gower was to play the lumbering fall guy to the nimble and free-spirited Chaucer. In his defense, Gower scholars reassessed his political actions and revalued his literary works, producing a Gower who acted with political integrity and whose integrity thoroughly informs his poetry. The *Biographia Britannica* in 1757 had already argued pointedly against the charges of base ingratitude and obsequiousness, describing a Gower of "steady attachment";[14] the defense of Gower's political and literary acumen has continued steadily, if relatively unheeded, picking up on the themes of morality and integrity set out in the *Britannica's* account of the poet.[15]

It is, though, the very insistence by scholars on some sort of rivalry that interests me here, even prior to the rivalry's particular terms. It must be noted that the *Britannica,* despite its strong defense of Gower, portrays him in a more familiar, patently negative light in its life of Chaucer, in which Gower's shameful triumphing over Richard's misfortunes is contrasted to Chaucer's innocence of such scurrilous behavior.[16] When the poet is profiled individually, there is nothing to fault, but when the two poets are brought together, a fetid air of disparagement and rivalry permeates the atmosphere. What strikes me here—a metaphor that itself should give us pause in the context I want to develop—is the critical assumption that seems to be operating: that aggression is necessary to the articulation or assertion of a strong, coherent character, an identity. Differentiating the two poets, after centuries of perceiving their harmonious complementarities and similarities, became crucial to late eighteenth- and espe-cially nineteenth-century scholars and poets nostalgically in search of a palatable medieval aesthetic; to formulate a coherent identity, at once liter-ary and political, and thus to substantiate a distinction between the two *required*, it seems, that scholars find a display of aggression between them. This structure of a rivalry that serves the articulation of individual identity while differentiating individuals from each other apparently has deep ex-planatory or truth value to some scholars; this is witnessed by the linger-ing appeal for those scholars of the quarrel legend, even in its genial and playful form.

But this assumption—that an articulation or assertion of strong, coher-ent individuality requires aggression—is a dangerous one. When indi-vidual identity is considered to be necessarily coherent and solid, its con-solidation depends on the eradication of any unity-threatening difference from within the self. And difference, in our male-dominated culture, is always gendered feminine. In Western culture masculine identity is a unity, and the feminine has been characterized as that difference from the coherent One which must be cast out as Other—pollution, uncertainty.[17] The violence with which such elimination of difference proceeds *precedes* the rivalry between men, as René Girard has argued; thus the rivalry itself serves the consolidation of identity on each side of the battle. Girard has suggested that violence allows the differentiation of two groups of men at war from each other, while it unites each individual group within itself, eradicating difference within; he speaks of a process of "violent undiffer-entiation" that consolidates identity and expels contamination in the form of a scapegoat.[18] The aggressive rivalry is thus generative: it provides the occasion for production of a pure, unified whole on each side via expulsion of difference. Girard does not analyze this scapegoating in gendered terms, but in an important rereading of Girard which has shaped my thinking here, Patricia Joplin has argued that the feminine is in fact what is violently expunged: the rivalry between groups of men is just an excuse, a "pretext" for this prior consolidation of masculine identity of each group.[19]

Such a gendered elimination of difference can be seen clearly operating in the formulation of the Chaucer-Gower "quarrel." The eighteenth- and nineteenth-century construction of the feud produced unconflicted mas-culine identities for the individual poets (in a time in which poetry itself was increasingly considered feminine and the robust masculinity of its male practitioners had to be asserted). Traditionally feminine traits—ti-midity, dependency, secondariness, sycophancy, insincerity, fickleness, dullness—were adduced only to be explicitly expelled, in order for scholars to assert the strength, independence, primacy, integrity, keenness of the poets; in order, that is, to establish both poets as serious, proper men. It was necessary that each poet be purged of feminine qualities, but most often the manly Chaucer was purged of Gower's femininity. According to *The English Poets* (1897), a good example of this latter phenomenon, Gower, "timid and a timeserver," was content to "follow, not lead; interpret, not modify opinion"; "possessing no originality," he wrote "under the spell of fashion and in the groove of imitation." But Chaucer, with "bold independence of his models," "mastery over his materials," and "keen" eye, "learned the necessity of self-criticism; of that severe process . . . which deliberates, sifts, tests, rejects, and alters."[20] Even Chaucer's admitted imitations are masculinized: Godwin (1803) argues that Chaucer's following Gower in constructing a story collection is in fact "a generous and manly emulation."[21] Gower, in turn, is invested by his defenders with "sever[ity]" and "courage," and with a forthrightness that contrasts with Chaucer's indirection and insincerity in "twice sarcastically allud[ing] to Gower's works."[22] In the assumption that Chaucer and Gower must have quarreled, eighteenth-, nineteenth- and twentieth-century readers have been following a notion Girard has articulated: that an aggressive rivalry is the productive occasion for each to "be at peace," to purge threats to his self-unity. But the further notion in force here—one Girard has not followed out—is that violence between men and the prior masculine identity formation are enabled by an unacknowledged violence against the feminine. To put it in stronger and more general terms: at the moments when these men seem most explicitly preoccupied with each other, they are most fundamentally misogynist.

II

There is no convenient or smooth transition for me to make between the construction of the Chaucer-Gower quarrel and rape, the former a trivial confection and the latter a horrifying, ongoing reality. The two phenomena seem—on the surface, at least—entirely different and incommensurate: one is an idea, concocted in the late eighteenth century and elaborated in the nineteenth, about two men in a rivalry, an idea that has no apparent consequences; there seems to be no victim, really, no violation, certainly no crime. The other is a violent offense, punished variously at different times in England.[23] But I want to argue that there is a significant connection. We have been trained out of seeing structural connections between minor habits of thinking, on the one hand, and sexual violence, on the other, by the persistent view of rape as an anomalous sex crime. But rape—heterosexual rape, the most prevalent kind and sometimes a model for male-male rape as well—is a violent act that intends to demonstrate man's power, an act that rearticulates, each time, the superiority of masculine over feminine. As Catharine MacKinnon has so clearly seen in this context, gender is a hierarchy of *power* that structures our society.[24] Western society is ordered by a logic that construes the world in terms of one sex and its lack or deviation, as Irigaray writes, and the act of rape forcibly puts this foundational logic into practice: it insists that woman is—and must be—only what man is not, man's Other, man's lack, a not-man, a no-thing.[25] If this is the case, rape can hardly be said to be an anomalous act but one, rather, that has much in common structurally with other Western cultural phenomena: Irigaray speaks of "*the sexual indifference that underlies the truth of any science, the logic of every discourse.*"[26] The act rejects any true difference from man, for that is a threat; it rejects female autonomy. Insisting that masculine identity is necessarily singular, rape seeks to enforce that oneness, eradicating the evidence of something threateningly other; in this way it can be said to be an act of violent indifference. And it is, indeed, often viewed with considerable affective indifference: once woman has been reduced to a no-thing by the logic of sexual indifference—a reduction motivated by fear, or rage, or both—violence against her can be regarded with utter indifference.[27]

This basic structure of indifference, I argue, is a constant from the Middle Ages through the eighteenth century to the present. This constancy is reflected in medieval laws that are more clearly concerned with family property than with women's persons;[28] in the mid-eighteenth-century laws "which still saw wives and children as patriarchal property," as Roy Porter writes, and in the eighteenth-century "court room practice [which] continued to treat rape as a crime to be settled man-to-man";[29] and in the twentieth-century studies that find that the one thing most rapists seem to have in common is the inability to see their victims as human beings.[30] When Chaucer and Gower scholars assume, then, that the poets' articulation of individual identity necessarily entailed aggression, that aggression, in other words, was *productive* of coherent, unified identity for each poet, they are operating by a structure similar to that which can be seen to underwrite a much more consequential thing: rape. In both situations—rape and the readerly construction of a quarrel between men—the primary aggression is against the feminine, an aggression that enacts the logic of sexual indifference.[31]

In seeing a relationship between very different kinds of phenomena—assumptions, on the one hand, and actions, on the other—with diverse practical consequences, I don't want to be understood to be suggesting that all men are rapists (or would be, if put in the "right" situation). Some men rape, others don't, and my quite abstract thesis can't explain why; many particular factors must be involved.[32] But my thesis does assert a similarity—indeed, a continuity—between these phenomena and I thereby intend to draw attention to the destructive misogyny of this apparently trivial habit of thought, this way of thinking that seems harmless and consequenceless and seems to be only about men. Women are scapegoated by such habits; and perpetuating the habits perpetuates a prior and unacknowledged victimization.

There are, however, other ways of imagining relationships between men, relationships that are really about men and not dependent upon surrogate victims and abjected Others. To suggest a preliminary step in the process of moving away from misogynistic relations between men such as that which scholars have constructed for Chaucer and Gower, I want to turn to Chaucer's and Gower's texts, to read them in an interaction that does not obfuscate but rather clarifies the fact and the threat of violence to women's bodies. I shall turn now to the legend of Philomela, that classical and classic tale of rape, as Gower uses it in the *Confessio Amantis* and then as Gower's treatment can be used to gloss *Troilus and Criseyde*. I shall first make two general comments on this classical tale, as Gower, quite unexceptionally in these regards, narrates it; I shall then, in the third and final part of this paper, turn to the innovation in Gower's rendition, using it to read Criseyde's dream in Book Two of *Troilus and Criseyde*. Such an interaction between texts, as I construe it, uncovers the rape in the nightingale's song.

The tale of Philomela occurs in Book Five of the *Confessio,* the book of avarice; it is the exemplum of "ravine" (*rapina*), of rape. Gower uses it here as rape's paradigm: the attack is isolated, extraordinary, by a barbarian, the Thracian Tereus. His behavior is described as mad (he was "so wod / That he no reson understod," 5.5639–40), bestial (he is like a wolf, 5.5633; a bird of prey, 5.5644–46), even madly bestial: he is "that wode hound" (5.5701; cf. 5.5684), absolutely without reason and therefore not even a man.[33] The woman's resistance is unquestioned—she calls out to her father and mother (5.5635–36), who are unable to hear her. All meaningful bonds of society are broken in the act and as a consequence of the act: Tereus breaks marriage vows, has incestuous relations with his sister-in-law, breaks the bonds of family relations; Procne breaks maternal bonds (she acts "Withoute insihte of moderhede," 5.5893); and Tereus, fed by Procne, violates the taboo against cannibalism.[34] *This is rape;* it is spectacularly anomalous.

But the spectacular anomaly of Tereus's rape of the one sister may serve to obliterate the structural or narrative resemblances between the passage of her from Pandion to Tereus and the passage of the other sister from Pandion to Tereus. Clearly, the intentions behind each transfer differ, and that makes a great deal of difference. And, of course, Philomela's sexual passage was actively resisted; but this should make us want to ask, in turn, if Procne wanted to marry Tereus in the first place. Maybe she did; Genius reports that he was a "worthi king," a "noble kniht," eligible indeed; but it is more than likely that Procne had no choice. Ovid tersely notes Pandion's bestowal of Procne; Gower elaborates here on Ovid by mentioning her father's intentions for her and thus makes even more visible the daughter's lack of say in the matter:[35]

The fader of his pourveance
His doughter Progne wolde avance,
And yaf hire unto mariage
A worthi king of hih lignage. (5.5563–66)

My point is not that marriage is no more than a legal form of rape; such a point, taking the form of an act for its intention, as Frances Ferguson has put it, leads to a reductive, overly formal account of sexual relations as necessarily oppressive.[36] My point is, rather, that rape is not anomalous; thus we must analyze the ways in which rape is nevertheless kept distinct from other gender-asymmetrical acts. The anomalous, "aggravated rape" definition is one way: it isolates one act and keeps us from seeing connections between, say, this and male rivalry; it is thus useful to male-dominated society.[37] The "anomalous" definition deflects attention from violations or evacuations of women's wills that are always potential—and potentially, even if reluctantly, sanctioned—in a society (ours) in which the power relations are between men, and women serve as conduits of power but not as themselves wielders of power, in a society in which women are used as things exchanged between men.[38] Any need to analyze such a system is obviated by making the rape seem unusual, the result of a single, even inhuman, desire.

Genius's language does suggest that rape is an offense by one man against another. It is a kind of "ravine," which is described as a man-to-man sin: "Ravine of othre mennes folde / Makth his larder and paieth noght" (5.5512–13). The "Raviner / Of love" takes possession ("the sesine," 5.5527) of goods which are understood to be another man's—a husband's, a father's. The same is true of the next sin, obviously related, of robbery of maidenhead (5.6075–6358): the thing stolen is seen as another man's.

Yee, though sche were a Scheperdesse,
Yit wol the lord of wantounesse
Assaie, althogh sche be unmete,
For other mennes good is swete. (5.6115–18)

But though the man-to-man structure of society is made explicit here, its implications for women are not drawn out. The relation of rivalry between the barbarian and the Greek in the tale of Philomela that used women as objects of exchange—even, as Patricia Joplin argues, as surrogate victims—goes unremarked and certainly unanalyzed in Gower.[39]

Similarly, in the tale of Geta and Amphytrion in Book Two of the *Confessio* (one of the exempla of Supplantation, a species of Envy) the focus is on the (broken) relationship between two men; the effect on the woman goes completely unnoticed. The sin of Supplantation in love occurs when one man improperly takes the place of another man in his love relationship with a woman. Here, Amphytrion supplants his best friend, Geta, taking Geta's beloved, Almeene; there is no narrative recognition of the rape of the woman when her lover's friend, disguised as her lover, sneaks into her bed.[40] The supplanter violates the rules of the circulation of women between men—the sinned-against, the explicit victim in this account, is Geta—but the violation of the woman by the very structure of exchange is not at issue. Both such tales, then, the tale of Philomela and that of Geta and Amphytrion, are useful to a conservative social vision such as that of the *Confessio,* a text that nostalgically yearns for proper Christian hierarchy and order.[41]

My second general point about the tale concerns Procne's hideous, and hideously appropriate, response to Tereus's act. After Philomela has been raped and mutilated, Tereus hypocritically communicates her death to Procne; Procne has found out about the deed and has cooked up, so to speak, a grisly revenge. This culinary vengeance, wreaked by the two sisters, can be read as an indirect, ironic critique of the use of rape in the reinforcement of masculine identity. As unforgettable as Philomela's severed tongue, just a stump after Tereus clips it "with a peire scheres" (5.5691), is Procne's gruesome stew, Ithis *à la maison.* Procne is, of course, trying to suggest the unnaturalness of Tereus's act in her rendering him an unwitting cannibal: he devours his son "ayein kinde, / As he that was tofore unkinde" (5.5905–6). But further, Tereus is said to love this son "as his lif" (5.5886); what he eats is "his oughne fleissh and blod" (5.5904). If his rape of Philomela asserts his superior power, his masculine identity and wholeness, Procne makes him ingest something of himself ("his oughne fleissh and blod")—makes him literally reinforce his self, his physical being—in the same act as that in which he destroys that flesh and blood.[42] A unified identity, a gender identity, acts to organize the body into an understandable whole; it thus acts as a certain hedge against mortality—against the disaggregation of the body, as Judith Butler and Elaine Hansen have suggested in different contexts.[43] Ithis is Tereus's life beyond his own life; when Tereus rapes, he may be imposing his masculine power and solidity, thus violently refusing mortality and disaggregation. But when Tereus is made to eat Ithis, Procne makes him defeat that purpose; he destroys his own legitimate chance at life beyond his own decay.

III

But Procne's "critique," if that is what to call it, is not allowed much force in the narrative. The crisis of metamorphosis ironically grants to all three an immortality of an unexpected kind, and the horrors of violation and mutilation are recast as sweet amorous suffering. I want now to look more closely at Gower's unusual ending of this tale and then to turn to *Troilus and Criseyde;* I shall look at the ways in which rape and dismemberment can be brought back into the reader's focus, beyond the socializing and reintegrative glare of each of these narratives.

Philomela's new life as bird is described in a long passage that is peculiar to Gower's version. She "makth hir pleignte and seith, 'O why, / O why ne were I yit a maide?'" (5.5978–79). Her song is not a mere lament for her lost "speche" and "virginite" (5.5749), however; it is also a celebration by the violated and shamed woman of the fact that she has an avian disguise.

> in hir song
> Sche makth gret joie and merthe among,
> And seith, "Ha, nou I am a brid,
> Ha, nou mi face mai ben hid:
> Thogh I have lost mi Maidenhede,
> Schal noman se my chekes rede." (5.5983–88)

So her song is a mixture of "joie" and "wo," "sorwe" and "merthe" (5.5989–90). In fact, this paradoxical lyric rendering of the experience and aftermath of rape and mutilation—there is nothing like it in Ovid—sounds just like a conventional courtly love song.

> Thus medleth sche with joie wo
> And with hir sorwe merthe also,
> So that of loves maladie

Sche makth diverse melodie,
And seith love is a wofull blisse,
A wisdom which can noman wisse,
A lusti fievere, a wounde softe:
This note sche reherceth ofte
To hem whiche understonde hir tale. (5.5989–97)

Sexual violation and bodily mutilation become "loves maladie"; these pains become metaphorical. This is the "unsely jolif wo" (1.88), the "sorwes glad" (4.1212), the "maladie" (1.128) of Amans, the courtly lover. The conventional discourse of love here converts the experience of forcible rape into desirable, idealized, elite love; those must be only a select few who "understonde hir tale" when Philomela sings it. The conventions of patriarchal love talk perform this conversion miracle: they in effect socialize rape, convert it into that exquisite pain called "love."

Gower's treatment of the nightingale's song is the perfect gloss on Criseyde's dream in Book Two of *Troilus and Criseyde*. In that dream she translates the startling news she has heard earlier in the day into corporeal terms, imagining how the strange new love Pandarus has told her about might be enacted upon or affect her person. Having finally gone to bed, she lies still, while

A nyghtyngale, upon a cedre grene,
Under the chambre wal ther as she ley,
Ful loude song ayein the moone shene,
Peraunter in his briddes wise a lay
Of love, that made hire herte fressh and gay.
That herkned she so longe in good entente,
Til at the laste the dede slep hire hente. (2.918–24)

The story of Philomela in fact lurks behind the story of Troilus and Criseyde, as I have suggested elsewhere: Pandarus is awakened by the swallow Procne's sorrowful song at the beginning of Book Two, whereupon he rises to begin the wooing of Criseyde. Procne's song is a "waymentynge" (*Troilus and Criseyde*, 2.65), and that musical motivation of Pandarus's actions should give the reader pause when considering what is to come.[44] The nightingale's song, conventionally, is sometimes mournful, sometimes sadly sweet; both are evidenced, for example, in Petrarch. But the nightingale's song here is thoroughly refreshing to Criseyde; it gladdens her heart and eases her into sleep.

And as she slep, anonright tho hire mette
How that an egle, fethered whit as bon,

Under hire brest his longe clawes sette,
And out hire herte he rente, and that anon,
And dide his herte into hire brest to gon—
Of which she nought agroos, ne nothyng smerte—
And forth he fleigh, with herte left for herte. (2.925–31)

She dreams of the violent invasion of her body, the removal of her will, her desire ("And out hire herte he rente, and that anon"), and the interposition of someone else's. But Criseyde feels neither fright nor pain; the nightingale's song has already converted violation and mutilation into love's pain, bittersweet and elite. That love is no doubt what Criseyde is foretelling. The exchanging of hearts ("herte left for herte") is thus a literal representation of what will come, the metaphoric romantic love talk in later books: Troilus calls Criseyde his "herte," and Criseyde refers to Troilus as her "herte" (4.1449, 1254). In this dream scene in Book Two, as read with Gower's text, courtly birdsong's reinterpretation—its metaphorization, its "disappearing"—of bodily pain is emphasized.

But the very literality of the dream puts the mutilation before our eyes. And Gower's text helps us analyze courtly love discourse, such as is spoken and lived by Troilus in Chaucer's poem; it is not only, as many critics have seen, gender asymmetrical and misogynist in its petrifying idealization of women. In Gower's narrative of Philomela it actually expresses the woman's experience of being violated and mutilated.[45] Paradoxes are breakings of logic, yoking two things that cannot be yoked together except by violence (to adapt Samuel Johnson—on the wit of the metaphysical poets—to my purposes here). I read them here as representing the experience of being broken into, broken up. Often enough the experience of being in love, for men and for women, is expressed in these terms, but what Gower's text helps us suggest is that at base, courtly discourse encodes the bodily violation and destruction of a woman.[46] Courtly love discourse is the discourse of sexual indifference *par excellence*, and its literal ground is revealed here to be the violation of the woman's body.

This analysis of courtly love talk is crucial in underlining the bodily threat to Criseyde throughout Chaucer's narrative. She is "allone," the narrator repeatedly remarks, and fearful, even "the ferfulleste wight / That myghte be" (2.450–51).[47] Her use as a counter in the war between Greeks and Trojans tends to make of her body an "abstraction," as Irigaray would put it, a mere "mirror of value of and for men," without matter and without particulars; an understanding of the bodily subtext of courtly discourse resists this abstracting of the matter of woman.[48] And such an understanding is useful in resisting the narrator's gradual movement away from the specificity of this woman, a movement that is charted in his increasingly distant treatment of Criseyde: vicarious participation in the first three books of the poem gives way to irritation and finally detachment and rejection in the last two books. In Book Five, even as he paints a portrait of her that seems to particularize her, the narrator ends with a character description that functions, in addition, as a description of her body as an enactment of the principles of patriarchal social organization. She is, he comments famously, "tendre-herted, slydynge of corage," where "corage," in proximity to "herte" here (as it often is in Middle English phrases) and with its manifest root in *cor* can refer not only to the immaterial "heart, spirit" or "disposition, temperament" (as the *MED* puts it) but draws on the physical connotations of "the heart as the seat of emotions, affection, attitudes, and volition."[49] This "corage" can be envisioned as a part of the body, and it is not intrinsically hers; it is, rather, in its sliding, a visible image, a "crystallization" or "objectivization" of man's activity of exchange.[50] And finally the narrator hardens into a view of her as a fickle thing of a fickle world: "Thus goth the world. God shilde us fro meschaunce, / And every wight that meneth trouthe avaunce!" (5.1434–35); in the Epilogue, Troilus's "lovyng of Criseyde" is assimilated to "false worldes brotelnesse" (5.1832–33).

But Gower's text, read with Chaucer's, can provide a context in which to bring back the matter of women, to read women's "oppressioun" (Chaucer's usual word for rape). In the *Confessio Amantis* Gower offers no perspective on this aspect of courtly discourse; Chaucer's text offers slightly more perspective, I think, through the frame of the distinctly characterized narrator. But when we read the interaction of these texts with each other we need not replicate the structures of rivalry that would elevate one text at the expense of the other; read in interaction, both can be opened to reveal and resist the violent obliteration of the feminine. This kind of thinking about interactions between texts points to the possibility that interactions between men can be changed. Attention to what enables—and what is enabling about—male rivalries can serve to return to us the matter of woman and can serve to insist that men's relations with one another not be formed at the expense of an Other.

So did Chaucer and Gower quarrel? Over my dead body.

NOTES

1. This article is reprinted with slight modifications from *Chaucer and Gower: Difference, Mutuality, Exchange,* ed. Robert F. Yeager, English Literary Studies Monograph Series 51 (Victoria, B.C.: University of Victoria, 1991), 130–52. An ear-

lier version was presented at the New Chaucer Society Congress, University of Kent at Canterbury, August 1990, where I benefited from many comments afterward. Thanks to the participants in my Feminist Theory and Medieval Literature seminar at Berkeley (Spring 1990), to the 1990–91 Fellows at the Doreen B. Townsend Center for the Humanities, and to Susan Schweik, H. Marshall Leicester Jr., Stephen Greenblatt, Robert Yeager, and Amy Scholder for bright ideas about this material.

2. Eberle recounts Tatlock's version of the quarrel hypothesis, then continues: "The grounds for this hypothesis are not firm, however; no other evidence for the supposed quarrel between Chaucer and Gower is extant" (Chaucer, *Riverside*, 854; all further references to Chaucer's poetry are to this edition). The explanatory notes on lines 77–89 then admit the possibility of a criticism of Gower by Chaucer (Chaucer, *Riverside*, 856); such a possibility has traditionally been converted into evidence indeed of a feud. The persistence of quarrel references such as Eberle's here is due not only to a sense of scholarly responsibility to account for critical tradition; critical traditions do die out, as other notes in the *Riverside* attest. As I argue, desires beyond the purely bibliographical are in force as well.

3. Fisher, *John Gower*, 1–36. My discussion of the critical reputations of Gower and Chaucer is indebted to Fisher's clear and acute account, which has pointed me to the rich literature of the "quarrel." See also Hammond, *Chaucer*, 278–79.

4. Phillips, *Theatrum Poetarum*, part 2, "Eminent Poets among the Moderns," 109.

5. "Life of Chaucer," by John Dart, rev. William Thomas, in Urry, *Works*, 1721, fol. [e]: Gower "basely insulted the memory of his murdered Master, and as ignominiously flattered his murderer"; *Biographia Britannica* 1747–66, 2:1293, in the entry on Chaucer: the author finds that Chaucer did not "triump[h] in the misfortune of his late kind master and generous benefactor, as others, and particularly Gower, who had been more obliged to that unfortunate Prince, and who at that time was both old and blind, most shamefully did."

6. Fisher, *John Gower*, 26–27.

7. Tyrwhitt's "Introductory Discourse," in Chaucer, *The Canterbury Tales*, clxxxviii.

8. Godwin, *Life of Chaucer*, 1:347, laments that the two poets, after such a long period of intimacy, "should afterward come to view each other with eyes of estrangement, indifference and distaste"; Browning (rpt. 1916, 630; see also the reprint in Furnivall, *Essays*, 155–64, with a running footnote quarrel of the editor "F. J. F." [Frederick James Furnivall] with "Miss Barrett"); Skeat, *Complete Works*, 3:413–17; Tatlock, *Development*, 173.

9. Howard, *Chaucer*, 420. See Nicholson, "Gower's Revisions," for a study that casts new light on the absence in various manuscripts of Gower's lines to Chaucer.

10. Fisher, *John Gower*, 27.

11. Courthope, *History*, 1:306–7.

12. E. Talbot Donaldson's famous description of "Chaucer the poet" depicts

such an ideologically free entity who "operates in a realm which is above and subsumes those in which Chaucer the man and Chaucer the pilgrim have their being" (*Speaking of Chaucer*, 11). John Ganim, contributing to the current effort of displacing such a notion, claims that "the presumption of a Chaucer, or a Chaucerian text, serenely removed from crisis and disruption is one rarely held now, despite the construction of such a presumption as a straw man by myself as well as others" ("Chaucer and the Noise," 71). But witness Pearsall's 1985 study, arguing that "the character of individual tales and the organization of the tales as a whole are constant in their determination not to press for or permit a systematic kind of moral or ideological interpretation" (*The Canterbury Tales*, xiv). Lee Patterson draws attention to this passage, also citing Donaldson and Robert K. Root as exemplifying the widespread critical belief "that the poet is a keen and genial observer of humankind who is himself emancipated from narrow self-interests" ("'No man'," 458). Patterson goes on to subject that liberal notion of the poet as "ideologically free-floating" (464) to critique.

13. Ritson, *Bibliographia Poetica*, 25; T. Arnold, "Gower," in Ward, *English Poets*, 1:102–6, esp. 103.

14. About Gower's reinscribing the dedication of the *Confessio*, the *Britannica* claims: "The author of the [Urry] life of Chaucer, and the plain spoken Thomas Hearne, blame him exceedingly for his conduct in this respect, and for his attacking the character of his old master Richard, very severely, on purpose to court the party of the house of Lancaster, when they became triumphant. But it may be, and indeed is more like to be the truth, that our author was ever averse to King Richard's administration, in consequence of his steady attachment to Thomas of Woodstock Duke of Gloucester" (*Biographia Britannica* 4:2244–45). And this political constancy was understood to underwrite his poetry: Gower's writings show that he had "the courage and virtue to attempt stemming the tide of corruption, by taking the only method left, of instilling principles of morality and good sense. . . . He was esteemed for his knowledge and integrity, even by those who had no great inclination to imitate either" (*Biographia Britannica*, 4:2243).

15. See Pearsall, "The Gower Tradition," which traces the critical tradition of "moral Gower" through 1981.

16. See Fisher, *John Gower*, 26.

17. For this by now commonplace analysis of androcentric Western culture many studies could be cited; Luce Irigaray, *This Sex Which Is Not One*, is still one of the most direct on the topic.

18. Girard, *Violence and the Sacred*, 223–49, esp. 246. Girard here talks about groups of men at war; I adapt his principles here to the discussion of individual men "at war," two men in a rivalry. In *Deceit, Desire and the Novel: Self and Other in Literary Structure* Girard analyzes such individual rivalries in terms that are related to his larger social analyses.

19. Joplin, "Voice," 25–53, esp. 41. Pointing to Girard's description of marriage rituals—"The ritual violence that accompanies the exchange of women serves a sacrificial purpose for each group. In sum, the groups agree never to be com-

pletely at peace, so that their members may find it easier to be at peace among themselves" (Girard, *Violence and the Sacred*, 249)—Joplin comments that Girard "tends to equate the male point of view with culture, so that he does not pause to see how the woman, in exchange, becomes the surrogate victim for the group" (36).

20. Arnold, "Gower," in Ward, *English Poets*, 1:103, 105; Ward, "Chaucer," in *English Poets*, 1:1–14, esp. 7–9.

21. Godwin, *Life of Chaucer*, 1:349. Cf. Skeat, *Complete Works*, 3:413–17, on Chaucer's originality.

22. "Gower," in *Biographia Britannica*, 4:2243: he "had a great genius for poetry, in which he sought to accommodate the severest sentiments to the sweetest language. . . . [He] had also the courage and virtue to attempt stemming the tide of corruption" in his tales; in the unsigned "John Gower and His Works," "friendly rivalry" between the two poets is understood to have turned into an ugly vendetta: "While Gower merely withdraws his eulogy on his late friend, Chaucer, in the *Man of Law's Tale*, twice sarcastically alludes to Gower's work, although he does not insert his name" ("John Gower and His Works," 11).

23. In the late Middle Ages, according to statute (Westminster II, 1285; the Statute of Rapes, 1382), rape was a capital offense, "regardless of the woman's consent," as Post notes ("Sir Thomas West," esp. 25). But conviction was rare and imposition of the full penalty "apparently remained unknown," according to Post, "Ravishment of Women," esp. 160. See Bashar for an account of this phenomenon of low conviction rate and unheard-of imposition of maximum penalty—"the contradiction or gap between what the law claimed to do, and what it actually did regarding the prosecution of rape" ("Rape in England," 41)—in the period 1550–1700. In Britain rape now carries a maximum penalty of life imprisonment (in regard to which Bashar notes the same contradiction).

24. MacKinnon in fact argues against discussions of rape (as well as of sexual harassment, pornography, and battery) that maintain that these are acts of power, not sex (or that they are violence, not sex). She insists that we must look at sex itself as at some times violence: "From women's point of view, intercourse, sex roles, and eroticism can be and at times are violent to us as women. . . . It seems to me that we haven't talked very much about gender *as* a hierarchy, as a division of power, in the way that's expressed and acted out, primarily I think sexually" ("Sex and Violence," 85–92, esp. 86, 90; emphasis in original). Where this leads MacKinnon, in relation to pornography in particular, has been hotly disputed by other feminists; for opinions on violence and the erotic addressing the politics and problematic of pleasure, see Ellis et al., *Caught Looking*, Vance, *Pleasure and Danger*, and my comments in note 36 on rape and marriage. But MacKinnon's general formulation of gender as a division of power enacted primarily sexually underwrites much that is basic in feminist social analyses. And she challenges us to interrogate the means by which acts of sexual violence are kept definitionally distinct from other gender-asymmetrical but socially sanctioned acts.

25. Irigaray, *This Sex*, 69 and passim.

26. Irigaray, *This Sex*, 69; emphasis in original.

27. The affectlessness of rapists in talking about their crimes is a commonplace. Such affective indifference, noted by the press in the highly publicized Central Park jogger case (see *Newsweek*, 23 July 1990, esp. 48–49, for example), was linked to rape (although made to seem anomalous) when the three defendants in the first trial—Antron McCray, Yusef Salaam, and Raymond Santana—were convicted in August 1990 of rape and first-degree assault with depraved indifference to human life (as well as three other assault charges, robbery, and riot). Scully, *Understanding Sexual Violence*, gets beyond affectlessness in her research based on interviews with convicted rapists in prison, and reveals deep-seated and far-ranging misogyny in various rapists' beliefs.

28. See Bashar, "Rape in England"; Brownmiller, "Against Our Will," 6–22, esp. 15; and Post, "Sir Thomas West" and "Ravishment of Women": "By interpretation and extension, therefore, the Statutes of Westminster turned the law of rape into a law of elopement and abduction, which inhibited the purposes of the woman herself—whether outrage at a sexual assault or the desire to further or avenge a consenting relationship—and fostered the interests of those who wanted material recompense for the material disparagement wrought by self-willed women-folk and suitors. . . . The history of the 1382 statute and its aftermath illustrates vividly the same priority of family fortunes over personal feelings" (Post, "Ravishment of Women," 160).

29. Porter (in Tomaselli and Porter, *Rape*) argues against Brownmiller's analysis of rapists as the "shock troops" of patriarchy, and against other feminists' apparent equations of patriarchy with rape (Susan Griffin, Mary Daly), writing that patriarchy "has a life of its own independently of rape, and a solidity which no amount of sloganizing will grasp or dissolve" (Porter, "Meaning," 236). Patriarchy doesn't *need* rapists, Porter maintains. I agree that, as he states, we must not "underestimate patriarchy" and its hold; but maintaining that rape is a "fringe" crime, a crime by patriarchy's outsiders, as Porter does, circumscribes and distances the crime, and thus refuses the possibility of analyzing rape's relation to other gender-asymmetrical uses and abuses of power in patriarchal society.

30. This is a thread that runs through many studies; see, for example, Fremont, "Rapists Speak."

31. In this context, another lingering Chaucerian biographical detail can be addressed. The connection between assertion of Chaucer's masculine identity and rape comes into focus when thinking about the *raptus* of Cecily Chaumpaigne: though various scholars from the beginning (the discovery of the documents in 1873) have tried to suggest Chaucer's innocence of sexual violation, there is another strain of scholarly treatment of this incident that without much distress (indeed, with some contentment, even at time with relish) accepts the idea that Chaucer raped; this is, I think, because it is just such an incident that will establish the robust masculine reputation of a national poet—the "father" of English poetry. For exculpating Chaucer, see, for example, Plucknett, "Escapade," 33–36; for relishing the idea that Chaucer raped (and delighting in the "literary implica-

tions"), see Baum, *Critical Appreciation*, 41–43; for contentedly accepting the possibility of a rape, see Howard, *Chaucer*, 317–20.

32. Research by Scully and Marolla, however, leads them to suspect that the key question is not "Why do men rape?" Considering the surrounding culture, they comment, "Perhaps we should be asking men who don't, 'Why not?'" See Scully and Marolla, "'Riding the Bull'," esp. 262. This study is incorporated into Scully's 1990 book, *Understanding Sexual Violence*.

33. All quotations from the *Confessio Amantis* are from Gower, *The English Works*.

34. It is such an abominable crime that it makes Chaucer's narrator's eyes sore in the *Legend of Good Women* upon just reading about it (2238–40). Chaucer's version concentrates on the weakness and consequent victimization of the women, as does the whole *Legend of Good Women* (see my remarks in *Chaucer's Sexual Poetics*, 65–87). Because Chaucer amputates the revenge and metamorphoses (in his effort to demonstrate feminine victimization), his version does not figure into my discussion here.

35. Ovid's description of the marriage transaction is more concerned with the relationship between the two kings Pandion and Tereus than is Gower's: "Threicius Tereus haec auxiliaribus armis fuderat et clarum vincendo nomen habebat; quem sibi Pandion opibusque virisque potentem et genus a magno ducentem forte Gradivo conubio Procnes iunxit" (Now Tereus of Thrace had put these to flight with his relieving troops, and by the victory had a great name. And since he was strong in wealth and in men, and traced his descent, as it happened, from Gradivus, Pandion, king of Athens, allied him to himself by wedding him to Procne; Ovid, 1:316–19, ll. 424–28). But, as Joplin points out, any development of the consequences of this relation of "violent rivalry between the two kings" in Ovid is deflected by the "cover story" of Tereus's desire for Philomela ("Voice," 33). Gower reduces even what *is* in Ovid of the traffic in women, thus reducing any suggested structural relation between Procne's marriage and Philomela's *rapina*. He omits the long Ovidian description of Tereus as he lustfully imagines taking Pandion's place in Philomela's daughterly arms (478–82). Ovid also hints at a potential similarity between those structures of marriage and rape, on the one hand, and father-daughter relations, on the other, a hint that Gower does not pick up: "et quotiens amplectitur illa parentem, / esse parens vellet; neque enim minus inpius esset" (and whenever she embraces her father he wishes he were in the father's place—indeed, if he were, his intent would be no less impious; 481–82). Yeager notes that Gower uses a new Middle English word for "rapist"; thus the effort to isolate the rapist functions on the lexical level as well (*Gower's Poetic*, 153n62). Yeager's argument—that Gower portrays Tereus as a split character, a different man as rapist from the "noble kniht" that he was initially (152–57)—supports my claim that Gower's narrative strategies work to throw attention away from any structural similarities between rape and other gender-asymmetrical social relations.

36. Ferguson argues that Susan Brownmiller and Andrea Dworkin, who critique patriarchal rape laws, in fact recapitulate the moves of such laws in that they all

stipulate "inexorable connections between the form of an action (intercourse) and the mental state of the individuals involved" ("Rape and the . . . Novel," 92). According to Ferguson, Saxon law "offered a raped virgin the possibility of extending retroactive consent to her rape" if she agreed to marry her attacker; both Saxon and ancient Hebrew law offered marriage as the legal recompense for rape, thus assuming that marriage "formally (in this case, legally) implies the consent to intercourse that was previously lacking" (92). Brownmiller and Dworkin, Ferguson argues, share "the tendency of the law to negate particular psychological states and to substitute formal states for them" (93): Brownmiller "derives the intention to rape from the physical capacity to do so," and Dworkin refuses the idea that women are able to consent or deny consent, because the form of the act of intercourse is itself an occupation, an inhabiting of the woman (93). Ferguson's analysis here of the extreme formality of Dworkin's thinking in particular is useful; what kind of political or social analysis of rape Ferguson would suggest in place of Brownmiller's or Dworkin's, though, is less clear.

37. Many recent studies of rape make this point. See, for one example among many, Russell: "One function of the myth that rape is only perpetrated by society's freaks is that rape then appears to have no further implications for the rest of society" (*Politics of Rape,* 260). Or Griffin, more radically: "Rape is not an isolated act that can be rooted out from patriarchy without ending patriarchy itself" ("All-American Crime," 35). Susan Estrich seeks to foster "an understanding of rape that recognizes that a 'simple' rape *is* a real rape" (*Real Rape,* 7, emphasis in original). Simple rape occurs between "friends, acquaintances, and neighbors," and thus operates within social relationships set up and sanctioned by society; a simple rape case is one in which no aggravating circumstances—"extrinsic violence (guns, knives, or beatings) or multiple assailants or no prior relationship between victim and defendant"—are present (7, 4).

38. My thinking here is informed by Gayle Rubin's pivotal essay, "The Traffic in Women: Notes on the 'Political Economy' of Sex," in Reiter, *Toward an Anthropology of Sex.* Eve Kosofsky Sedgwick has adapted the analysis of the traffic in women to literary discourse in her *Between Men.* See also Fisher and Halley, *Seeking the Woman.*

39. Joplin, "Voice," 31–43, esp. 33.

40. I am indebted to Barbara Anscher of the English Department, University of California at Berkeley, for this point about the invisible rape in the tale of Geta and Amphytrion.

41. For a different view of Gower's involvement in analyzing women's victimization, see Wetherbee, "Genius and Interpretation."

42. Cf. Yeager on Antiochus in *Confessio Amantis,* Book Eight, whose incest is figured as eating his child: "The wylde fader thus devoureth / His oghne fleissh, which non socoureth" (8.309–10). Yeager interestingly argues here that cannibalism is a radically disjunctive human act: Antiochus is "a man horribly divided," at once rejecting his consanguinity and confessing his awareness of the sin of consuming his own "fleissh." Yeager comments that "only a 'whole' man avoids

reduction to cannibal status"; Apollonius, in stark contrast to Antiochus, recognizes "one-ness" (*Gower's Poetic*, 228). The differences between Antiochus and Apollonius in the narrative are as clear as Yeager suggests here; so clearly drawn, in fact, that I would want to ask in this case (as I have done in the case of marriage and rape in the tale of Philomela) what purpose that unproblematic differentiation might be serving.

43. See Judith Butler's provocative work, which develops an idea of gender as a "performative construction of an original and true sex" (Butler, *Gender Trouble*, x) and thus argues against the commonplace theoretical distinction made in feminist analyses between biology and gender (gender produces sex, she argues; gender in fact functions to identify a body as male or female in the first place). Elaine Hansen, in her stimulating *Chaucer and the Fictions of Gender*, argues in a medieval context for the reassuring properties of fixed gender roles: the myth of fixed gender difference, she suggests, serves to allay many fears, prime among them being that there is at bottom *no* difference between male and female, and thus that the mortality of the body is indeed unavoidable.

44. See Dinshaw, *Chaucer's Sexual Poetics*, 81–82.

45. Benson comes close to making this point in relation to Book Three of the *Confessio Amantis:* Canacee's final letter to Machaire before she stabs herself to death is full of courtly diction: "Canacee's oxymorons are an exact description of her present state, which reflects that division which Gower had identified in the Prologue as the root of all misery on earth" ("Incest and Moral Poetry," 106). But the point here concerns the (im)moral state of Canacee, whereas I am interested in the courtly oxymoron as expressive of the actual physical state of the woman; her state, as I see it, signifies not in moral but rather in social terms.

46. Beyond the scope of this paper but clearly relevant here is the *Roman de la rose*, where an elaborate narrative of courtly desire finally comes down to, or is consummated in, an act of rape (see Cahoon, "Raping the Rose," for some thoughts on this issue). Christine de Pizan addresses related concerns in her part of the quarrel over the *Rose* (a quarrel which, this time, takes misogyny as its explicit concern), especially in her comments about the woman whose husband, feeling himself authorized by Jean de Meun's work, beats her; see Hicks, "Le Débat," esp. 139–40.

47. See, for example, 1.97, 1.178, 2.450–51, 4.671, 5.727–28. For discussions that focus on Criseyde's position in Trojan and Greek society, see in works cited Fries; Aers; and Diamond.

48. "Women on the Market," in Irigaray, *This Sex*, 170–91, esp. 175, 177.

49. *Middle English Dictionary*, "corage," noun 1 (a).

50. See Irigaray, *This Sex*, 179; further, she writes, the "properties," the particulars of the woman's body, "have to be suppressed and subordinated to the exigencies of its transformation into an object of circulation among men" (187).

WORKS CITED

Aers, David. "Chaucer's Criseyde: Woman in Society, Woman in Love." Chap. in his *Chaucer, Langland, and the Creative Imagination*. London: Routledge and Kegan Paul, 1980.

Bashar, Nazife. "Rape in England between 1550 and 1700." In *The Sexual Dynamics of History*, London Feminist History Group, 28–42. London: Pluto Press, 1983.

Baum, Paull F. *Chaucer: A Critical Appreciation*. Durham, N.C.: Duke University Press, 1958.

Benson, C. David. "Incest and Moral Poetry in Gower's *Confessio Amantis*." *Chaucer Review* 19 (1984): 100–109.

Biographia Britannica; or, the Lives of the Most Eminent Persons Who Have Flourished in Great Britain and Ireland . . . . 6 vols. London: W. Innys, 1747–66.

Browning, Elizabeth Barrett. "The Book of the Poets." In *The Poetical Works of Elizabeth Barrett Browning*. London: Oxford University Press, 1916. First published in *Atheneum* (4 June 1842): 499.

Brownmiller, Susan. *Against Our Will: Men, Women and Rape*. New York: Simon and Schuster, 1975; rpt. New York: Bantam Books, 1976.

Butler, Judith. *Gender Trouble: Feminism and the Subversion of Identity*. New York and London: Routledge, 1990.

Cahoon, Leslie. "Raping the Rose: Jean de Meun's Reading of Ovid's *Amores*." *Classical and Modern Literature* 6 (1986): 261–85.

Chaucer, Geoffrey. *The Canterbury Tales of Chaucer*. Ed. Thomas Tyrwhitt. London: T. Payne, 1775–78.

———. *The Complete Works of Geoffrey Chaucer*. 7 vols. Ed. Walter W. Skeat. Oxford: Clarendon Press, 1900.

———. *The Riverside Chaucer*. Ed. Larry D. Benson. 3d ed. Boston: Houghton Mifflin, 1987.

———. *The Works of Geoffrey Chaucer*. Ed. John Urry. London: Bernard Lintot, 1721.

Courthope, W. J. *A History of English Poetry*. 1895–1910; rpt. New York: Russell and Russell, 1962.

Diamond, Arlyn. "*Troilus and Criseyde:* The Politics of Love." In *Chaucer in the Eighties*, ed. Julian N. Wasserman and Robert J. Blanch, 93–103. Syracuse, N.Y.: Syracuse Univ. Press, 1986.

Dinshaw, Carolyn. *Chaucer's Sexual Poetics*. Madison and London: University of Wisconsin Press, 1989.

Donaldson, E. Talbot. *Speaking of Chaucer*. New York: Norton, 1970.

Ellis, Kate, et al., eds. *Caught Looking: Feminism, Pornography and Censorship*. New York: Caught Looking Inc., 1985.

Estrich, Susan. *Real Rape*. Cambridge, Mass. and London: Harvard University Press, 1987.

Ferguson, Frances. "Rape and the Rise of the Novel." *Representations* 20 (Fall 1987): 88–112.

Fisher, John H. *John Gower: Moral Philosopher and Friend of Chaucer.* New York: New York University Press, 1964.

Fisher, Sheila, and Janet E. Halley, eds. *Seeking the Woman in Late Medieval and Renaissance Writings: Essays in Feminist Contextual Criticism.* Knoxville: University of Tennessee Press, 1989.

Fremont, Jack. "Rapists Speak for Themselves." In *The Politics of Rape: The Victim's Perspective,* ed. Diana E. H. Russell, 243–56. New York: Stein and Day, 1975.

Fries, Maureen. "'Slydynge of Corage': Chaucer's Criseyde as Feminist and Victim." In *The Authority of Experience: Essays in Feminist Criticism,* ed. Arlyn Diamond and Lee R. Edwards, 45–59. Amherst: University of Massachusetts Press, 1977.

Furnivall, Frederick James. *Essays on Chaucer, His Words and His Works.* Part 2, Chaucer Society Publications, ser. 2, no. 9. London: Kegan Paul, Trench, Trübner, 1874.

Ganim, John. "Chaucer and the Noise of the People." *Exemplaria* 2 (1990): 71–88.

Girard, René. *Violence and the Sacred.* Trans. Patrick Gregory. Baltimore and London: Johns Hopkins University Press, 1977.

———. *Deceit, Desire and the Novel: Self and Other in Literary Structure.* Trans. Yvonne Freccero. Baltimore and London: Johns Hopkins University Press, 1965.

Godwin, William. *Life of Chaucer.* 4 vols. London: Richard Phillips, 1803.

Gower, John. *The English Works of John Gower.* Ed. G. C. Macaulay. Early English Text Society, e.s. 81, 82. London: Oxford University Press, 1900.

Griffin, Susan. "Rape: The All-American Crime." *Ramparts* (September 1971): 35.

Hammond, Eleanor Prescott. *Chaucer: A Bibliographical Manual.* 1906; rpt. New York: Peter Smith, 1963.

Hansen, Elaine. *Chaucer and the Fictions of Gender.* University of California Press, 1992.

Hicks, Eric, ed. *Le Débat sur* Le roman de la rose. Paris: Champion, 1977.

Howard, Donald R. *Chaucer: His Life, His Works, His World.* New York: Dutton, 1987.

Irigaray, Luce. *This Sex Which Is Not One.* Trans. Catherine Porter. Ithaca, N.Y.: Cornell University Press, 1985.

"John Gower and His Works." *British Quarterly Review* 27 (1858): 3–36.

Joplin, Patricia Klindienst. "The Voice of the Shuttle Is Ours." *Stanford Literature Review* 1 (1984): 25–53.

MacKinnon, Catharine A. "Sex and Violence: A Perspective." In her *Feminism Unmodified: Discourses on Life and Law,* 85–92. Cambridge and London: Harvard University Press, 1987.

"The Mind of the Rapist." *Newsweek.* 23 July 1990: 48–49.

Nicholson, Peter. "Gower's Revisions in the *Confessio Amantis.*" *Chaucer Review* 19 (1984): 123–43.

Ovid, *Metamorphoses.* Ed. and trans. Frank Justus Miller. 3d ed. Cambridge, Mass.: Harvard University Press, 1934.

Patterson, Lee. "'No man his reson herde': Peasant Consciousness, Chaucer's Miller, and the Structure of the *Canterbury Tales.*" *South Atlantic Quarterly* 86 (1987): 457–95.

Pearsall, Derek. "The Gower Tradition." In *Gower's* Confessio Amantis: *Responses and Reassessments*, ed. A. J. Minnis, 179–97. Cambridge: D. S. Brewer, 1983.

———. *The Canterbury Tales.* London: George Allen and Unwin, 1985.

Phillips, Edward. *Theatrum Poetarum, or A Compleat Collection of the Poets, Especially the Most Eminent of All Ages.* London: Charles Smith, 1675.

Plucknett, Theodore F. T. "Chaucer's Escapade." *Law Quarterly Review* 64 (1948): 33–36.

Porter, Roy. "Rape—Does It Have a Historical Meaning?" In *Rape: An Historical and Social Enquiry*, ed. Sylvana Tomaselli and Roy Porter, 216–36. New York and Oxford: Basil Blackwell, 1986.

Post, J. B. "Sir Thomas West and the Statute of Rapes, 1382." *Bulletin of the Institute of Historical Research* 53.127 (1980): 24–30.

———. "Ravishment of Women and the Statutes of Westminster." In *Legal Records and the Historian*, ed. J. H. Baker, 15–164. London: Royal Historical Society, 1978.

Reiter, Rayna R., ed. *Toward an Anthropology of Sex.* New York: Monthly Review Press, 1975.

Ritson, Joseph. *Bibliographia Poetica: A Catalogue of Engleish [sic] Poets, of the Twelfth, Thirteenth, Fourteenth, Fifteenth, and Sixteenth, Centurys.* London: G. and W. Nicol, 1802.

Rubin, Gayle. "The Traffic in Women: Notes on the 'Political Economy' of Sex." In *Toward an Anthropology of Women*, ed. Rayna R. Reiter, 157–210. New York: Monthly Review Press, 1975.

Russell, Diana E. H. *The Politics of Rape: The Victim's Perspective.* New York: Stein and Day, 1975.

Scully, Diana. *Understanding Sexual Violence: A Study of Convicted Rapists.* Boston: Unwin Hyman, 1990.

Scully, Diana, and Joseph Marolla. "'Riding the Bull at Gilley's': Convicted Rapists Describe the Rewards of Rape." *Social Problems* 32 (1985): 251–63.

Sedgwick, Eve Kosofsky. *Between Men: English Literature and Male Homosocial Desire.* New York: Columbia University Press, 1985.

Skeat, Walter W. See Chaucer, Geoffrey. *The Complete Works of Geoffrey Chaucer.*

Tatlock, John S. P. *The Development and Chronology of Chaucer's Works.* Chaucer Society Publications, ser. 2, no. 37. London: Kegan Paul, Trench, Trübner, 1907.

Tyrwhitt, Thomas. See Chaucer, Geoffrey. *The Canterbury Tales of Chaucer.*

Urry, John. See Chaucer, Geoffrey. *The Works of Geoffrey Chaucer.*

Vance, Carole S., ed. *Pleasure and Danger: Exploring Female Sexuality.* Boston: Routledge and Kegan Paul, 1984.

Ward, Thomas Humphry, ed. *The English Poets: Selections with Critical Introductions.* 4 vols. London and New York: Macmillan, 1897.

Wetherbee, Winthrop. "Genius and Interpretation in the *Confessio Amantis.*" In *Magister Regis: Studies in Honor of Robert Earl Kaske,* ed. Arthur Groos with Emerson Brown et al., 241–60. New York: Fordham University Press, 1986.

Yeager, Robert F. *John Gower's Poetic: The Search for a New Arion.* Rochester, N.Y. and Suffolk, England: Boydell and Brewer, 1990.

8

Gender Subversion and Linguistic Castration in Fifteenth-Century English Translations of Christine de Pizan

Jane Chance

In his sixteenth-century English translation of Christine de Pizan's *Livre de la Cité des Dames*, Bryan Anslay imposes punctuation on a passage of dialogue between Christine and Dame Ryghtwysnesse concerning reasons for male criticisms of women. His punctuation makes it sound as if it is Christine who is remiss (rather than male writers) in her blame of male writers for misogynous attacks on women. Compare the English of this passage, spoken by the character Reason, in which Anslay translates incorrectly the subject, "se yceulx eussent quis," as "If thou [Christine] should have sought," and separates it from the preceding clause with a stop:

> . . . *yet as thou haste sayd other tymes ynowe. If thou sholde have sought* the wayes to withdrawe these men from folye and to kepe them that they laboure not in vayne to blame the lyfe and the condycyons of theym the whiche sheweth them vycyous and lyght / as there is nothyng in [the] worlde [that] maketh one more to fle to say the ryght trouthe / as dothe a shrewde woman / lyght and cursed as it showeth whiche is a thynge counterfayte & out of her propre condycyon natural whiche ought to be symple / pryvy / and honest I consente well that they sholde have buylded soveraynely a good and fayre worke / but to blame all where there ben so many ryght excellent I promyse [that] that it came never of me. (Dd.ij.v, cited Curnow, ed., *Cité des Dames,* 126; my emphasis).

> (*But just as you have said elsewhere, if these writers had only looked for* the ways in which men can be led away from foolishness and could have

been kept from tiring themselves in attacking the life and behavior of immoral and dissolute women—for to tell the straight truth, there is nothing which should be avoided more than an evil, dissolute, and perverted woman, who is like a monster in nature, a counterfeit estranged from her natural condition, which must be simple, tranquil, and upright—then I would grant you that they would have built a supremely excellent work. But I can assure you that these attacks on all women—when in fact there are so many excellent women—have never originated with me.) (Richards, trans., *City of Ladies*, 1.8.3, p. 18; my emphasis)

Literary translation, in its transformation of one language to another, according to postmodern theoreticians involves a vexed relationship between self and Other. An attempt to navigate the difference between two texts, the original of which itself is a product of an often indefinable intertextuality, the translation mediates between the translator and the author and between two languages and therefore two cultures.[1] From the point of view of the original author and the author's text, any translator must be a traitor, as the old adage *traduttore, traditore* reflects in miniature, no matter what kind of translation is involved. Another adage, dating from the seventeenth century, misogynously suggests that translations, which should be either beautiful or faithful, resemble women, *les belles infidèles*, but because in French the word *traduction* is feminine, translation will inevitably always remain unfaithful (Chamberlain, "Gender and Metaphorics," 58).

In a recently published postmodern "Roundtable on Translation" in which Jacques Derrida participated, Patrick Mahoney identifies three types of translation, based on the definitions of Roman Jakobson (*On Translation*): paraphrase, or intralingual translation; translation in the most common sense, or interlingual translation; and the re-encoding of verbal signs in nonverbal sign systems, or intersemiotic translation (Derrida, *Ear of the Other*, 95). Because translation in all three depends on transformation, for Derrida (writing in *Positions*), "In the limits to which it is possible or at least *appears* possible, translation practices the difference between signified and signifier. But if this difference is never pure, no more so is translation, and for the notion of translation we would have to substitute a notion of *transformation:* a regulated transformation of one language by another, of one text by another" (cited in Derrida, *Ear*, 95). The process of transforming the original is the translation contract, for Derrida "a question of neither representation nor reproduction nor communication; rather, the contract is destined to assure a survival, not only of a corpus or a text or an author but of languages"

(*Ear,* 122). In his model of the diversity of language, or Babel (confusion), Derrida holds out for the messianic character of translation, in that it promises to reconcile different tongues, but he qualifies this promise by saying that "the event of a translation . . . is not that they succeed" (*Ear,* 123). Translation, by postmodern definition, will always fail and disappoint.

The role of translation as cultural transformation is complicated by the theoretical nature of text as itself a translation, or so Terry Eagleton argues: specifically it is "a set of determinate transformations of other, preceding and surrounding texts of which it may not even be consciously aware; it is within, against and across these other texts that the poem emerges into being. And these other texts are, in their turn, 'tissues' of such pre-existent textual elements, which can never be unraveled back to some primordial moment of 'origin'" ("Translation and Transformation," 73). Because of the nature of this mythical "primary text," or "metatext," the search for its existence functions as an analogue for the hunt for the origin of language itself (73). But according to Eagleton, in the beginning was nothing, or there was no beginning. Hence, "translation from one language into another may lay bare for us something of the very productive mechanisms of textuality itself—may figure as some kind of model or paradigm of the very secret of writing" (73).

In this general context of cultural and metatextual dissociation in the practice of translation, I would like to consider the example of translation offered by fifteenth-century author Christine de Pizan, who wrote ironically and hence subversively in Middle French in the first three decades of the fifteenth century. Writing in a century in which, thanks to print technology, writing would become for the first time both commercially profitable and also democratized—that is, accessible to a wider readership that included women (Bennett, *English Books;* Hutchison, "Devotional Reading")—Christine authorized many manuscript copies of her works in order to present them to different patrons, who were usually royal and male but sometimes female, whether or not French. Because of her widespread fame in the early years of the fifteenth century, she came to be translated into other languages. But in another sense Christine was translated doubly or triply. First, she was born into an Italian family whose members lived much of their lives in France, and hence was herself translated culturally as an author. Second, her writings in Middle French—what might be termed her father tongue, or her adoptive tongue—exist in multiple and varied manuscripts, some copied by other scribes not authorized by Christine and then themselves translated into other languages, chiefly Middle English and Portuguese. Third, her translators and printers in England were male English scholars whose cultural orientation may have led them to resent French hegemony in letters, if only because of the larger wars taking place between the two countries and because of the fact that she was female, being translated by male scholars concerned about her femaleness.

The possibility of mistranslation in such an environment figures in every new reading offered by a translator. While it is true that authors would come to assume greater control of the dissemination and printing of their texts in France by the beginning of the sixteenth century for a variety of reasons related to the centralization of the publishing process, the use of the lawsuit as a tool in assertion of proprietary rights, and the development of a concept of authorship as ownership, such control did not and could not exist in this earlier, fluid period of transition between the manuscript culture of the Middle Ages and the print culture of the Renaissance in early modern Europe (Brown, *Poets, Patrons, and Printers,* esp. 1–59). This control certainly did not exist for women writers, such as Christine de Pizan, whose legal rights in France were reduced and diminutive to begin with; nor did it exist in transnational situations of migration of texts through the copying and translating of manuscripts.

The purpose of this essay, then, is twofold: to examine how widespread in late medieval and early modern England was translation of Christinian texts, like the one by Bryan Anslay, and to explain theoretically such skewed and misogynous translation practice. Such practice distorts the woman writer's authority and also inserts what it assumes to be the essential nature of women, thereby failing to perceive the irony inherent in and necessary to her text. This practice functions as a gendered form of what has been termed by Barbara Johnson, as we shall see later, "linguistic castration."

Christine de Pizan Translated

Translation into Middle English was generally reserved for the most canonical, influential, and learned of authors, as we can observe in the example of Geoffrey Chaucer's translation of Boethius's *De consolatione Philosophiae,* entitled *Boece,* and of Guillaume de Lorris' *Roman de la Rose,* entitled *Romaunt of the Rose.* Canonization, then as now, was often determined by French fashion and reflected or was influenced by the legitimation conferred by print. Yet, despite the importance of Christine de Pizan in France as early as 1404, and even though many manuscripts of her more didactic works were available at that time in France and England, according to P. G. Campbell this Franco-Italian poet was received in fifteenth-century England primarily as writer of light verse rather than as serious poet-scholar: "Therefore there is no doubt that, since 1400, Christine enjoyed an honorable reputation at the English court as author of light verse; her more serious works, in verse or in prose, had not appeared yet."[2] If it was true that she was regarded primarily as writer of light verse and not as a scholar, why was this so?

Reasons for her diminished reception can be traced in part to the civil wars dividing both England and France and the subsequent politicization of the literary scene; in part to the circulation (or noncirculation) of manuscripts of her works, especially those belonging to the French nobility, and their passage into England; and at least in part to the very production of translations and paraphrases by male scholars and poets.

Out of her entire prolific outpouring of more than twenty works during her lifetime, specifically available in the French original in England at some point during the fifteenth century, according to the testimony of library listings and catalogues, were five copies of the *Epistre Othea* (ed. Loukopoulos), two of the *Livre de la Cité des Dames* (ed. Curnow), three of the *Livre des Trois Vertus* and one of the *Corps de policie* (ed. Lucas), four of the *Fais d'armes et de chevalerie*, one of the *Enseignements*, and finally, the very important anthology, the handsomely illustrated British Library manuscript Harley 4431.

These works by Christine entered England by three means. First, several copies originally prepared in France by Christine for French royalty passed to England through English nobles with French marital connections or involvement in foreign campaigns. Most important was the anthology collection of Harley 4431, presented to Isabeau of Bavaria, queen of France, in 1407. One of the books in the library of Charles V and VI sold in 1425 to the duke of Bedford, Harley 4431 was given by the duke to his wife Jaquette de Luxembourg, who passed it at death to her son Anthony Wydeville, Earl Rivers. From the Harley text, William Caxton in 1478 published the translation of *The Morale Proverbes of Christyne* by Anthony Wydeville, who explicitly noted that "Of these sayynges Christine was the aucteuresse, / Which in makynge hadde such intelligence / That therof she was mireur and maistresse" (cited by Campbell, "Christine en Angleterre," 667). Earlier, in 1445, British Library manuscript Royal 15 E VI (with the *Fais d'armes*) had been presented to Margaret of Anjou, wife of Henry VI, by Jean Talbot, first earl of Shrewsbury. Second, some of the copies of her work were produced in England. In 1469 *The Paston Letters* records the copying of the *Epistre Othea* by scribe William Ebesham as "Othea Pistill" (Campbell, "Christine en Angleterre," 665). Third and finally, Christine herself may have presented copies of her works to English nobles like the earl of Salisbury.

From these copies circulating in England translations were made. It is likely that Christine's *Epistre au Dieu d'Amours* had traveled to England through her son, who served as a page to the earl of Salisbury before the earl's execution for treason (Laidlaw, "Christine de Pizan, the Earl of Salisbury, and Henry IV"). The earl, Jean de Montacute, had traveled to France in 1396 to arrange the marriage to Richard II of Isabella, daughter of Charles VI. After the marriage had taken place in November of 1396, Christine's son Jean de Castel accompanied the earl to England in 1397. However, because Jean de Montacute was decapitated in 1400 for having taken arms against Henry IV, Christine's son turned to Henry for protection and was returned to France (perhaps along with a copy of Chaucer's *Legend of Good Women*). From one of these trips, *L'Epistre au Dieu d'Amours* (May 1399) might also have arrived for Hoccleve to translate (May 1402). Later on, Sir John Fastolf was believed to have brought back from France between 1440 and 1459 some French manuscript of the *Epistre Othea*—perhaps acquired during a war campaign and probably begun during the first decade of the century—which his stepson and ward Stephen Scrope (1396–1472) used as a model for his various copies of his translation (Bühler, "Sir John Fastolf's Manuscripts," 123–28). In imitation of Christine's practice of dedicating her works to different nobles, one of the English translations accordingly was dedicated to Fastolf and one to Duke Humphrey of Gloucester, patron of the library at the Bodleian (Bühler, "Revisions and Dedications"). Fastolf's secretary was William Worchester, who also translated *Fais d'armes* as *Boke of Noblesse*.

Generally speaking, of Christine's works the most heavily scholastic and learned—those intended or marked for a masculine audience of royal patrons—were translated into English, chiefly the *Epistre Othea* but also other works dealing with the moralization of classical mythology and legendary history, political theory, chivalry and martial strategy, and proverbial wisdom. At some later point they would be printed in French or English editions (after the end of both the civil wars and also the dispute between France and England). Among these were the *Epistre Othea*, published in France by Philippe Pigouchet in 1499–1500, by Jean Trepperel around 1518, by Philippe Le Noir in 1522, and by Raulin Gaultier before 1534; and translated into English by Stephen Scrope in 1440–50 (ed. Bühler), by Anthony Babyington in the second half of the fifteenth century (ed. Gordon), and by printer Robert Wyer in 1540. The *Corps de policie* was translated by an unknown translator (in Cambridge University Library MS Kk. 1.5, ed. Bornstein) and published in England in 1521. The *Fais d'armes*, printed by Vérard in one early French edition of 1488 as *L'Art de chevalrie*, then reprinted 1527, was translated by William of Worchester and then published by William Caxton in 1489 or 1490 (ed. Byles); the *Proverbes moraux* was translated by Anthony Woodville, Earl Rivers, and printed by Caxton in 1477 or 1478; and the *Livre de paix,* by an anonymous translator and publisher. The *Corps de policie* was published by John Skot. Published in France was the *Trésor de la Cité des Dames,* by Antoine Vérard (1497), Michel le Noir (1503), and Jean André and Denis Janot (1536); the *Chemin de Long Estude de Dame Christine de Pise* was published in Paris in 1549.

Christine's works specifically about women, however, *Le Livre de la Cité des Dames* and its sequel, *Le Livre des Trois Vertus,* also enjoyed a wide audience, with the former appearing in a Dutch translation, "Die Lof der Vrouwen" (British Library MS Additional 20698), and afterward in two French printed editions (1497 and 1503), a Portuguese translation and edition (1518), and a Dutch edition (the Hague Royal Library MS 131, 26). Only then was it translated into English by Bryan Anslay and printed at the request of Earl Grey by Henry Pepwell in 1521; a third French edition would follow in 1536. A courtly exception to this scholarly list is the loose translation of Christine's early poem, *L'Epistre au Dieu d'Amours,* or *Letter from Cupid* (in *Poems of Cupid,* ed. Fenster and Erler), by Thomas Hoccleve, in his *Letter of Cupid to Lovers, His Subjects* (1402).

Given the circulation among, and copying of her works for, English nobles, it is surprising, then, that scholars, translators, and poets of the period tended to accord Christine less importance, especially in the reception of her most famous, most copied, and most scholarly work, the *Epistre Othea à Hector* (1399), but also of the early courtly poem, the *Epistre au Dieu d'Amours* (1399). In some cases translators and illustrators masculinize her *Epistre Othea* by attributing it to a male poet whose education might indeed have produced such an erudite work. In the two examples of translations of Christine's *Epistre Othea*—one by Stephen Scrope (ca. 1440, according to Bühler, ed., *The Epistle of Othea,* xviii), stepson of Sir John Fastolf, and one by Robert Wyer, in an early printed edition (1540)—there are unmistakable signs of such "immasculation," to borrow a term from Judith Fetterley, as there are in the translation of Christine's *Fais d'armes* by Fastolf's secretary, William Worcester. The term *immasculation* is used by Fetterley in the introduction to *The Resisting Reader* (entitled "On the Politics of Literature") to refer to the scholastic process of making women read and think as if masculine, out of the misogynistic belief that the norm is male and the female is different, other. This term can be applied here to the earlier but similar scholastic situation of depriving women of their authorship and authority because of the philosophical and scientific belief in their natural inferiority and inability to write or think in the same way as men.[3]

Thus Scrope, in the dedication to Humphrey Stafford of Gloucester (made duke of Buckingham in 1444 but slain in 1460) found in the Morgan and St. John's MSS, excises Christine's authorship while borrowing, from her attribution of her small intellectual gift to her father, her modesty topos and her metaphor of the paternal—patriarchal—literary banquet from which she stole a few crumbs. First, in the preface to Longleat MS 253 dedicated to Fastolf, Scrope describes this as his little book, "The poure effecte of my litell connyng" (line 25) (Bühler, ed., *The Epistle of Othea*, 4). Then, in the preface to *The Boke of Knyghthode* (a portion of which is appended to *The Epistle of Othea* edition by Bühler), Scrope attributes authorship to the doctors of Paris: "And this seyde boke, at the instaunce & praer off a full wyse gentyl-woman of Frawnce called Dame Cristine, was compiled of the most excellent in clerge the nobyl Vniuersyte off Paris, made to the ful noble famous prynce and knyght off revonne in his dayes, beyng called Jon, Duke of Barry, thryd son to Kyng Jon of Frawnce, that he throwe hys knyghtly labourys, as welle in dedys of armes temporell as spirituell exercisyng by the space and tyme of C yeerys lyvyng, flowrid and rengnyd in grete wor-chip and renounne of chivalry" (Bühler, ed., *The Epistle of Othea*, 122–23). The tripartite process of composition and production merely begins with Dame Cristine's prayers, but is in fact implemented by those men capable to take up such a learned labor and intended for the exemplar of chivalry himself, the duke of Berry. One copy of Christine's French text in England, Oxford Bodleian Library MS Laud 570, is also dedicated to the duke of Berry (Bühler, "Sir John Fastolf's Manuscripts," 125); it may have been the source manuscript from which Scrope translated. It was probably owned by Fastolf, brought back from France by him (Bühler, "Revisions and Dedications"). In a similar attempt to castrate the feminine, in his translation of the text Scrope also masculinizes several gods—Phoebe (fable 10) and Echo (fable 56)—for no apparent reason, certainly out of ignorance of classical mythology, in that they are not masculinized in Christine's original.

In addition, even in the English translation of her *Fais d'armes*, Worcester (secretary to John Fastolf), suppresses Christine's authority as woman poet and scholar. Declaring he had heard of a "Dame Christyn" in *Arbre des batailles* (Campbell, "Christine de Pisan en Angleterre," 662), he notes in the margin of a copy of his *Boke of Noblesse* (1487) that "Christine was a well-known and virtuous lady who supported [*exhibuit*] many clerical students in the Parisian university and did so to collect [*compilare*] many virtuous books"; that is, the books were actually written by her students.[4] A similar excision of Christine's authorship also occurred in one later group of manuscripts of *Fais d'armes*, including the sixteenth-century French printings of Vérard and Philippe Le Noir.[5] This excision does not take place in another, earlier, and finer group in which her authorship is noted and which contain many miniatures of Christine as author, including the original used by Caxton in his late fifteenth-century printing.[6] The later group extinguishes her name and any reference to female authorship in the first, introductory, chapter; feminine forms of adjectives are changed to masculine and deleted is her address to Minerva, in which she identifies with the Italian matron of warfare ("I am as thou were, a woman ytalien") (Byles, ed., *Faytes of Armes*, xiv–xv). The editor of the modern edition of the Middle English translation explains the excision of authorship in the anonymous group of later manuscripts as a reaction to scribal anxiety that "prejudice against a woman writing on a manly subject might detract from the book's appeal" (Byles, ed., *Faytes of Armes*, xvi). In his description of London British Library MS Royal 15 E vi, however, editor Byles also notes as appropriate deletions made because of its nature as a gift from John Talbot, first earl of Shrewsbury, to the new queen, Margaret of Anjou, married to Henry VI—negative references to the English invaders (*Fais* 1.5; Byles, ed., *Faytes of Armes*, xvi).

This unwillingness to permit Christine to be an author—the denial of her authority—is also witnessed in the most famous English "translation" (more accurately, paraphrase) of Christine, in Hoccleve's *Letter of Cupid* (1402). To this most important free "translation" of a work by Christine, Hoccleve adds a male voice, and hence male subjectivity, in the changes he makes to her lines and approach.[7] Her feminism in the *Epistre au Dieu d'Amours* is undercut by his subversive antifeminism and hostility of tone, her irony interfaced with his literalism. The *Letter of Cupid*, written for (or at the behest of) Duke Humphrey of Gloucester like Scrope's translation of the *Epistre Othea* (according to Hoccleve's later *Dialogue*), offers his patron another poem about courtly love and women (a male bonding experience of sharing a female text). Hoccleve's *Letter* supposedly "defends" women by demeaning them—by using scatalogical or sexual metaphors for the female, such as a chamber pot a man has just finished using ("whan the man the *pot* hath by the stele / And fully of hire hath possessioun," Hoccleve, *Letter*, ed. Furnivall, 50–51; my emphasis), or a horse he "rides" ("As a hors fro day to day [she] is hyrid. . . . Now *prike* on faste," 103, 106, my emphasis). Woman is so sexually voracious that Hoccleve advises, "qwikly of an othir take a *snak*," (109, my emphasis). Hoccleve's antifeminism is noted by modern critic Diane Bornstein in both the content and style of his poem; in his omission of the French knights in Christine, such as Oton de Graunson, who support women, and of other arguments in favor of women; and in his transformation of Cupid from moral god to jester (Bornstein, "Anti-Feminism," 7–14). Most important, Hoccleve's introduction of Chaucer as literary authority (in place of Penelope, in Christine's triad of female victims of love, Dido, Medea, and Penelope) masculinizes what had been a feminization of history (just as Hoccleve also subtly shifts focus from Dido to Aeneas, Medea to Jason, even while acknowledging the male figures' lack of trustworthiness as lovers). That Hoccleve also adds St. Margaret to figures who include the Virgin Mary, in what Bornstein sees as a sanctification of the natural Woman that real women are not permitted to be, may have been intended as homage to a new, female, and French patron, Margaret of Anjou, queen of England and wife of Henry IV.

Hoccleve displays a barely concealed scholarly anxiety about the authority of this woman poet-scholar, borne out by his omission of Christine's name, or in other words, her learning, her authorship—as if he wished to erase her, and real women, altogether. In the literary criticism from the 1970s on Hoccleve's relationship as translator to Christine as author, the gender subversion (if not erasure) by fifteenth-century scholars and translators is continued in what might be regarded as a modern "Quarrel of the Rose." John Fleming argues that Hoccleve preserves Christine's tenor, one of *anti*-antifeminism, but that Hoccleve is laughing, not at all women but at one woman—Christine—for being a "bad literary critic" and for "making a public fool of herself" (Fleming, "Hoccleve's *Letter of Cupid*," 26). Situating Christine's poem (1399) and Hoccleve's (May 1402) within the scholastic and university-centered Quarrel of the Rose, Fleming can then show that Hoccleve is attempting to counter both Christine and Gerson (the latter, "unquestionably the more interesting mind") and support Jean de Montreuil and the Col Brothers. For Fleming, Hoccleve, by introducing as witness Chaucer (who had also translated the *Roman de la Rose*) in stanza 46, can reveal Christine's attacks on Jean de Meun's *Roman* as a "blunder": declares Fleming, "Chaucer had anticipated Christine in presenting Cupid as a literary critic presiding over a Star Chamber for the suppression of naughty books" (30). Further, according to Fleming, speaking on behalf of Hoccleve, it is inappropriate (for Christine) to apply "canons of courtesy" to Jean de Meun in regard to his depiction of female sexuality. Christine's "Victorian propriety" marks her, and her ally Gerson, as "obtuse and naive" in responding to the *Roman*-poems described by Fleming carnally as "moist chivalry." (Fleming also calls her desexualized rose in the *Dit de la Rose* "fumigated.") Fleming ultimately regards Christine not as a person at all, much less an author, but as a mindless female body (or body part) symbolized by her text: "Her allegorical veil is spun of fine transparent silk; it richly adorns, but barely conceals" (35), he smirks, in a literal undressing of Christine's carnal text.

Such scholastic misogyny colors other kinds of "translation" of Christine's works. Illustration, like translation, also represents an interpretation of a text and therefore can measure the author's or the artist's own assessment of an author's importance, or a translator's mistake or bias. For examples of the former, manuscript illustrations of Christine herself in the fifteenth century show an increasing richness of dress that traces her growth of importance as an author (Dufresne, "A Woman of Excellent Character"). But when such illustrations were not zealously copied from originals authorized by the writer—as many of Christine's were in fact authorized (Hindman, *Painting and Politics*)—they could reflect the scribe's or illustrator's program: for example, Jean Miélot, a scribe working around 1460 in the service of Philippe le Bon, duke of Burgundy, supplemented a new mythographic commentary with new illustrations which, because of his additions from Boccaccio's *Genealogia gentilium libri* and Guido delle Colonne's *Historia destructionis Troiae*, literalized Christine's more moral and allegorical purpose through his dominant visual preoccupation and focus on the biographical narrative in the text (Brown-Grant, "Illumination as Reception").

Such adaptation-qua-interpretation is also true of Robert Wyer's 1540 printed English translation of Christine's *Epistre*, the *C. Hystoryes of Troye*, which, clearly in imitation of a text Wyer admires, incorporates the woodcuts from the earlier French edition (1490) by Philippe Pigouchet. Woodcuts, found frequently as well in early printed devotional works, some of which were intended for a female readership (Driver, "Pictures in Print"), translated from parchment to paper extant images authorized by the manuscript form of a text. Some of the woodcut figures in Christine's printed editions were not only translated but masculinized—that is, made male—from their form as empowered females in Christine's texts and from their illuminations in the original manuscripts. Among these are, for example, in fable 1 a much-reduced Othea presenting her book to a grown and manly fifteen-year-old Hector (see fig. 1), in contrast to Christine's depiction of the dominant Othea and the puerile Hector in Harley 4431 (see fig. 2). There is also Thamaris in fable 57, the Amazonian Queen who beheads bloodthirsty King Cyrus of Persia and his Barons, depicted as male (see fig. 3) or omitted entirely. In fable 73 diminished and kneeling goddesses Juno, Minerva, and Venus are judged by a dominant Paris (fig. 4). Chatterbox Echo in fable 86 is presented as Queen Margaretha to King Henry VI's Narcissus, in a curiously misogynistic (or ironic) depiction, given the text (fig. 5). In fable 99 appears the masculinization of the normally female figure of Ino scattering her grain uselessly (fig. 6), no doubt fabulizing in this context what we might call the writer's dissemination of her text. At the end, in fable 100, as in the beginning, in fable 1, masculine figures (Caesar Augustus, see fig. 7, like Hector) are enlarged and female ones diminished (the Sybil, like Othea) or expunged (the Virgin Mary). That is, the diminutive Sibyl, whose power both Christine's text and also illustration (for example, in Harley 4431) celebrate by means of her standing position and her size, is squeezed into the left-hand box at the top, while the kneeling and humble Caesar Augustus in Christine's illustration is magnified into the regnant figure dominating the center of the illustration, facing forward (fig. 8). This posture ignores the text's delineation of Augustus's vision of the Virgin and child and his obeisance to the female component in Christianity. In Christine, the large Virgin holding the babe Christ is the focus of both text and illustration. In Wyer's English translation, the Virgin has been apparently erased and the babe enlarged to the figure of the naked Christ ready for crucifixion.

Almost, we might imagine, in order to prevent this woman from entering the domain of the teacher-scholar, her translators in large part silenced her by excising her authority and her authorship. Thereby they (as it were) circumcised her from her own text. That is, in translating her language, so associated with the domination of the French court, they reinscribed her text into their own mother tongue and in some cases assumed her position as author—excised her authority. In this examination of what might be considered an early instance of female reception, that is, in several translations and paraphrases of some of her scholarly and even courtly works, scholastic and masculine poetic misogyny in addition circumcises her intellectual and literary importance—her gender and authority are denied and, in Hoccleve's loose translation of her *Epistre au Dieu d'Amours,* her ideas parodied and mocked, her sex abused. To adapt Judith Fetterley's term, Christine is first immasculated: that is, male translators and scholars, after erasing her dedicatory prologues, replace them with their own and take credit for her authorship. Or they immasculate her by suggesting her as source of inspiration for the male cleric who was believed to have authored the text. Or they altogether erase what might be termed signs of her feminizing influence. Second, they "circumcise" her power, so to speak—cut away that which she offers as female empowerment.

The power relationship of the controlling (male, English) translator over the controlled (female, French) leads to a reversal: the triumph of a masculinized nationalism over a feminized intertext. Indeed, when Scrope wishes his patron to judge his translation favorably he appeals to Duke Humphrey's *mankyndlynes* (line 140), his nature as a man. That this triumph can be accepted as normal practice by poets and scholars does not imply that it cannot also be interpreted as literary violence against a woman when set against a cultural and literary environment of violence against women. In early French romances by Chrétien de Troyes (for example, *Erec et Enide*), and the later Old French romances such as *Silence*, women are raped or drawn and quartered without another thought. In Chaucer's *Reeve's Tale* the rapes of mother and daughter by the two clerics are depicted as quasi-consensual and apparently a respite (according to the narrating Reeve) from their quotidian sexual tedium. Kathryn Gravdal, in *Ravishing Maidens*, has documented the kinds of normalizing influences that made rape acceptable to medieval society. Accordingly, then, within the context of translation, rape or drawing and quartering, when the authorial power is as considerable as that of Christine de Pizan, become troped—a form of scholastic violence against women, its force concealed by the distancing offered by language and verbalization. What we find here, additionally, is that the national enmities coloring the cultural relationship project into the gender difference between the male translator and the female text, or intertext, a normalizing violence of suppression and linguistic castration. As Lori Chamberlain has shrewdly noted, "In the metaphorics of translation, the struggle for authorial rights takes place both in the realm of the family . . . and in the state, for translation has also been figured as the literary equivalent of colonization, a means of enriching the language and the literature appropriate to the political needs of expanding nations. . . . For the Romans, Nietzsche asserts, 'translation was a form of conquest'" ("Gender and Metaphorics," 61).

To explore the reasons for such hostility toward the female text and author it is necessary to look more closely at contemporary postmodern translation theory and the ways in which the violence of misogyny works to resist and erase gender difference itself.

The Translator and the Return to the Mother (Tongue): The Linguistic Castration of the Female

Although there has been little written on gender difference in translation, George Steiner acknowledges the act of translation as a form of erotic penetration and likens the exchange of words from one language to another to the exchange of women and goods (*After Babel*, 298, 302). Christine Brooke-Rose picks up on the power issue in the male fantasy of the mute dream woman as defined by the writer Debax, in "Et voilà pourquoi votre femme est muette." Debax declares, "To reduce woman to silence is to reduce her

There begynneth the Epistle, whiche Othea the Goddes sende vnto Hector of Troye, when he was of the age of.xv.yeres.

The fyrste texte.

Thea goddes of Prudence
whiche doeth adresse
good hertes in valyaunce

I.iij. ⁂ To

1. A diminutive Othea presents her book to a grown and manly fifteen-year-old Hector, in the frontispiece to Robert Wyer's 1540 printed English translation of Christine's *Epistre Othea*, entitled *The C. Hystoryes of Troye*, which incorporated the woodcuts from the 1490 French edition by Philippe Pigouchet. Reproduced by permission of the British Library (C21a34).

2. A supernal and large Othea at the opening (fable 1) of Christine's *Epistre Othea* presents her book to a young and diminutive Hector, in London, British Library MS Harley 4431, fol. 95v. Reproduced by permission of the British Library.

The.lvii.Hystorie.

Therfore sayth saynt Peter.

Sobzii estote et vigilate quia al uersarius
vester diabolus tanch leo / rugiens circuit que-
rens quem deuozet. Secundo petri vltimo ca.

The.lvii.Hystorie.

The.lvii.Texte.

BE not Thamarys, of the despysed

Thoughe she a woman, and to Armes set her entent

M.v.   Remem-

---

3. Masculinized Thamaris, the Amazonian Queen who beheads blood-thirsty King Cyrus of Persia and his Barons, in fable 57 of Robert Wyer's 1540 printed English translation of Christine's *Epistre Othea, The C. Hystoryes of Troye*. Reproduced by permission of the British Library (C21a34).

The .lppii. Allegorie.

to empeſſhe hỹ oz be abaſſhed, and leſſe
whan he dzaweth mento hisloue, than
whan he gyueth occaſion to be deſpiſed
To this purpoſe ſayth Jhoñ the Euan
gelyſt in his fyzſt Goſpell.

Si quis diligit mundum non eſt cari̇s
tas patris in eo. pzimo Joḥañ.ii.ca.

The .lppiii. Hyſtozie.

The .lppiii. Texte.

IN Judgement lyke Paris,
no ſentence out caſte
foz

4. Diminished and kneeling goddesses Juno, Minerva, and Venus in fable 73 are judged by a dominant Paris, in Robert Wyer's 1540 printed English translation of Christine's *Epistre Othea, The C. Hystoryes of Troye*. Reproduced by permission of the British Library (C21a34).

The.lxxxvi. Texte.

Gladly to Echo, her reque∫
∫tes attroye
Be thou not in wyll, her playn
tes to augmente
If thou haue power, to ∫et her
harte in ioye
Thou knoweﬅ not what For∫
tune is vnto the lente.

S iij.   Echo

5. Chatterbox Echo in fable 86 depicted as Queen Margaretha to King Henry VI's Narcissus, in Robert Wyer's 1540 printed English translation of Christine's *Epistre Othea, The C. Hystoryes of Troye*. Reproduced by permission of the British Library (C21a34).

The.lxxxpix.Texte.

Thou oughtest not to showe
wyse parables and fayre
To them that lacketh reason/
them to vnderstande
Of this by yno , take good ex-
amplayre

U.b.   Whiche

6. A masculinized Ino in fable 99 scatters her grain uselessly, in Robert Wyer's 1540 printed English translation of Christine's *Epistre Othea, The C. Hystoryes of Troye*. Reproduced by permission of the British Library (C21a34).

7. The masculine figure of Caesar Augustus in fable 100 is enlarged and the female figures are diminished (the Sybil) or expunged (the Virgin Mary), in Robert Wyer's 1540 printed English translation of Christine's *Epistre Othea*, *The C. Hystoryes of Troye*. Reproduced by permission of the British Library (C21a34).

8. A standing and dominant Sibyl explains the supernal Virgin and her small baby Jesus (depicted as the sun) to a Caesar Augustus kneeling and eager to learn, in fable 100 of Christine's *Epistre Othea*, in London, British Library MS Harley 4431, fol. 141. Reproduced by permission of the British Library.

to powerlessness; that is how the masculine will to castrate operates. Thus—perhaps because of this—women's will to revolt necessarily passes through the use of language, the tongue [*la langue*]. Language, the tongue, is woman's weapon" (cited in Brooke-Rose, "Woman as Semiotic Object," 310). After marriage, Debax suggests, the mute virgin encounters sex (masculine) and thus if she continues to speak, becomes a shrew—another example of how the power of language is always denied to woman.

Yet the act of translation, especially when attempted by a male translator from a language that is Other, is one of return to the mother, or the mother tongue. For this reason, to return to the mother tongue by necessity involves violence—linguistic castration, in the act of silencing the woman. In an identification with the (male) translator, Barbara Johnson argues, in "Taking Fidelity Philosophically," that

> We tear at her syntactic joints and semantic flesh and resent her for not providing all the words we need. . . . If we are impotent, it is because Mother is inadequate. In the process of translation from one language to another, the scene of *linguistic castration*—which is nothing other than a scene of impossible but unavoidable translation and normally takes place out of sight, behind the conscious stage—is played on center stage, evoking fear and pity and the illusion that all would perhaps have been well if we could simply have stayed at home. (In Graham, *Difference in Translation*, 143–44; my emphasis)

The image Johnson uses is centered on the castration of the father (tongue, text) and the impotence of the mother (tongue, Otherness), with the translation as product, child, mediating between.

The translator, like the author, resembles his intertextual text, that is, he is himself his own parents, for whom he writes. In his reflection on translation, Derrida recognizes the text in which Nietzsche says, "I am two, my father and my mother," in that he has inherited from them and writes *for* them (Derrida, *Ear*, 53). The translator writes for both past and future—looking back to the one and ahead to the other—and sometimes for two genders. For Derrida, the power of the mother in language is exerted in the concept of the mother tongue: there is a law that "creates obligations with regard to language, and particularly with regard to the language in which the law is stated: the mother tongue. This is the living language (as opposed to Latin, a dead, paternal language, the language of another law where a secondary repression has set in—the law of death). There has to be a pact or alliance with the living language and language of the living feminine against death, against the dead" (Derrida, *Ear*, 21). For Eugenio

Donato, another participant in the roundtable discussion on translation, the "mother language" lives, whereas the father (the constituted meaning) is dead, to be revived in translation. Therefore, "The tear in the mother's living body must always give birth to and must always abort the memory of the father who is always dead" (in Derrida, *Ear,* 129). Continuing these gender tropes, roundtable discussant Eugene Vance notes that "through libidinal translation, nature manifests itself, over time, in its totality. To refuse translation is to refuse life" (in Derrida, *Ear,* 137). Here Vance bases his process on medieval systems of human psychology, specifically, the impelling of action by means of language and its energy. The latter can force man to "translate anger (*ira*) into a libidinal form (*concupiscentia*)" and "transport" men to women "in *hymene,* allowing for a translation of semen" (in Derrida, *Ear,* 137). Conversely, Donato offers the Derridean possibility of invagination, "in which nothing would remain but edges or borders" (129): that is, he fantasizes that "Translation can be thought of as a speculative *mise en abîme* of each text" (129). A useful translation here of what Donato means is exemplified in the painting of a gallery wall on which is hung the painting of the gallery wall (Derrida, *Ear,* 62n.). Because of the etymological and semantic associations of translation with what Mahoney in the roundtable discussion terms "metaphor, transfer, transference, and transport" (94), it is easy to understand the androcentric slide into gender as trope in postmodern translation theory.

But what happens when the translated is herself female—when translation involves an author who is, because of gender difference, Other, a passive victim of the translator's desire to return to the mother (tongue)? At the end of the "Roundtable on Translation," Monique Bosco first remarks that when a man translated her book it became a completely different book, then asks Derrida a question that he evades answering: "Do you agree that there is a problem of sexual difference which enters in at the level of translation?" (Derrida, *Ear,* 153). The misogyny apparent in postmodern translation theories arises from the Freudian hostility toward the mother, the eternal feminine: Derrida does reserve space for the mother, for "the mother is the faceless figure of a *figurant,* an extra. She gives rise to all the figures by losing herself in the background of the scene like an anonymous persona. Everything comes back to her, beginning with life; everything addresses and destines itself to her. She survives on the condition of remaining at bottom" (38).

In the more specific context of academe, writing, and translation, women for Derrida theoretically and literally do not and cannot exist. In relation to the role of the ear in teaching, given that the ear is an invaginated symbol, Derrida notes of woman that she "never appears at any point along the umbilical cord, either to study or teach. She is the great 'cripple,' perhaps. No woman or trace of woman," which results in the vulgar procedure of seduction in all courtrooms (or courtships), or "gynegogy." Woman is either literally silent, excised, or existent merely as a trope. And to respond to Monique Bosco's pertinent question, when there is a male translator of a female text, she is doubly excised, hidden, closed off.

Johnson also notes that "translation is a bridge that creates out of itself the two fields of battle it separates" (Graham, *Difference in Translation*, 162). As such, the relationship is based as well upon a transfer of power from one entity to the other, which can deteriorate into abuse—castration, ripping, violence. The violent transaction stems from the imposition of authority by one, ruling, entity or class, upon another, according to Hannah Arendt. But, she cautions, "politically speaking, it is insufficient to say that power and violence are not the same. Power and violence are the opposites; where the one rules absolutely, the other is absent. Violence appears where power is in jeopardy, but left to its own course it ends in power's disappearance. . . . Violence can destroy power; it is utterly incapable of creating it" (Arendt, *On Violence*, 56). Power depends upon the acting in concert of a group ("without a people or group there is no power"); strength is a property inherent in an object or person: "The almost instinctive hostility of the many toward the one has always, from Plato to Nietzsche, been ascribed to resentment, to the envy of the weak for the strong, but this psychological interpretation misses the point. It is in the nature of a group and its power to turn against independence, the property of individual strength" (44). Authority, vested in persons or offices, depends upon "unquestioning recognition by those who are asked to obey," its greatest enemy therefore existing in the form of "contempt, and the surest way to undermine it is laughter" (45).

This is not so different from the weapon identified as that of women in gender wars. According to Claude Lévesque, turning to Hegel on Sophocles' *Antigone* and femininity's position in a transition to *Sittlichkeit* (morality), "the all-powerful weapon of the impotent, the unalienable stroke of woman is irony. Woman, 'internal enemy of the community,' can always burst out laughing at the last moment. She knows, in sorrow and in death, how to pervert the power that represses her" (Derrida, *Ear*, 75).

Although in this essay there is not time to explore all the ways in which Christine de Pizan perverted the power that attempted to repress and silence her within her own culture, nevertheless within the context of the feminization of literary reception—her own, of the traditions she inherited and those of her literary heirs—laughter and its more sophisticated rhetorical cousins demonstrate the literary subversion of that power. What we find is her use of the rhetorical figure of irony—antiphrasis—as a gender weapon in the war between the sexes, and, more to the point, an acceptance of her literary prominence among those women writers who succeeded her.

Christine's Gendered Textuality and Feminized Literary Reception of Her Authority

Christine's frontispiece illustration for the *Epistre au Dieu d'Amours* in Harley 4431 depicts the God of Love as receptive to, not suppressive of, a (female) text—after all, the God of Love receives *Christine's* book from a messenger and presumably will read it receptively as well (fig. 9). Further, even though Christine excises herself from the frontispiece, a sign of her authority remains in the symbol of the book, her antimisogynist *Epistre au Dieu d'Amours*, presented to divinity. Her identification of her self as a book, or letter, is mirrored in the acrostic of her name at the end of her poem, Christine as Christ and Christine as Word, CREINTIS ("fearful," see Laennec, "Christine *Antygrafe*," 27; Nouvet, "Writing (in) Fear," 296–99), but nevertheless also Christine as *female* word, *female* text. In this instance I would not agree that Christine herself was so ambivalent about her own status as woman author that she described herself as an *antygrafe* (antiwriter, from the Latin *antigrafus*), as a means of both affirming and denying her authority (Laennec), and thus using anagrams for her own name to conceal her identity. She was an antiwriter in writing *against* the patriarchal writing tradition to which so many scribes, scholars, and translators belonged, and consciously distinguished herself from them as a writer of female, or feminizing, texts.

That Christine did influence English literary conventions, indeed, even *feminize* poetic output, can be recognized through her impact on female subjectivity and authority in at least two late fifteenth-century anonymous poems possibly written by women, the *Floure and the Leafe* and the *Assembly of Ladies* (ed. Pearsall) and possibly also the Findern anthology of courtly love lyrics (ed. Robbins), filled as they are with poems illustrative of a female perspective (Hanson-Smith, "A Woman's View,"), an argument that I have traced elsewhere (Chance, "Christine as Literary Mother"). Further, literary echoes of her *Epistre Othea* (or its Middle English translation) appear in the anonymous late fifteenth-century poem once attributed to John Lydgate, the *Assembly of Gods*, a poem that appears in its only authoritative form (that is, in a manuscript source that is not copied from a printed edition, as was in fact the case with the only other extant manuscript, Brit-

9. A seated God of Love receives from a messenger Christine's poem, *L'Epistre au Dieu d'Amours,* or a letter of complaint (which of course Christine's *Letter* also is) about the cavaliers' treatment of women; or the God of Love hands his *Letter* to a messenger. Christine de Pizan's *Epistre au Dieu d'Amours.* London, British Library MS Harley 4431, fol. 51. Reproduced by permission of the British Library.

ish Library MS Royal 18 D, fols. 167a–180b, from a copy of Wynken de Worde's print, British Library G. 11587; Triggs, ed., *Assembly of Gods*, viii) in the same manuscript as that of the feminized *Assembly of Ladies*, Cambridge Trinity College MS R. 3.19 (fols. 67b–97b).[8] This Trinity manuscript was owned by John Stowe at one point and can be dated around 1463 at the earliest (Triggs, ed., *Assembly of Gods*, vii) and the last quarter of the fifteenth century at the latest (Pearsall, ed., *Floure*). Here Christine's mythical *Epistre* goddess, Othea, appears in a catalogue of gods assembling to hear a complaint.

It is no accident that the author of the *Assembly of Gods* borrows from Christine the fictional Othea, the goddess who writes her letter of mythological morality and allegory to her fifteen-year-old nephew Hector in the *Epistre Othea*, possesses a name consisting of O plus *thea*, "goddess" (Mombello, "Déesse Othea"). The other Christinian elements in the *Assembly of Gods* include the female gods Diana, Ceres, and Isis. Diana is central to the *Dit de la Rose* as well as to the *Epistre Othea* and the *Cité des Dames*, the latter two being works which also showcase Ceres (Kellogg, "Feminist Myth") and Isis (Chance, "Christine as Literary Mother"). I would argue that these female divinities are important for understanding her scholarly influence: the anonymous (female?) *Assembly*-poet, while adding these central female figures to the poem, does so as a corrective to the standard (male poet's) catalogues of gods (found most fully in the school-text of Martianus Capella's *De nuptiis Philologii et Mercurii*). Indeed, the central issue in the *Assembly of Gods* allegory also seems scholastic and educated— that is, whether reason and sensuality can coexist. The question is appropriately framed (and perhaps answered) by the appearance of the guide Morpheus, god of sleep and dreams. If subjectivity, imagination, fancy, represent a faculty more useful than reason, then it is no surprise that the subsequent rational assembly of gods to discuss the complaints of Diana (earth) and Neptune (water) against Aeolus (air) finally authorizes the female components of Nature (Diana, earth). In this way the *Assembly* underscores Christine's own feminine authority in the *Epistre Othea*. The *Assembly*-poet also preserves Christine's determined feminist reading of the Fate Atropos, signifying Death, as male rather than female. After all, why should the power to take away life be associated with the life-bestowing female?

While the excision of feminine influence and authority by male translators, editors, poets, scholars, and printers—this immasculation of texts—in the early to mid–fifteenth century may have stymied modern tracings of the actual literary influence of Christine de Pizan on England, it has also revealed cultural and class differences in the way authors are received. The male and female aristocrats who patronized Christine in France or England did not feel as threatened by her, it appears, as did the *male* secretaries and scholars who were themselves presumably vying for position, prestige, and patronage. These men therefore had more of an interest in appropriating for themselves the gifts of Christine's innovative reading of classical mythology and the scholastic exegetical or literary tradition. To return to an examination of the signs of her presence in fifteenth- and sixteenth-century England, as in the case of the *Assembly of Gods,* will open the door to the rediscovery of a female literary tradition that is cross-cultural, multilingual, and, of course, unmistakably and essentially gendered.

NOTES

An earlier version of this essay was delivered as "Gender Subversion and Erasure in Fifteenth-Century English Translations of Christine de Pizan" in a session on "Translation, Interpretation, and the Symbolism of Gender" organized by Professor Jeanette Beer for the International Courtly Literature Society at the annual meeting of the Modern Language Association, New York, December 30, 1992. I am grateful to the dean of humanities at Rice University for the summer research grant in 1994 that helped defray expenses incurred in reading manuscripts in London while serving as visiting research fellow at the University of Edinburgh Institute for Advanced Studies in the Humanities and for the summer research grant in 1995 that subsidized the cost of the illustrations used in this study.

1. See Derrida, "Living On/Border Lines" (1979), on the problems of translation, especially from the French. There is a whole volume devoted to *Difference in Translation,* edited by Joseph F. Graham (1985), trained especially on Derrida's views both on difference and on translation. See also Gavronsky, "The Translator," on cannibalism and translation.

2. "Donc nul doute que, dès 1400, Christine jouissait à la cour anglaise d'une honorable réputation comme auteur de poésie légère; ses oeuvres plus sérieuses, soit en vers, soit en prose, n'ont pas encore paru" (Campbell, "Christine de Pizan en Angleterre," 661).

3. "Though one of the most persistent of literary stereotypes is the castrating bitch, the cultural reality is not the emasculation of men by women but the *immasculation* of women by men. As readers and teachers and scholars, women are taught to think as men, to identify with a male point of view, and to accept as normal a male system of values, one of whose cultural principles is misogyny" (Fetterley, *Feminisms,* 497). There is a long bibliography now available on feminist reader-response theory and gender difference in reading and writing practice and the medieval scholastic practice of misogyny: see Chance, introduction to *Gender and Text,* 1–21. See also Blamires, Pratt, and Marx, eds., *Woman Defamed,* and Cadden, *Meanings of Sex Difference.*

4. "Cristina domina praeclara . . . et ita virtuosa fuit quod ipsa exhibuit plures clericos studentes in universitate parisiensi, et compilare fecit plures libros virtuous" (Campbell, "Christine de Pisan en Angleterre," 669).

5. See these two English MSS, Oxford Bodleian 824 and Brussels Bibliothèque Royale MS 10205, and the French MSS Paris Bibliothèque Nationale 585, 1242, 1243, 23997 (Byles, ed., *Faytes of Armes,* xv).

6. See these English MSS, London British Library Royal 15 E vi, Royal 19 B xviii, Harleian 4605; Brussels Bibliothèque Royale MSS 9009–11, 10476; and the French MSS at Paris, Bibliothèque Nationale, 603, 1183, 1241, and the fragmentary Collection Duchesne 65 (Byles, ed., *Faytes of Armes,* xv).

7. Walter Skeat's notes compare lines in the *Epistre au Dieu d'Amours* with the English lines of Hoccleve's version (in Hoccleve, ed. Furnivall, 243–48).

8. See Bühler, "The *Assembly of Gods* and Christine de Pisan," 251–54. I am preparing an edition of *Assembly of Gods* for the Middle English Texts Series edited by Russell Peck under the auspices of TEAMS (Consortium for the Teaching of the Middle Ages, Inc.), which will appear through the Medieval Institute of Western Michigan University.

Works Cited

Arendt, Hannah. *On Violence.* New York: Harcourt, Brace, and World: 1969, 1970.

Bennett, H. S. *English Books and Readers, 1475 to 1557.* Cambridge: Cambridge University Press, 1970.

Blamires, Alcuin, with Karen Pratt and C. W. Marx, eds. *Woman Defamed and Woman Defended: An Anthology of Medieval Texts.* Oxford: Oxford University Press, 1992.

Blanchard, Joel. "Christine: Tradition, expérience, et traduction." *Romania* 111 (1990): 200–235.

Bornstein, Diane. "Anti-Feminism in Thomas Hoccleve's Translation of Christine de Pizan's *Epistre au Dieu d'Amours.*" *English Language Notes* 19 (1981): 7–14.

Brooke-Rose, Christine. "Woman as Semiotic Object." In *The Female Body in Western Culture,* ed. Susan R. Suleiman, 305–16. Cambridge, Mass.: Harvard University Press, 1986.

Brown, Cynthia J. *Poets, Patrons, and Printers: Crisis of Authority in Late Medieval France.* Ithaca and London: Cornell University Press, 1995.

Brown-Grant, Rosalind. "Illumination as Reception: Jean Miélot's Reworking of the 'Epistre Othea'." In *The City of Scholars: New Approaches to Christine de Pizan,* ed. Margarete Zimmerman and Dina De Rentiis, 260–71. Berlin and New York: Walter de Gruyter, 1994.

Bühler, Curt F. "The *Assembly of Gods* and Christine de Pisan." *English Language Notes* 4 (1967): 251–54.

———."The Revisions and Dedications of the *Epistle of Othea.*" *Anglia* 76 (1958): 266–70.

———. "Sir John Fastolf's Manuscripts of the *Épître d'Othéa* and Stephen Scrope's Translation of this Text." *Scriptorium* 3 (1949): 123–28.

Cadden, Joan. *Meanings of Sex Difference in the Middle Ages: Medicine, Science, and Culture*. Cambridge: Cambridge University Press, 1993.

Campbell, P. G. C. "Christine de Pisan en Angleterre." *Revue de littérature comparée* 5 (1925): 659–70.

———. "Christine de Pizan—A Publisher's Progress." *Modern Language Review* 82 (1987): 35–75.

Chamberlain, Lori. "Gender and the Metaphorics of Translation." In *Rethinking Translation: Discourse, Subjectivity, Ideology*, ed. Lawrence Venuti, 57–74. London and New York: Routledge, 1992.

Chance, Jane. "Christine de Pizan as Literary Mother: Women's Authority and Subjectivity in 'The Floure and the Leafe' and 'The Assembly of Ladies.'" In *The City of Scholars: New Approaches to Christine de Pizan*, ed. Margarete Zimmerman and Dina De Rentiis, 245–59. Berlin and New York: Walter de Gruyter, 1994.

———, ed. *Assembly of Gods*. Middle English Texts Series. Kalamazoo: TEAMS (Consortium for the Teaching of the Middle Ages, Inc.) Medieval Institute Press of Western Michigan University. Forthcoming.

———, ed. *Gender and Text in the Later Middle Ages*. Gainesville: University Press of Florida, 1996.

———, ed. *The Mythographic Art: Classical Fable and the Rise of the Vernacular in Early France and England*. Gainesville: University of Florida Press, 1990.

Chaucer, Geoffrey. *The Legend of Good Women*. Trans. Ann McMillan. Houston: Rice University Press, 1986.

Christine de Pizan. "Works." MS Harley 4431. British Library, London, England.

———. *Lavision-Christine: Introduction and Text*. Ed. Sister M. L. Towner. 1932; rpt. New York: AMS Press, 1969.

———. *Les Cent Histoires de Troye*. Paris: Philippe Pigouchet [1499–1500].

———. *S'ensuyt L'Epistre de Othea, deese de Prudence, moralisee . . . par Christine de Pisan*. Paris: La Veuve Trepperel [1518?].

———. *Les Cent Hystoires de Troye*. Paris: Philippe Le Noir, 1522.

———. *L'Epistre de Othea*. Rouen: Raulin Gaultier [before 1534].

———. *L'Epistre Othea*. In "Classical Mythology in the Works of Christine de Pisan, with an edition of *L'Epistre d'Othea* from the Manuscript Harley 4431." Ed. Halina Didycky Loukopoulos. Ph.D. Diss., Wayne State University, 1977.

———. *Here foloweth the C. Hystoryes of Troye, Lepistre de Othea deese de Prudence envoyee a l'esprit chevalereux Hector de Troye*. Trans. Robert Wyer. With illustrations from the earlier French edition (1490) by Philippe Pigouchet. London: Robert Wyer, 1540.

———. *The Epistle of Othea to Hector, or the Boke of Knyghthode: translated from the French of Christine de Pisan, with a dedication to Sir John Fastolf, K. G., by Stephen Scrope esquire*. Ed. G. F. Warner. Trans. Stephen Scrope. London: J. B. Nichols and Sons, 1904.

———. *The Epistle of Othea to Hector: A 'Lytil Bibell of Knyghthod,' edited from the Harleian Manuscript 838*. Trans. Anthony Babyington. Ed. James D. Gordon from the Harleian MS 838. Philadelphia: n.p., 1942.

————. *The Epistle of Othea.* Trans. Stephen Scrope. Ed. Curt F. Bühler. Early English Text Society, 264. London, New York, Toronto: Oxford University Press, 1970.

————. *The Letter of Othea.* Trans. Jane Chance. Newburyport, Mass.: Focus Information Group, 1990.

————. "The *Livre de la Cité des Dames de Christine de Pisan:* A Critical Edition." Ed. Maureen Cheney Curnow. 2 vols. Ph.D. diss., Vanderbilt University, 1975.

————. "Die Lof der Vrouwen." British Library MS Additional 20698. British Library, London.

————. *The Boke of the Cyte of Ladyes [by] Christine Du Castel.* Trans. Bryan Anslay. London: H. Pepwell, 1521.

————. *The Book of the City of Ladies.* Trans. Earl Jeffrey Richards. New York: Persea, 1982.

————. *L'Art de chevalerie selon Végèce.* Paris: Antoine Vérard, 1488; rpt. *L'Arbre des batailles et fleur de cheualerie.* Paris: Philippe Le Noir, 1527.

————. *The Boke of the Fayt of Armes and of Chyualrye.* Westminster: William Caxton, 1489 or 1490.

————. *The Book of Faytes of Armes and Chyvalrye.* Ed. A.T. P. Byles. Translated and printed by William Caxton from the French original by Christine de Pizan. Early English Text Society, Old Series 189. London: Humphrey Milford–Oxford University Press, 1932, 1937.

————. *Boke of Noblesse: addressed to King Edward the Fourth on his Invasion of France in 1475.* Trans. William Worchester from the *Faits d'armes.* Ed. J. G. Nichols. London: Nichols, 1860.

————. *Oeuvres poétiques de Christine de Pisan.* Ed. Maurice Roy. 3 vols. Société des Anciens Textes Français. Paris: Firmin Didot, 1886–96.

————. *The Body of Polycye.* London: John Skot, 1521.

————. *Le Livre du Corps de policie.* Ed. R. H. Lucas. Geneva: Librairie Droz, 1967.

————. *The Middle English Translation of Christine de Pizan's "Livre de Corps de policie,"* ed. *from MS C[ambridge] U[niversity] L[ibrary] Kk. 1.5.* Ed. Diane Bornstein. Heidelberg: Carl Winter, 1977.

————. *Le Livre des Fais et bonnes meurs du sage roy Charles V.* Ed. Suzanne Solente. 2 vols. Paris: Champion, 1936, 1940.

————. *Le Chemin de Long Estude de Dame Christine de Pise ou est descrit le debat esmeu au parlement de Raison, pour l'election du Prince digne de gouverner le monde. Traduit de langue Romanne en prose Françoyse, par Jan Chaperon, dit lassé de Repos.* Paris: Estienne Groulleau, 1549.

————. *Le Livre du Chemin de Long Estude.* Ed. R. Puschell. Berlin: Damkolher; Paris: Le Soudier, 1881; rpt. Berlin: Hettle, 1887; Geneva: Slatkine, 1974.

————. "An Edition of Christine de Pisan's *Livre du Chemin de Long Estude.*" Ed. P. B. Eargle. Ph.D. diss., University of Georgia, 1973.

————. *Le Livre de la Mutacion de Fortune.* 4 vols. Paris: Picard, 1959–66.

————. *Le Livre de la Paix.* Ed. Charity Cannon Willard. The Hague: Mouton, 1958.

————. *The Morale Proverbes of Christyne.* Trans. Earl Rivers, Anthony Woodville.

Westminster: William Caxton, 1477–78[?] Rpt. "Moralle Prouerbes of Christyne." In *Here begynneth the Boke of Fame by Geoffrey Chaucer.* London: R. Pynson [1926].

———. "The Morale Prouerbes of Cristine." In *Typographical Antiquities,* 72–77. London: William Savage, 1810.

———. "The Morale Proverbes of Cristyne." In *Biblioteca Spenceriana* 4, 218–24. London: Shakespeare Press, 1815.

———. *The Morale Prouerbes of Christyne.* Amsterdam and New York: Da Capo Press, Theatrum Orbis Terrarum, 1970.

———. *Le Trésor de la Cité des Dames.* Paris: Antoine Vérard, 1497.

———. *Le Trésor de la Cité des Dames.* Paris: Michel Le Noir, 1503.

———. *Le Trésor de la Cité des Dames.* Paris: Jean André and Denis Janot, 1536.

———. *Le Livre des Trois Vertus: Edition critique.* Ed. Charity C. Willard and Eric Hicks. Paris: Champion, 1989.

———. *O espelho de Christina.* Lisboa: Hernao de Campos, 1518; rpt. Lisbon: Biblioteca Nacional, 1987.

———. *Christine de Pisan: Buch von den drei Tugenden in portugiesischer Uberstetzung.* Ed. D. Carstens-Grokenberger. Muenster: Aschendorffische Verlag, 1961.

———. Dutch edition. MS 131, 26. Royal Library. The Hague.

Curnow, Mauren Cheney. "*The Boke of the Cyte of Ladyes,* an English Translation of Christine de Pisan's *Le Livre de la Cité des Dames.*" *Les Bonnes Feuilles* 3 (1974): 116–37.

Derrida, Jacques. *The Ear of the Other: Otobiography, Transference, Translation. Texts and Discussions with Jacques Derrida.* English edition by Christie V. McDonald, based on French by Claude Lévesque and Christie V. McDonald. Trans. Peggy Kamuf. New York: Schocken, 1985.

———. "Living On/Border Lines." In *Deconstruction and Criticism,* trans. James Hulbert, 75–176. New York: Continuum, 1979.

Driver, Martha W. "Pictures in Print: Late Fifteenth- and Early Sixteenth-Century English Religious Books for Lay Readers." In *De Cella in Seculum: Religious and Secular Life and Devotion in Late Medieval England,* ed. Michael G. Sargent, 229–44. Cambridge: D. S. Brewer, 1989.

Dufresne, Laura Rinaldi. "A Woman of Excellent Character: A Case Study of Dress, Reputation, and the Changing Costume of Christine de Pizan in the Fifteenth Century." *Dress* 17 (1990): 104–17.

Eagleton, Terry. "Translation and Transformation." *Stand* 19 (1977): 72–77.

Fenster, Thelma S., and Mary Erler, eds. *Poems of Cupid, God of Love.* Leiden: E. J. Brill, 1990.

Fetterley, Judith. "Introduction: On the Politics of Literature." In *The Resisting Reader,* 1977. Rpt. *Feminisms: An Anthology of Literary Theory and Criticism,* ed. Robyn W. Warhol and Diane Price Herndl, 492–501. New Brunswick, N.J.: Rutgers University Press, 1991.

Fleming, John V. "Hoccleve's *Letter of Cupid* and the Quarrel over the *Roman de la Rose.*" *Medium Aevum* 40 (1971): 21–40.

Gavronsky, Serge. "The Translator: From Piety to Cannibalism." *SubStance* 16 (1977): 53–62.

Graham, Joseph F., ed. *Difference in Translation*. Ithaca and London: Cornell University Press, 1985.

Gravdal, Kathryn. *Ravishing Maidens: Writing Rape in Medieval French Literature and Law*. Philadelphia: University of Pennsylvania Press, 1991.

Hanson-Smith, Elizabeth. "A Woman's View of Courtly Love: The Findern Anthology," *Journal of Women's Studies in Literature* 1 (1979): 179–94.

Hindman, Sandra L. *Christine de Pizan's 'Epistre Othéa': Painting and Politics at the Court of Charles VI*. Studies and Texts 77. Toronto: Pontifical Institute of Medieval Studies, 1986.

Hoccleve, Thomas. "To the Duke of Bedford." In *Thomas Hoccleve: Selected Poems*, ed. Bernard O'Donoghue, 67–68. Carcanet, Manchester, England: Fyfield Books, 1982.

———. "The Letter of Cupid to Lovers, His Subjects." *Works*, vol. 1: *The Minor Poems*, ed. Frederick J. Furnivall, 72–91. London: Early English Text Society, 1892.

Hutchison, Ann M. "Devotional Reading in the Monastery and in the Late Medieval Household." In *De Cella in Seculum: Religious and Secular Life and Devotion in Late Medieval England*, ed. Michael G. Sargent, 215–27. Cambridge: D. S. Brewer, 1989.

Kellogg, Judith. "*Le Livre de la Cité des Dames:* Feminist Myth and Community." *Essays in Arts and Sciences* 18 (1989): 1–15.

Kelly, Joan. "Early Feminist Theory and the *Querelle des Femmes*, 1400–1789." *Signs* 8 (1982): 4–28.

Laennec, Christine Moneera. "Christine *Antygrafe:* Authorial Ambivalence in the Works of Christine de Pizan." In *Anxious Power: Reading, Writing, and Ambivalence in Narrative by Women*, ed. by Carol J. Singley and Susan Elizabeth Sweeney, 35–49. Albany: State University of New York Press, 1993.

Laidlaw, J. C. "Christine de Pizan—An Author's Progress." *Modern Language Review* 78 (1983): 532–50.

———. "Christine de Pizan, the Earl of Salisbury and Henry IV." *Feminist Studies* 36 (1982): 129–43.

Lewis, Philip. "Vers la traduction abusive." In *Les fins de l'homme: A partir du travail de Jacques Derrida*, ed. Philippe Lacoue-Labarthe, 253–61. Paris: Editions Galilée, 1981.

McLeod, Glenda L., ed. *The Reception of Christine de Pizan from the Fifteenth through the Nineteenth Centuries: Visitors to the City*. Lewiston, Queenston, and Lampeter: Edwin Mellen Press, 1991.

Mombello, G. "Recherches sur l'origine du nom de la Déesse Othea." *Atti della Accademia delle Scienze di Torino, II, Classe di Scienze Morali, Storiche e Filologiche* 103 (1969): 343–75.

Nouvet, Claire. "Writing (in) Fear." In *Gender and Text in the Later Middle Ages*, ed. Jane Chance, 279–305. Gainesville: University Press of Florida, 1996.

Pearsall, Derek, ed. *The Floure and the Leafe and The Assembly of Ladies*. Nelson's Medieval and Renaissance Library. London and Edinburgh: Thomas Nelson, 1962; rpt. Manchester University Press, Old and Middle English Texts Series, 1980.

————. *The Flower and the Leaf, The Assembly of Ladies, The Isle of Ladies*. Kalamazoo, Mich.: Medieval Institute Publications, 1990.

Quinn, William A. "Hoccleve's Epistle of Cupid." *Explicator* 45 (1986): 7–10.

Richards, Earl Jeffrey. "'Seulette a parte'—The Little Woman on the Sidelines Takes Up Her Pen." In *Dear Sister: Medieval Women and the Epistolary Genre*, ed. Karen Cherewatuk and Ulrike Wiethaus, 139–70. Philadelphia: University of Pennsylvania Press, 1993.

Robbins, Rossell Hope. "The Findern Anthology." *Publications of the Modern Language Association* 69 (1954): 610–42.

Schaefer, Lucie. "Die Illustrationen zu der Handschriften der Christine de Pizan." *Marburger Jahrbuch für Kunstwissenschaft* 10 (1938): 119–208.

Steiner, George. *After Babel*. London and New York: Oxford University Press, 1975.

Triggs, Oscar L., ed. *The Assembly of Gods*. Early English Text Society, 69. London: K. Paul, Trench, Trübner, 1896; rpt. Oxford University Press, 1957.

Walters, Lori. "The Woman Writer and Literary History: Christine de Pizan's Redefinition of the Poetic *Translatio* in the *Epistre au Dieu d'Amours*." *French Literature Series* 16 (1989): 1–16.

Willard, Charity Cannon. "Christine de Pizan on Chivalry." In *The Study of Chivalry*, ed. Howell Chickering and Tom Seiler, 511–28. Kalamazoo, Mich.: Medieval Institute Publications, 1988.

————. "Christine de Pizan's Treatise on the Art of Medieval Warfare." In *Essays in Honor of Loris Francis Solano*, ed. R. Cormier and U. T. Holmes, 179–91. Chapel Hill: University of North Carolina Press, 1970.

————. "A New Look at Christine de Pisan's *Epistre au Dieu d'Amours*." In *Seconda Miscellanea di Studi e Ricerche sul Quattrocentro Francese*, ed. Franco Simone, 73–92. Chambéry and Turin: Centre d'Etudes Franco-Italien, Jonathan Beck and Gianni Mombello, 1981.

————. "A Portuguese Translation of Christine de Pisan's *Livre des Trois Vertus*." *Publications of the Modern Language Association* 78 (1963): 459–64.

Domesticating the Spanish Inquisition

Deborah S. Ellis

Just as both men and women today prefer to think of rape as something inflicted by strangers—ignoring the prevalence of both date rape and domestic abuse—so the Middle Ages privileged the image of the home as refuge over its equally potent role as threat to the women who sheltered within it. The ambivalent realities of women at home spanned the Middle Ages to create a paradoxical image of the enclosed woman, a figure thought simultaneously to foment domestic discord and to preserve domestic tranquillity, seen as imprisoned as much as protected. It is this tension within medieval interpretations of women's space that allowed strategies of domestic violence to expand into strategies of domestically based and condoned institutional violence. In this essay I show that the violence against suspected women judaizers in the early years of the Spanish Inquisition derives from a long tradition of medieval unease with women's domestic roles, and that displaced anxieties about female sabotage in the home are at the heart of inquisitorial strategies against women.

Uneasiness with the home as refuge resonates throughout the Middle Ages. In the twelfth century, an English treatise urging virginity warns potential wives that a house with a husband would offer them no sanctuary, for when the husband arrives home "all your wide rooms seem to you too narrow" (Millett and Wogan-Browne, *Medieval English Prose*, 28). This destabilizing perspective is not what we might expect from the Middle Ages, which was an age of firmly established homes. Business went on within the home, war was waged between homes, and even royal terminology—the English office of chamberlain, for instance—reflects the essential domesticity of medieval monarchy. Yet this reminder that wide walls could narrow in on women evokes a home in which gender as much as space defined the limits of safety and power. Such a fundamentally ambivalent domesticity has (almost) always been associated with women. To be "domesticated" has frequently been seen in a pejorative sense: houses confine rather than empower their female inhabitants. Yet homes have always offered people, women and men, more than either restrictions or shelter.

Homes provide a fundamental measure of human identity and integrity. But this link was complicated in the Middle Ages by a threatening patriarchal ideology in which women were thought to be virtuous only within the confines of enclosed bodies and closed doors. Leaving the house or even unlocking those doors could be construed as signs of deviancy. In a polarized society in which women represented evil, the woman-associated house itself becomes a locus of evil. This sense of dichotomies extends naturally to the architecture which enclosed women, since architecture is generally seen as enabling such dialectical oppositions as inner and outer or public and private. Architecture becomes a way to reveal—to unmask, in inquisitorial terms—the woman "hiding" within. The house can sanctify violence because ultimately it serves both as a locus of anxiety about gender and as a setting for restrictions of women.

Privacy issues in particular can reveal clear examples of these tensions. Both men and women in the Middle Ages rarely achieved the privacy we now associate with autonomy and safety; their frustrated quest for privacy has been well documented. Medieval depositions and literature refer to adulteries occurring in the brewhouse, the gatehouse, and even over a latrine, while private conversations are recorded as occurring in the garden, a field, or the corner of a crowded room; and these are all, obviously, ploys that failed.[1] Hanawalt observes that a "concern for privacy was almost an obsession among the peasantry" (*Ties That Bound*, 44), and among the gentry that concern was as much on avoiding privacy for their dependents as on achieving it for themselves. Late fifteenth-century manuals of behavior evoke the possibility of secret associations right in front of the lord: "And at the tabylle loke þou make goode chere / Loke þou rownde not in nomannys ere" (at the table be sociable; don't whisper in anybody's ear; Furnivall, *Manners*, 269). And for men, woman's privacy was especially threatening, with even her psychic privacy seen as potentially seditious. Goldberg cites a representative fifteenth-century Spanish text reminding men that they can never know a woman's secrets: "There will always be a secret corner of her heart not subject to his will or control" ("Commonplaces," 89–90).[2] The private revolt of a woman's thoughts, when magnified by the private revolt of forcibly converted Jews and set within the assumed privacy of a woman's home, could condemn a woman to charges of heresy.

The Inquisition's persecution of Jewish women and *conversas* reveals the threatening ambiguities inherent in gendered domestic space. The idea of a more private refuge that we expect from the home was in many ways gendered female, not just ideologically but also architecturally (see Wood, *Medieval House,* and Lámperez y Romea, *Arquitectura Civil*). It was most associated in the Middle Ages with the residential upper-story solar block, the part of the home most associated with women and such female domestic activities as sewing, reading, birthing, tending the sick, childcare, sexual activities, and laying out the dead (solars, chambers, and bowers were all names for women's rooms). Women were as closely associated with the chamber as men with the hall: "knights sat in the hall / Ladies in the chamber all" (Zupitza, quoted in Girouard, *English Country House,* 46). Women in medieval literature, even queens, are most commonly associated with bowers and kitchens.[3] Modern architectural history, though generally treating the chamber as peripheral to the main interests of the family, offers structural evidence of its centrality: halls were not always defended, but the solar wing—often in the form of a residential tower—was (Faulkner, "Manor House Plans"; Wood, *Medieval House,* chap. 12).

The separate spaces of women, however, were shared rather than truly private, refuges from external rather than internal threats. The precariousness of women's refuge was complicated by their internal dangers, since women often personified threats to domestic sanctuary. The "angel in the house" that we know from nineteenth-century England and America was in earlier times much more likely to be the devil in the house, both cause and emblem of social and household dissolution. Chaucer frequently refers to the biblical proverb that a man can be destroyed by a smoky house, a leaky roof, and a nagging woman, conjoining all three into one vision of a domestic/social hell where the woman is a compressed version of the architectural imagery.[4] Samuel Johnson makes a similar casual connection between anarchy, architecture, and women: "Here falling houses thunder on your head, / And here a female atheist talks you dead."[5] The women were permanently poised between their domesticated version of the rock and the hard place, for if the home was a setting for their diabolical flourishes, the outside world was even worse. This hostile attitude coexisted with dependence on the wife's extensive household responsibilities, which, especially in the manorial class, encompassed tasks such as overseeing agricultural and domestic workers, arranging lawsuits and fines in the manorial courts, currying favor with more powerful noble families, arranging for the military defense of threatened houses, producing the clothes for the entire extended household, and arranging for meals, food storage, and the purchases of supplies. Women knew how many candles were needed in winter and summer, where the midwives and healers were and how (with or without those specialists) to prepare medical potions, where to buy the best trimming for cloaks, and how much repair the tenants' houses had to have. Town women like Margery Kempe often ran supplemental brewing or baking businesses out of their homes, in addition to working in their husbands' shops or crafts and supervising the necessary apprentices and servants. This is the sort of scope that H. S. Bennett had in mind when he wrote, "If we want to see the medieval woman rightly, it is in her home we must view her. All other things in her life were subservient to her housekeeping" (*The Pastons*, 52).[6] Nevertheless, this medieval home was also thought to embody the threats that women, subversive since Eve, posed to men.

Those whose hold on security was most tenuous—Jews, for instance— found the homes they depended on particularly susceptible to outward treachery. Jewish families in Spain were said to stay so close to home that in 1482, Queen Isabella's secretary "pleaded for a Christian education for the younger generation of conversos, citing those thousands of boys and girls in Andalusia who never left their homes and thus saw nothing but their parents' ways" (Beinart, "The Conversos and Their Fate," 107). People were said to cling to their homes and customs, to the point where a defense witness (!) at an Inquisition trial claimed that the accused woman "did not appear as a good Christian for she had grown up among the Conversos of Cordova": state and Church could not compete with home and family (Beinart, *Conversos on Trial*, 166n.205).[7] Yet these homes were anything but secure. Sometimes their privacy was violated unexpectedly, as we learn from an Inquisition investigation into alleged kosher slaughter, where the witness watched "por un agujero" [through a hole] as a group of alleged conversos examined an animal carcass in the corral, part of the inner courtyard fenced off from casual observation (Beinart, *Conversos on Trial*, 263n.112). The inner sanctuaries of bedrooms seem to have been even more vulnerable. An Inquisition defendant in Puebla de Montalbán in 1490 who made a list of his enemies (a maneuver meant to disqualify hostile witnesses) included an incident of lodging in someone's house "and, while I was in bed, [his host] and his son . . . came to kill me with swords"; and ambush in his own bed: "one night when I went to bed, I found [another enemy] lurking in the dark and, imagining him to be a thief, drew my sword, cried out, and threatened him" (Gilman, *Spain of Fernando de Rojas,*

245–46). A witness in another trial offers more subtle violations of privacy in the *cámara:*

> Yten, dixo que oyo este testigo çiertas vezes, en amaneçiendo, cantar a los dichos sus amos a so bos, estandose acostados en la cama, e que estaban este testigo al pie de la escalera de vna camara donde ellos dormian, que esta la dicha escalera por de dentro de la cozina, donde los podia oyr. (Beinart, ed. *Records of the Trials,* 3:387).

> (Item, this witness said that at certain times at daybreak he heard his masters singing aloud, being still in their bed, and that this witness was at the foot of the ladder [or staircase] that went from their bedroom where they used to sleep to down inside the kitchen, where he could hear them.)

But Spanish houses were so given to gendered polarities that they focused as centers of inward betrayal as much as of outward treachery. Whether the typical Spanish patio, for instance, was seen chiefly as the source of fresh air for semicloistered women (as it was in *morisco* households) or as another version of the hall or *sala* (as in Christian households), it was primarily dedicated to the use of one gender. Especially in the preservation of such Islamic features as the patio and the *reja* or iron window grille, Spanish architecture is said to preserve "the protection and seclusion of the women" (Mack and Gibson, *Architectural Details,* n.p.). The Spanish architectural historian Lámperez y Romea emphasizes the "retirada y doméstica" (retired and domestic) life of women, due to "la influencia mahometana [que] estableció una mayor separación entre hombres y mujeres" (the Muslim influence which established a major separation between men and women; *Arquitectura Civil,* 211). Spanish women shared in the general Southern European practice of allocating certain common areas, like house-yards, to women and children, but "las españolas" seem to have been valued not just for keeping to their place but for achieving invisibility within it.[8] Spanish women are "encerradas en sus habitaciones" (enclosed in their dwellings), to the point that a major importance of domestic chapels in large houses was that pious women could stay away from the public areas of church.[9]

In Spain, we might see the entire house, rather than simply areas within it, associated with women. Lámperez y Romea refers to a "coro de vituperios" (chorus of vituperative critics; 117) who disdain what they see as the notably ugly exteriors of pre-Renaissance Spanish houses. We are told that in Seville, for instance, "todo el edificar era dentro del cuerpo de las casas, sin curar de lo exterior" (all the building was within the body of the houses, without attention to the exterior; 117). The Spanish house may re-enact, or at least reinterpret, the behavior of the "good," virtually clois-tered, Spanish woman, who rarely ventures out even for church and is reluctant to be seen from outside the home. The house that in effect turns its back on the street can thus be seen as gendered female. This house's secluding, interiorized aspect is further reinforced by the indirect connec-tion between street and house: "Desde la calle penétrase en un zaguán en el que las puertas nunca están fronteras, sino opuestas, para evitar la vista, desde la calle, del interior" (One penetrates from the street by an entrance in which the doors never are facing, but opposed, to avoid the view of the interior from the street; 168).[10] Can this architectural language, of *cuerpos* (bodies) and penetration, be accidental? We might well find the Spanish "closed" response to be particularly interesting, intensifying a pattern that genders houses throughout European thought.

To both men and women in the Middle Ages, the woman *was* her house, and so patriarchal ideology tried to force each of these two aspects of what they saw as one subversive entity into a diminished stillness. As Stally-brass comments about the Renaissance, "the surveillance of women con-centrated upon three specific areas: the mouth, chastity, the threshold of the house. These three areas were frequently collapsed into each other. . . . Silence and chastity are, in turn, homologous to woman's enclosure within the house. . . . This 'Woman,' like Bahktin's classical body, is rigidly 'fin-ished': her signs are the enclosed body, the closed mouth, the locked house" ("Patriarchal Territories," 126–27). Such an identification between the two aspects of exteriorized woman—house and body—carries inward by logical force into judgments of her virtue and her soul. As we have seen in the image of the "good" Spanish woman, women who stayed within-doors were, by medieval standards, inherently more virtuous than those who wandered. It is not merely that the Wife of Bath is an inveterate gossip or that Celestina is a bawd or that Margery Kempe is given to public hys-terics that make their wanderings so threatening to their societies and to their husbands: it is the very act of leaving the house that implies their potential deviance.

There is a powerful medieval fear that women are corrupted merely by contact with the outside world. We hear particularly how women looking out of or speaking out of their windows open themselves to sin and cor-ruption: widows, for instance, who instead of praying for their dead hus-bands or doing their housework "pass time at the window, laughing and joking in front of everyone, and they display their venality to whoever wants them or gives them the most."[11] Indeed, to quote Casagrande (a wonderfully appropriate name), "Women did not have to wander very far, nor join particularly suspicious gatherings, to commit a sin; it was enough to go to the door or window. Standing in the doorway or leaning out of the window was 'going out'—a limited, but still dangerous, attempt to establish a rapport with the outside world and to abandon oneself to the desire to go out and join the world of men."[12] Criseyde's falling in love with Troilus as she watches him out of her window architecturally embodies the sexual vulnerability ascribed to any medieval women who were domiciled rather than immured. Men resisted recognizing that the home in which "their" women were confined was a liminal rather than a limiting boundary, and their fears and distrust of the corrupting potential of the home extend from literature through laws. Such men thought that protecting women by keeping them at home could be only a stopgap measure against incorrigible female wanderlust and corruption. Whether we see the Wife of Bath's "walkynge out by nyghte" (l. 397) or Griselda's plea not to have to "lyk a worm go by the weye" (l. 880), we see that the very condition of being out of the house is potentially dangerous for women. But if it is bad enough that medieval women were subject to ideological violence merely by leaving their houses, it was far worse that they could be subject to institutionalized violence by staying inside.

This intensification of danger occurred because during the fourteenth and fifteenth centuries, when most Jews were exiled from Spain, whatever covert practices of Judaism continued did so mostly within the homes of purportedly converted families. This relapse of conversos into Jewish practices and beliefs was known as "judaizing," and the Inquisition punished it as heresy by confiscation of property, loss of rights, torture, and sometimes by burning at the stake. We can never know the true extent of judaizing, but the Inquisition was convinced it was a widespread phenomenom, and thousands of Jews or suspected Jews suffered horrific penalties.[13] Although the integrity of both Jews and women was consistently being compromised by such external threats, the woman in the home— especially the Jewish woman in the home—was particularly subject to threats from within.

Common Inquisition testimony reveals a world in which people were constantly examining other people's houses with a view toward uncovering evidence of heresy. Christian neighbors making allegations of judaizing breached the privacy and security of the home by watching the activities of the people—particularly the women—within. They looked for damning evidence of special candles on Friday nights or clean clothes on

Saturdays, and the women's work that might produce a Sabbath meal or special housecleaning for the Sabbath could condemn the entire family. The woman's activities of cooking and cleaning could alone define the house as a Jewish or a Christian one. In addition, there are several rituals (including lighting the Sabbath candles and ritual bathing) that in the eyes of the Church established the heresy of practicing Jewish women.

Suspected judaizers who were accused of keeping the Sabbath were so accused on the basis of what they did in their doorways and courtyards, what they wore, how and when they cooked, and even how clean their houses were. The women's activities of cooking and cleaning were repeatedly stressed in Inquisition testimony. In a typical instance, one woman was accused of treating Saturdays differently from other days in which she "entendía en las cosas de su casa cosiendo y labrando, y en otras cosas de su casa" (was involved in the things of her home [household activities], sewing and working, and other affairs of her home; Gómez-Menor Fuentes, "Judío Converso," 49). A cobbler accused of working on a Sunday is particularly condemned by the activities of his wife and daughters; he "cosya çapatos e su muger e yjas trabajauan como entre semana, la puerta enparejada" (was sewing shoes and his wife and daughter worked as though it were a weekday, the door ajar; Beinart, ed., *Records of the Trials*, 1:252). That partly opened door is the perfect metaphor for the momentary lapse of caution that could expose Jewish women to the violating gaze of the other, here both a gendered and a religious threat. Even a closed door offered women little protection; a witness in the trial of Juan de Lucena condemned him because "venian muchas parientas e amigas del dicho Juan de Luçena á se holgar en su casa los dias de los sábados con sus hijas e su hogauan muy vestidas é ataviadas á puerta çerrada" (many women relatives and friends of the said Juan de Luceno came to his house on Saturdays with their daughters to amuse themselves, and they had a good time, all dressed up, behind the closed door; Serrano y Sanz, "Noticias biográficas," 285).

The trials of specific women accused of violating household sanctity—or, rather, of creating their own household sanctity—reveal the lack of sanctuary their homes offered them. At Teresa de Lucena's trial in 1530, she was accused of lighting candles on Friday night, with the interesting further accusation that she "vistió ropas linpias en los tales dias y en otros" (wore clean clothes on those days and on others; Serrano y Sanz, "Noticias biográficas," 259n.2). Diego Gómez's wife, in a typically formulaic accusation, was said to wear better clothes and to clean her house for the Sabbath: "los viernes en las tardes linpiavan e lavavan e adereçavan la casa" (they cleaned and washed and straightened the house on Friday afternoons; Gómez-Menor Fuentes, "Judío Converso," 49). A woman's defense in another trial was to deny that she kept the Sabbath: "she in fact worked in the morning and put her house in order" (Beinart, *Conversos on Trial,* 175–76). Women accused of judaizing were said to "prepare two separate dinners on Friday evenings, the meat dinner that was considered appropriate for the Sabbath and also a fish dinner, in case an outsider happened by" (Gerber, *Jews of Spain,* 121). Some women confessed that in trying to keep the Sabbath secretly, they would carry around their distaffs and pretend to work, a disguise they practiced both at home and on walks (Beinart, *Conversos on Trial,* 243). One woman confessed that although she kept the Sabbath in her thoughts, she had to work because her daughters and husband might have turned her in: "siempre en su intençion e pensamiento e guardado los sabados, aunque por la obra non la guardava, porque no osava, por no ser sentida de su marido e sus fijas" (she always kept the Sabbath in her intention and her thought, even though she didn't keep it in deed, because she didn't dare, for fear of being discovered by her husband and her daughters; 274n.160).

Thus women could sometimes not depend on their own husbands, daughters, or other family members. They were particularly vulnerable because of the number of individual-centered Sabbath rites, which included such activities as "candle-lighting, baking and cooking, cleaning and dressing up" (Levine, "Women in Spanish Crypto-Judaism," 57). It is important to note that most of the individual activities Levine-Melammed lists here are not only associated with women's normal activities, as we have seen, but are also *gendered* female. That is, they are not only characteristic of but also definitive of woman, in terms of her domestic sphere. They do not lend themselves to gender overlap; both men and women might kasher meat, for instance (although it was primarily a male job), but men did not usually make themselves responsible then, any more than now, for putting a clean tablecloth on the table. Thus the choice of these particular activities to define heresy meant in effect that women's domesticity became their vulnerability. The house was not a stronghold but a trap.

Nowhere is this more apparent than in an odd case cited by Levine-Melammed, in which an obviously compulsive woman named Mayor Meléndez is said to flee from unclean foods: "sy veya asar toçino se apartaba de alli e sé metia en una camara, en donde se ençerraua e atapaua todos los agujeros porque non héntrase el olor de toçino; lo mismo hazia quando veya derretir manteca de puercos (if she saw roast bacon, she removed herself and went into a room, where she closed it up and covered up all of the holes so that the smell of the bacon would not enter; she did the same thing when she saw pork lard dissolve; Levine, "Women in Spanish Crypto-Judaism," 169 and 169n.55; her translation). But even the solid houses of the Middle Ages were pervious to smells; one cannot block air. Similarly, other Inquisition testimony points to the uselessness of people's attempts to block the holes in their rooms to keep light from seeping out when they were trying to pray (for example, Beinart, ed., *Records of the Trials*, 3:32). Their rooms—the chambers so closely identified with women—intensified the vulnerability of the whole house. Inquisition records are full of the failed attempts of the accused to achieve real privacy in houses that were in effect open books.

Perhaps the customs of Jews who were in mourning reflect an acceptance of the failed sanctuary of the house. Much testimony accuses mourners of *guayas*, or sitting behind closed doors for seven days, a version of what we now call sitting shiva. But the testimony discussed by Beinart and Levine-Melammed shows that, in fact, these closed doors were balanced by open doors. Mourners are said to sit with "una puerta çerrada e otra abierta" (Levine, "Women in Spanish Crypto-Judaism," 227n.111). Levine-Melammed comments that one door must remain open to signal the accessibility of the mourner's house to all consolers. However, some evidence at least suggests that it was resignation rather than welcome that produced this paradoxical symbol. For instance, a clergyman in 1514 testified that he saw a house in mourning, "que la una puerta de la calle tenya çerrada e la otra avierta" (one door at the street was closed and another open; Levine, "Women in Spanish Crypto-Judaism," 231n.115). A recognition of the permeability of the house's walls and the inherent vulnerability of its inhabitants would account for the street door being closed while another, presumably interior door, was open: the mourners would attempt to maintain privacy although their very symbolism demonstrates their inability to attain it. We may be reminded of another group of heretics, those of Montaillou in an earlier century, whose proverb "If you don't want the walls of your house knocked down, keep your mouth shut" recognized the frail protection of their houses against institutionalized domestic espionage (LeRoy Ladurie, *Montaillou*, 37).

Another revealing case is that of Isabel López (Levine-Melammed, "Sixteenth Century Justice"). Testimony from 1518 suggests that López was a quarrelsome woman, firing servants who later testified that she engaged in many crypto-Jewish activities, including the usual array of accusations: she kashered her meat, dressed up for the Sabbath, prayed in a Jewish way, avoided unkosher foods, and cooked Jewish foods (in her defense, López denied even knowing what Jewish foods were). Of these five major heads of accusation, three concern food and one concerns clothes; only the accusation of prayer is gender-free. This trial seems a particularly clear example of how women were betrayed by their houses. Isabel is accused of keeping her house too clean, and her defense is that, far from making special Sabbath preparations, she always had a clean house; similarly, her defense against the accusation that she cleaned her meat carefully in a kashruth way is that she is just generally clean and fastidious. A key witness against her, on the other hand, her former servant Madalena, testifies out of grievance: her employers "had beaten and castigated Madalena because this servant did not want to do housework" (65). One woman is accused of keeping the house too clean, and the other of keeping it too dirty. In some ways, the anguish of this trial stems from the struggle between women in a household over the control and even the *idea* of the house. Domestic cleanliness becomes the absolute measure of good versus evil.

A common complaint of Old Christians against conversos was that their church-going was hypocritical, merely an evil empty gesture masking their true Jewishness (Coronas Tejada, *Conversos and Inquisition*, 34; Gilman, "Case of Alvaro de Montalbàn" and *Spain of Fernando de Rojas*). Whatever the validity of such accusations, the very idea of cloaked hypocrisy in church underlines the naked vulnerability of behavior at home. There was nowhere a conversa could hide from the dissection of the "cosas de su casa," the things of her home. Since the family home was the site for both the personal and social identities of women, its betrayal by forces from without and within provides the clearest focus for the institutionalized anxiety that assaulted all the Inquisition's victims, especially victimized women. If, as Levine-Melammed argues, "crypto-Judaism found the home to be its only refuge" ("Women in [Post-1492] Spanish Crypto-Jewish Society," 160), then we see its danger intensified by being set within that inadequate home. Whether the women targeted by the Inquisition on the basis of their domestic behavior were truly Jews or not, they still were crushed by the sabotage of the houses meant to protect them. The woman who was demonized in and by her own home had nowhere left to go.

NOTES

1. For the brewhouse and gatehouse: Owen, "White Annays," 335–36. For the latrine: Wunderli, *London Church Courts*, 39. For the crowded room: Cozens-Hardy, *Norwich Depositions*, no. 2, f. 3. For the garden: Smyser, "Domestic Back-

ground," 300–301 (re. *Troilus* 2.1114–17). For the field: Davis, ed., *Paston Letters*, 1:476. Compare Margery Kempe, when she and her husband are accused of resorting "to woodys, grouys, er valeys to vsyn þe lust of her bodijs þat þe pepil xuld not aspyin it" (Meech and Allen, *Margery Kempe*, 180).

2. She cites Martínez de Toledo, *Arcipreste de Talavera*, 146.

3. Even when royalty was concerned, women were associated with kitchens and butteries. A building contract from 1268 includes orders "to build a long house for a pantry and buttery for the use of the queen and of Eleanor the consort of Edward the king's eldest son; and a kitchen for the queen's use, with a passage from the kitchen to the queen's chamber" (Literate R. 52 Hen. III, quoted in Salzman, *Building in England*, 387, appendix A).

4. See Chaucer, *Melibee* 1086, *Wife of Bath's Prologue* at 278, and *Parson's Tale* at 631; compare Shakespeare's *1 Henry IV* 3.1.158 ff.

5. "London," 17.

6. H. S. Bennett's work on the domestic responsibilities of medieval women has been updated by much recent scholarship; see, for instance, Judith M. Bennett; Gies and Gies; Hanawalt; Klapisch-Zuber; Labarge; and Uitz. The regular bibliographic updates in the *Medieval Feminist Newsletter* are also very helpful, especially number 10 (Fall 1990).

7. See also Beinart, *Conversos on Trial*, 265n.116.

8. On allocation to women and children, see Pipponier, "World of Women," 334. She cites activities in Montaillou and in "the fortified Sicilian village of Brucato." Compare Lámperez y Romea, who cites a contemporary description of a lady of Rouen, who "tenia su gentil morada aparte de la del Almirante: pasaba entre la una posada y la otra una puente levadiza: a más las posadas eran dentro de una cerca" (had her noble dwelling apart from the Admiral's: a drawbridge ran between the two dwellings: besides, [both] dwellings were within one enclosure; *Arquitectura Civil*, 210).

9. Lámperez y Romea, *Arquitectura Civil*, 211, citing Hernando de Talavera.

10. See also Feduchi, who shows rural homes repeating the pattern of medieval urban homes, with very small street windows and homes "fac[ing] inwards on to courtyards" (*Spanish Folk Architecture*, 152).

11. A citation from Francesc Eiximensis's *Libro de les dones*, c. 1388; quoted in Piera and Rogers, "Widow as Heroine," 326. Compare *Much Ado about Nothing*, where Hero is rejected at the altar as a fallen woman, accused of "talk[ing] with a ruffian at her chamber-window" (4.1.91); it is this imagined architectural moment, rather than the other false accusations, that condemns her.

12. Casagrande, "Protected Woman," 86. She cites particularly Francesco of Barberino and Conrad of Megenburg.

13. There has been a great deal of scholarly interest recently around the issue of the Jews in Spain, especially since 1992 marked the 500th year of their exile. For general information, see, for example, Gerber; Kedourie; and Mann. Specifically, scholars have fallen into two camps about the critical question of whether Spanish conversos were crypto-Jews (that is, continued to practice Judaism secretly). Beinart in several works (some cited here) represents one extreme, suggesting

that all the inquisitorial testimony about secret Jewish practices ("judaizing") was true. The other side is presented rather more convincingly by, for instance, Netanyahu, *The Origins of the Inquisition* and *The Marranos of Spain*.

WORKS CITED

Beinart, Haim. "The Conversos and Their Fate." In *Spain and the Jews: The Sephardi Experience, 1492 and After*, ed. Elie Kedourie. London: Thames and Hudson, 1992.

———. *Conversos on Trial: The Inquisition in Ciudad Real*. Jerusalem: Magnes Press of Hebrew University, 1981.

———, ed. *Records of the Trials of the Spanish Inquisition in Ciudad Real*. 4 vols. Jerusalem: Israel Academy of Science and Humanities, 1981.

Bennett, H. S. *The Pastons and Their England: Studies in an Age of Transition*. 2d ed. Cambridge: Cambridge University Press, 1932; rpt. 1977.

Bennett, Judith M. *Women in the Medieval English Countryside: Gender and Household in Brigstock Before the Plague*. New York: Oxford University Press, 1987.

Casagrande, Carla. "The Protected Woman." Trans. Clarissa Botsford. In *A History of Women in the West: II. Silences of the Middle Ages*, ed. Christiane Klapisch-Zuber, 70–104. Cambridge, Mass.: Belknap Press, 1992.

Chaucer, Geoffrey. *The Riverside Chaucer*. Ed. Larry D. Benson. 3d ed. Boston: Houghton Mifflin, 1987.

Coronas Tejada, Luis. *Conversos and Inquisition in Jaén*. Trans. Stephanie Nakache. Jerusalem: Hispania Judaica VII, 1988.

Cozens-Hardy, Basil. *Norwich Consistory Court Depositions, 1499–1512 and 1518–1530*. Norwich: Norfolk Record Society, 1938.

Davis, Norman, ed. *Paston Letters and Papers of the Fifteenth Century*. 2 vols. Oxford: Clarendon Press, 1971, 1976.

Faulkner, P. A. "Manor House Plans of the Twelfth to Fifteenth Centuries." Lecture presented at Society of Antiquaries of London, 12 March 1981.

Feduchi, Luis. *Spanish Folk Architecture: The Northern Plateau*. Trans. Diorki. Barcelona: Editorial Blume, 1977.

Furnivall, F. J., ed. *Early English Manners and Meals*. Early English Text Society, Old Series 32. London 1868; rpt. 1894.

Gerber, Jane S. *The Jews of Spain: A History of the Sephardic Experience*. New York: Free Press, 1992.

Gies, Frances, and Joseph Gies. *Marriage and the Family in the Middle Ages*. New York: Harper and Row, 1987.

Gilman, Stephen. "The Case of Alvaro de Montalbán." *Modern Language Notes* 78 (1963): 113–25.

———. *The Spain of Fernando de Rojas: The Intellectual and Social Landscape of 'La Celestina.'* Madison: University of Wisconsin Press, 1956.

Girouard, Mark. *Life in the English Country House: A Social and Architectural History*. New Haven: Yale University Press, 1978.

Goldberg, Harriet. "Two Parallel Medieval Commonplaces: Antifeminism and Antisemitism in the Hispanic Literary Tradition." In *Aspects of Jewish Culture in the Middle Ages,* ed. Paul E. Szarmach, 85–119. Albany: State University of New York Press, 1979.

Gómez-Menor Fuentes, J. "Un Judío Converso de 1498: Diego Gomez de Toledo (Semuel Abologia) y su Proceso Inquisitorial." *Sefarad* 33 (1973): 45–75.

Hanawalt, Barbara. *The Ties That Bound: Peasant Families in Medieval England.* New York: Oxford University Press, 1986.

Kedourie, Elie, ed. *Spain and the Jews: The Sephardi Experience, 1492 and After.* London: Thames and Hudson, 1992.

Klapisch-Zuber, Christiane, ed. *A History of Women in the West: II. Silences of the Middle Ages.* Cambridge, Mass.: Belknap Press, 1992.

Labarge, Margaret Wade. *A Small Sound of the Trumpet: Women in Medieval Life.* Boston: Beacon Press, 1986.

Lámperez y Romea, Vicente. *Arquitectura Civil Española de Los Siglos I al XVIII.* Vol. 1. Madrid: Editorial Saturnino Calleja, 1922.

LeRoy Ladurie, Emmanuel. *Montaillou: The Promised Land of Error.* Trans. B. Bray. New York: Braziller, 1978.

Levine, Renee C. "Women in Spanish Crypto-Judaism 1492–1520." Ph.D. diss., Brandeis University, 1982.

Levine-Melammed, Renée. "Sixteenth Century Justice in Action: The Case of Isabel López." *Revue des études juives* CXLV (Jan.–June 1986): 51–73.

———. "Women in (Post-1492) Spanish Crypto-Jewish Society." *Judaism* 41:2 (Spring 1992): 156–68.

Mack, Gerstle, and Thomas Gibson. *Architectural Details of Southern Spain.* New York: William Helburn, 1928.

Mann, Vivian B., Thomas F. Glick, and Jerrilyn D. Dodds, eds. *Convivencia: Jews, Muslims, and Christians in Medieval Spain.* New York: Braziller, 1992.

Martínez de Toledo, Alfonso. *Arcipreste de Talavera o corbacho.* Ed. J. González Muela. Madrid: Clásicos Castalia, 1970.

Meech, Sanford B., and Hope E. Allen, eds. *The Book of Margery Kempe.* Early English Text Society, Old Series 212. Oxford: Oxford University Press, 1961.

Millett, Bella, and Jocelyn Wogan-Browne, eds. *Medieval English Prose for Women.* Oxford: Clarendon Press, 1992.

Netanyahu, Benzion. *The Marranos of Spain, from the late XIVth to the early XVI century, according to contemporary Hebrew sources.* 2d ed. New York: American Academy for Jewish Research, 1966; rpt. New York: Kraus, 1973.

———. *The Origins of the Inquisition in Fifteenth Century Spain.* New York: Random House, 1995.

Owen, Dorothy. "White Annays and Others." In *Medieval Women,* ed. Derek Baker, 331–46. Oxford: Blackwell, 1978.

Piera, Montserrat, and Donna M. Rogers. "The Widow as Heroine: The Fifteenth-Century Catalan Chivalresque Novel *Curial e Guelfa.*" In *Upon My Husband's*

Death: Widows in the Literature and Histories of Medieval Europe, ed. Louise Mirrer, 321–34. Ann Arbor: University of Michigan Press, 1992.

Pipponier, Françoise. "The World of Women." Trans. Arthur Goldhammer. In *A History of Women in the West: II. Silences of the Middle Ages,* ed. Christiane Klapisch-Zuber, 323–35. Cambridge, Mass: Belknap Press, 1992.

Salzman, L. F. *Building in England to 1540: A Documentary History.* 2d ed. Oxford: Clarendon Press, 1967.

Serrano y Sanz, Manuel. "Noticias biográficas de Fernando de Rojas, autor de LA CELESTINA, y del impresor Juan de Lucena." *Revista de Archivos, Bibliotecas y Museos* 6 (1902): 14–299.

Smyser, H. M. "The Domestic Background of *Troilus and Criseyde.*" *Speculum* 31 (1956): 297–315.

Stallybrass, Peter. "Patriarchal Territories: The Body Enclosed." In *Rewriting the Renaissance: The Discourses of Sexual Difference in Early Modern Europe,* ed. Margaret W. Ferguson, Maureen Quilligan, and Nancy Vickers, 123–42. Chicago: University of Chicago Press, 1986.

Uitz, Erika. *The Legend of Good Women: Medieval Women in Towns and Cities.* Trans. Sheila Marnie. New York: Moyer Bell, 1990.

Wood, Margaret. *The English Mediaeval House.* London: Phoenix House, 1965.

Wunderli, Richard. *London Church Courts and Society on the Eve of the Reformation.* Cambridge, Mass.: Medieval Academy of America, 1981.

—————10—————
Violence, Silence, and the
Memory of Witches

Jody Enders

Barbaric. Disgusting. "An unbelievable monstrosity filled with spiritual muck." "The most vicious and yet childish and, even so, the most damaging book in all of world literature."[1]

Those are the descriptions cited by editor Günter Jerouschek in his preface to one facsimile edition of the *Malleus maleficarum* or *Hammer of Witches*, first published in Latin in 1486 by the German inquisitor Heinrich Kramer.[2] "Since the beginning of printing," asserts Jerouschek, "few books have received such devastating condemnation" as this work, composed of three books and occupying two large volumes with its legal philosophies, procedures, and interpretations. It may well be that "critics spare themselves no pain in expressing their horror at this 'nauseating product of religious delusion' (dieser eklen Ausgebut religiösen Wahns)": but among the more sinister contributions of the *Malleus* to religiosity is its painstaking investigation into a unique kind of delusion: the memory phantasm.[3] Kramer offers a remarkable if troubling response to a question that has long preoccupied scholars of the Middle Ages, the Renaissance, and the early modern period and that continues to haunt contemporary feminist scholars: why were there so many more female witches than male witches?[4]

Touching on questions of anthropology, pedagogy, and the cultural construction of gender, Kramer explains that there are more female than male witches because women "*have weak memories; and it is a natural vice in them not to be disciplined, but to follow their own impulses without any sense of what is due; this is her whole study, and all that she keeps in her memory*" (Quantum insuper defectum in memorativa potentia, cùm hoc fit

in eis ex natura virium [sic], nolle regi; sed suos sequi impetus, sive qua-
cunque pietate: ad hoc studet, & cuncta memoria disponit; Kors and Peters, eds., *Witchcraft in Europe*, 124; *Malleus*, 1:44). He conflates illusions,
imagination, persecutions, power, impulse, deceit, and the Devil within
one and the same faculty: the fourth canon of the rhetorical tradition, *memoria:*

> By the power of devils, with God's permission, mental images long
> retained in the *treasury of such images*, which is the *memory*, are drawn
> out, *not from the intellectual understanding* in which such images are
> stored, but from the *memory, which is the repository of mental images,
> and is situated at the back of the head*, and are presented to the imagina-
> tive faculty. And so strongly are they impressed on that faculty that a
> *man* has an inevitable impulse to imagine a horse or a beast, when the
> *devil* draws from the memory an image of a horse or a beast; and so
> he is compelled to think that he sees with his external eyes such a
> beast when there is actually no such beast to see; but it seems to be so
> by reason of the impulsive force of *the devil working by means of those
> images*. (Kors and Peters, *Witchcraft*, 146–47; emphasis mine)

> (Quia virtute Daemonum, species sensibiles dudum reservatae *in
> thesauro* specierum sensibilium, ut est *memoria, non illa intellectiva*, in
> qua species intelligibiles conservantur, *sed memoria*, quae est *conserv-
> atrix* specierum sensibilium, quae etiam est in posteriori parte capi-
> tis, *educuntur* virtute Daemonum, *Deo interdum permittente*, ad sen-
> sum communem imaginativum. Et tam fortiter *imprimuntur*, quòd
> sicut necesse habet imaginare equum vel bestiam per impetuosum
> actum, quo Daemon *educit de memoria* speciem equi vel bestiae: ita
> necesse habet aestimare, se videre per oculos exteriores tantùm talem
> bestiam, quae in re ab extra non est bestia: sed per impetuosam Dae-
> monis operationem mediantibus illis speciebus, sic videtur. (*Malleus*,
> 1:128)

Here and throughout the *Malleus*, Kramer's numerous invocations of
such terms as *memoria, thesaurus, effigies*, and *imagines* call up the lexicon of
mnemotechnics as a body of knowledge with special relevance to diabolical acts as well as to the legal redress that might be effected to regulate and
punish them.[5] The question is why. What does a gendered memory have to
do with the prosecution and persecution of witches?

In this essay, I respond to that question by turning to the rhetorical representation of mnemotechnics in the "great European witch-craze."[6] As we

shall see, Kramer's recontextualization of the art of memory serves to anathematize and, literally, to "demonize" the female memory as the birthplace of intellect and speech.[7] He does considerably more than insist on the literal Latin meaning of "education" (*educere*) as "leading out," with the woman as the passive receptacle of her own education and the Devil doing the leading.[8] When Kramer targets the female memory, his intervention is scarcely confined to epistemology: he also attacks the female bodies that house that faculty, conveniently somaticized above as a bodily organ.[9] His vision of the female memory then helps to create a philosophical model that justifies, naturalizes, and normalizes violence against women—and all with God's permission (*Deo interdum permittente*), which then extends to the persecution of women.

According to a long rhetorical tradition richly elaborated from antiquity through the sixteenth century, *memoria* was described by the pseudo-Ciceronian author of the widely disseminated *Rhetorica ad Herennium* as the "*treasure-house* of the ideas supplied by Invention [and] the guardian of all the parts of rhetoric" (nunc ad *thesaurum* inventorum atque ad omnium partium rhetoricae *custodem*, memoriam, transeamus; *Ad Herennium*, 3.28); and, in John of Salisbury's twelfth-century *Metalogicon* as the "mind's treasure chest, a sure and reliable place of safe-deposit for perceptions" (1.11.35). More important, such theorists as Longinus, Augustine, Martianus Capella, Geoffrey of Vinsauf, and Hugh of Saint Victor all stressed its capacity for performance. The purpose of the mnemonic treasure chest and its imagistic contents was to "engender speech" (Longinus, "On the Sublime," chap. 15, 1–2); or, as Geoffrey of Vinsauf had it, to translate "wandering images" into "languages [that] should be heard in reciting" (*Poetria Nova*, verse 2036). Memory was a virtual performance, even a virtual reality: "the arrangement and disposition of the images [is] like the script" (*Ad Herennium*, 3.30).[10] So, perhaps most important of all, if its canonized rhetorical function was to "set the stage" for the delivery of legal or literary speech, *memoria* was also a primordial cultural script for the performance of social control and civilized behavior. That had been the case ever since Plato equated lawyers to dramatists by reason of their shared capacity to create memorable illusions that influenced both judicial and poetic communities.[11] As he explains in the *Laws*, memory was a chief means by which to control and correct the misguided mental pictures of society by "persuad[ing] people that their notions of justice and injustice are illusory pictures" (663b–c). One of the things that the *Malleus* provides is a clear statement about who wields the power to generate the illusions that replace other illusions: evil devils or good men.

Since *memoria* was a virtual performance, it was but a step in inquisitorial paralogic to move from virtual to actual persecution. That did not occur, however, without the apparent resolution of the following anomaly: although memory had been institutionalized as the birthplace of speech, it was not desirable that women (who naturally possessed memories) should speak or act in the various arenas of law, politics, education, religion, and literature. Rhetorically speaking, the faculty designed to engender speech was *not* to engender it in women. Whence the dark, ideological struggle encouraged by Kramer and the exposures of his strategy depicted in this essay.

Mnemotechnics had always had a dark underside, which can be traced all the way back to the legend of its apocryphal founder, Simonides. As the story goes, Simonides originated the *techne* when he tapped his own excellent memory in order to identify and name the dismembered victims of a gruesome accident.[12] Thus, while contemporary critics have tended to focus on the beauty of the mnemonic *imagines agentes* so carefully imagined by the Pseudo-Cicero as garbed in crowns and purple cloaks, it is equally meaningful to review the second half of his well-known description. Orators could turn to *disfiguration* as efficaciously as they might to figuration "as by introducing one [figure] stained with blood or soiled with mud or smeared with red paint, so that its *form* is more striking (aut si qua re *deformabimus*)" (*Ad Herennium*, 3.37).[13] Notwithstanding the later propensities of certain modern commentators to associate spirituality with "muck," there was nothing innocuous or murky about the interplay between memory and violence. For example, when Saint Augustine cites the words of Paulinus, bishop of Nola, to describe the tortured bodies of martyrs, he invokes memory as the treasure house of violence in general and of religious violence in particular:

> "Lord, let me not be *tormented* (*excrucier*) for gold and silver, for thou knowest where all my possessions are." He kept all his possessions where he had been taught to *store* and *treasure* (*condere et thesaurizare*) them by him who had foretold that these evils would come to the world. Consequently, those who had obeyed their Lord when he counselled them where and how they should lay up *treasure* (*thesaurizare*), did not lose even their earthly treasures in the invasion of barbarians. (*City of God*, book 1, chap. 10)

It is the teleology of that darker side that plays itself out in the *Malleus*. For Augustine's martyrs, a true, Christian, spiritual treasure remains intact, a treasure in which they might ultimately derive some comfort from their torture.[14] And Kramer does believe in torture, which he advocates throughout the *Malleus:*

> But if neither threats nor such promises [to spare her life] will induce her to confess the truth, then the officers must proceed with the sentence, and she must be examined. . . . And while she is being questioned about each several point, *let her be often and frequently exposed to torture,* beginning with the more gentle of them; for the Judge should not be too hasty to proceed to the graver kind. . . .

> And note that, if she confesses under torture, she should then be taken to another place and questioned anew, so that she does not confess only under the stress of torture.

> The next step of the Judge should be that, if after being fittingly tortured she refuses to confess the truth, he should have other engines of torture brought before her, and tell her that she will have to endure these if she does not confess. If then she is not induced by terror to confess, the torture must be continued on the second or third day, but not repeated at that present time unless there should be some fresh indication of its probable success. (Kors and Peters, *Witchcraft,* 166–68)

> (Quòd si nec minis, nec talibus promissis fateri voluerit veritatem, tunc ministri sententiam latam exequantur, & *quaestionetur.* . . . Et dum *quaestionatur* de certis articulis super quibus *quaestionatur,* & hoc saepè & frequenter à levioribus incipiendo: quia citius concedet levia quàm graviora. . . .

> Et nota, quòd si fatetur *per tormenta,* ducatur postea ad alium locum, ut denuò recognoscat, & quòd non tantummodò vi *tormentorum* cognoverit.

> Quartò stat actus in isto, quòd si *quaestionatus* decenter noluerit fateri veritatem, ponantur *alia tormentorum genera* coram eo, dicendo, quòd oporteat eum haec sustinere, nisi fateatur veritatem. Quòd si nec sic poterit *ad terrorem* vel etiam ad veritatem induci, tunc pro secunda aut tertia die *quaestionanda* ad continuandum *tormenta,* non ad iterandum: quia iterari non debent, nisi nova supervenissent indicia. (*Malleus,* 1:245)[15]

Nor is any Augustinian or hagiographic comfort available to Kramer's witches, who are abused, disenfranchised, and de-intellectualized—even as it is they who are accused of abusing, absconding with property, compromising the male intellect, and stealing male organs in the middle of the night "in great numbers, as many as twenty or thirty" (Kors and Peters, *Witchcraft*, 151).[16]

Kramer's vision constitutes a stunning reversal of victim for victimizer of the very sort that has been identified by Elaine Scarry as a premier ideology of torture (*Body in Pain*, 27).[17] Women are persecuted as witches: yet it is they who are configured as powerful tormenters while exercising a power they do not really have. Even the presumably sympathetic Jules Michelet subscribed to that notion, advancing in his *Sorcière* sweeping statements that link male fears and psychosomatic symptoms to real female power: "les sorcières régnaient. Elles exerçaient sur le pays une terreur d'imagination incroyable. Nombre de personnes se croyaient leurs victimes, et réellement devenaient gravement malades" (2:35–36; the Sorceresses reigned supreme, exercising over the country an almost incredible domination by means of the terrors of the imagination. Numbers of persons came to believe themselves their victims, and actually fell seriously ill, *Satanism and Witchcraft*, 153).[18] In fact, one of the more disturbing aspects of Michelet's presentation is the presumed historical actuality that women participated in the torture and persecution of their own, as when one particularly corrupt girl was recruited to conduct bodily surveillance upon alleged witches:

> Ils confièrent à cette fille corrompue, légère, enrageé la charge terrible de chercher sur le corps des filles et garçons l'endroit où Satan aurait mis sa marque. Cet endroit se reconnaissait à ce qu'il était insensible, et qu'on pouvait impunément y enfoncer des aiguilles. Un chirurgien martyrisait les vieilles, elles les jeunes, qu'on appelait comme témoins, mais qui, si elle les disait marquées, pouvaient être accusées. (*La sorcière*, 2:37)

> (They actually entrusted this vicious, irresponsible, passionate girl with the grim task of searching the bodies of young women and boys for signs of the spot where Satan had put his mark. The place was recognised by the fact of its being insensible to pain, so that needles could be driven into it without extracting a cry from the victim. A surgeon tortured the old women, Margarita the younger ones, who

were called as witnesses, but who, if she declared them marked in this way, might easily find their way to the bench of the accused.) (*Satanism and Witchcraft*, 154–55)

Agency becomes passivity, birth becomes death, natural becomes unnatural, desire becomes fear, preservation becomes extermination.[19] In the larger context of memory, Kramer's frightening strategy offers a method of vilifying female witches by reversing the positive valence of the very category being used to understand them: the memory. What the histories of rhetoric and memory show, however, is that these are only *apparent* reversals: violence, passivity, fear, the unnatural, and extermination have eternally been part and parcel of memory. In order to discipline and punish the misrepresented behaviors of women, such a theorist as Kramer returns to memory as the source of the behaviors he deems most deserving of discipline and punishment.[20]

As it happens, the very notion of a mnemonic treasure-house for women posed a series of truly thorny problems in rhetoric, law, politics, religion, and literature. It was perfectly clear—even to Kramer—that women possessed memories theoretically capable of engendering speech. Under certain grim medieval circumstances like those of the Black Death, their memories even functioned as a kind of village register.[21] Long before that, Aristotle had distinguished humankind from animals based on the rationale that "the animals other than man live by appearance and memories, and have but little of connected experience; but the human race lives also by art and reasoning" (*Metaphysics*, book 1, sections 980a–b). Nor is it any surprise to anyone familiar with misogynistic literature to learn from the presumably romantic perspective of the *Poissance d'amor* (once attributed to Richard de Fournival) that the female memory was a perceived source of recalcitrance, rebelliousness, lack of discipline, and failure to submit. Women's bodies take their cues from their unruly memories:

> Et pour chou ke femme connoist et entent raison, ele se set et doit savoir garder d'omme. Par coi on voit souvent avenir ke, quant hom prie une femme k'ele soit acline a se volenté, li *memoire* et li raisons de cheli ne s'i acordera mie. (Speroni, ed., 237–40)

> (And since she has knowledge and understands rationally, she knows how to guard herself from man. Thus it is that often it happens that when man bids woman to yield to his will, her memory and reason do not agree.) (Solterer, *Master and Minerva*, 53)[22]

Be that as it may, a significant change has occurred between the twelfth and the fifteenth centuries. Richard's recalcitrant feminine memory is at least associated with knowledge, reason, and intellect; whereas Kramer's main feat of ratiocination is the dissociation of memory from those very faculties. Richard's woman has an intellect; Kramer's does not. Nor is that the only shift: silly superstition has also become legally actionable heresy.[23] As Alexander Murray writes in a persuasive early essay on "Medieval Origins of the Witch Hunt," there has been a "fateful shift" from John of Salisbury's earlier view that only women, simple men, and those "less firm in the faith" would believe such nonsense as the Black Mass to the later view of the *Malleus*, in which the first duty is to establish that "to *dis*believe in these magical meetings was heretical" (247–48).[24] Noting that the *Malleus* was published "with letters of approval from a pope and a faculty of theology," Murray surmises that the shift derives in part from an increasingly regularized and aggressive university life (257–58). The rhetorical memory was part of that life and part of the larger theoretical universe of scholastic disputation, pedagogy, theology, and the persecution of witches. It was the cultural custodian of that life.

So it is that, in a casuistic sleight of hand, Kramer constructs a rationale according to which an active male memory is a good thing while the presumably identical entity in women is a danger. He manages to transmute the theoretically *active* faculty of memory into one that is necessarily *passive* if possessed by women. Since female power was effective, since the behavior of the alleged witch was difficult to control, and since men fell victim to her illusions, Kramer must attribute that power not to the women who exercise it but to the Devil. So he simultaneously disempowers and neutralizes a feminine faculty that is clearly exploitable enough and powerful enough to render it a desirable candidate for appropriation (even though, in retrospect, it is men and not women who are engaged in diabolical appropriations). As the creator of pernicious memory images, woman is recast as the passive, mnemonic receptacle of the Devil, which renders any power she herself might possess diabolical:

All these things are caused by devils through an illusion or glamour, in the manner we have said, by confusing the organ of vision by transmuting the mental images in the imaginative faculty. . . . And the reason is that they effect this thing by an easier method, namely, by *drawing out an inner mental image from the repository of the memory, and impressing it on the imagination.*

And if anyone wishes to say that they could go to work in a similar way, when they are said to converse with witches and other men in assumed bodies; that is, that they could cause such apparitions by changing the mental images in the imaginative faculty, so that when men thought the devils were present in assumed bodies, they were really nothing but an illusion caused by such a change of the mental images in the inner perceptions. (Kors and Peters, *Witchcraft*, 151–52)

(Haec omnia utique praestigiosa illusione fieri à Daemonibus modis supra tactis, organum visus per transmutationem specierum sensibilium in imaginativam potentiam turbando. . . . Ratio est, quia faciliori modo, videlicet per motum interiorem localem specierum sensibilium *ex conservatoria seu memorativa potentia ad imaginativam ista facere possunt.*

Et si quis dicere vellet, quòd etiam simili modo facere possent, ubi in assumptis corporibus afferuntur maleficis aut alijs hominibus conversari, ut videlicet tales apparitiones facerent per transmutationem specierum sensibilium in imaginativam potentiam: ut homines dum putarent Daemones in assumptis corporibus esse praesentes, tunc non essent nisi tales specierum sensibilium in interioribus potentiis immutationes.) (*Malleus*, 1:130–31)

The only way man is seduced is because of woman.

Kramer has acknowledged the power of the female memory to confuse and frighten men—but only in order to argue that it is *because* of her weak and undisciplined memory that woman is really disempowered. As in so many medieval retellings of the Fall with its simultaneously persuasive and scapegoated Eve, Kramer finds a way to argue that a potent female mnemonic faculty really has no potency at all.[25] It is a "disempowered power" of which woman is both origin and non-origin. If she does possess a memory, it is opposed to intellectual understanding, relegated to governance by the diabolical imagination, and dangerous to the men who are exposed to the Devil in her. Violence, torture, and even death thus become legitimate responses to the manufactured problem about her memory. Since the witch's memory is the bedeviled birthplace of noxious illusions, speech, and behavior, then such an inquisitor as Kramer seeks to ensure that her undesirable speech and behaviors never occur by attacking her through it and it through her.

From the classroom beatings endured by Heloise to the domestic violence of farce to the prosecution and persecution of witches, few things compare to the violence inflicted upon woman's memory and body, both of which are commonly eroticized, ridiculed, and beaten into passivity or oblivion.[26] In contexts as varied as the condemnation of gossips and the persecution of witches, her memory is trivialized as her tongue is literally bridled by means of a gendered implement of torture like the brank or gossip's bridle (figs. 10–12).[27] Described by William Andrews as "an instrument employed by our forefathers for punishing scolds," the brank possessed all the potential for public humiliation of the pillory. Identifying himself at least subconsciously with his "forefathers," Andrews displays all the even-handed sensitivity to female pain as the medieval writer of farce:

> The brank may be described simply as an iron framework; which was placed on the head, enclosing it in a kind of cage; it had in front a plate of iron, which, either sharpened or covered with spikes, was so situated as to be placed in the mouth of the victim, and if she attempted to move her tongue in any way whatever, it was certain to be shockingly injured. With the brank on her head she was conducted through the streets, led by a chain, held by one of the town's officials, an object of contempt, and subjected to the jeers of the crowd and often left to their mercy. In some towns it was the custom to chain the culprit to pillory, whipping-post, or market-cross. She thus suffered for telling her mind to some petty tyrant in office, or speaking plainly to a wrong-doer, or for *taking to task a lazy, and perhaps a drunken husband.* (*Old-Time Punishments*, 39)

There is, of course, a mighty tradition of bridling the tongue. Karen Cunningham recalls that images of "rhetorical dissection" abound in Marlowe, as in Tamburlaine's promise to "bridle all . . . tongues / And bind them . . . with burnished steel."[28] Much earlier, Gregory Nazianzen wrote that "with measured words, I learn to bridle rage."[29] But the brank bridled women as an outlet for male rage, tortured them with the heightened brutality of one extant object in the Ludlow Museum catalogued by W. J. Bernard Smith: "The powerful screwing apparatus seems calculated to force the iron mask with torturing effect upon the brow of the victim; there are no eye-holes, but concavities in their places, as though to allow for the starting of the eye-balls under violent pressure. There is a strong bar with a square hole, evidently intended to fasten the criminal against a wall, or perhaps to the pillory."[30]

In one horrific display, the brank brings together a number of traditions. It concretizes the wisdom of Jean de Meun's Vieille that "A woman should

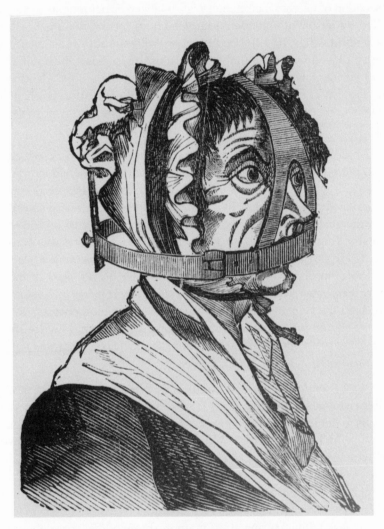

10. A woman wearing a brank. Reproduced from William Andrews, *Old-Time Punishments* (London: Simpkin, Marshall, Hamilton, Dent, 1890).

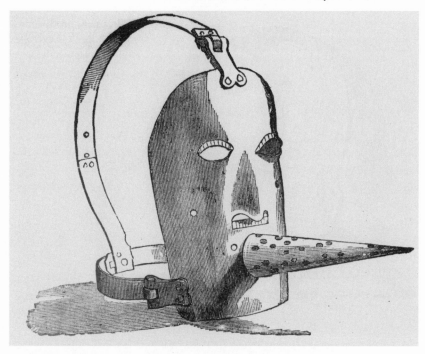

11. Brank (Doddington Park). Reproduced from Andrews, *Old-Time Punishments.*

always laugh with her mouth closed, for the sight of a mouth stretched like a gash across the face is not a pretty one" (Fame doit rire a bouche close / Car ce n'est mie bele chose / Quant el rit a goule estendue, / Trop semble estre large et fendue; *Roman de la Rose*, ll. 13359–62).[31] It evokes the ferocious images from hagiography and romance of such martyred heroines as Saint Christine and Philomela, whose tongues are plucked out.[32] And it crystallizes another conceptual shift from an earlier image like Hildegard of Bingen's of the eyes as windows to surgeon Henri de Mondeville's vision that the eyes are "cages, opening on the outside through an arbour (the eyelids)."[33] The brank is a gendered torture device, which sometimes blinds a woman's eyes, blocking out the visual component of her *phantasia*, and which forces her to "hold her tongue" by physically pinning it. Her mouth becomes both gash and cage in this ominous culmination of the regulation and punishment of the female memory as the birthplace of speech. Whether the brank was employed frequently, seldom, or not at all, it remains, at the very least, a hyper-real, iron incarnation of a threat to sever the cerebral connection between memory and speech—the same rupture advocated by Kramer in the *Malleus*.

12. Brank. Reproduced from Andrews, *Old-Time Punishments.*

It is in that sense that the status of memory as virtual performance most forcefully illustrates the important qualifiers articulated by Elaine Scarry, Herbert Blau, and Barbara J. Eckstein against the ideology of deconstruction. Denouncing as pernicious the critical tendency to exalt language above all things, all three insist that the infliction of physical pain cannot and should not be reduced to a series of linguistic or aesthetic constructs, as when Scarry asserts that "pain is pain, and not a metaphor of pain";[34] or Eckstein that "the daily assault on human flesh and all physical facts of life are not simply battles of words" (*Language of Fiction,* 181). In the final analysis, all the examples considered here of invasion, intervention, and repression conflate three interrelated means of eradicating woman's speech. First, the torture of witches targets the female memory as an origin of speech as it forces its victims to leave intelligible language behind by reverting to prelinguistic cries of pain. (That, of course, is one of Scarry's principal contentions about torture, in which "physical pain does not simply resist language but actively destroys it, bringing about an immediate reversion to a state anterior to language, to the sounds and cries a human being makes before language is learned" [*Body in Pain*, 4]). Second, a gendered implement of discipline and punishment like the brank painfully pins a woman's tongue and hypercorrects the very connection between female intellect and speech that Kramer denies. And third, the voices of the thousands of women who were killed after receiving questionable death sentences during the European witch-craze were permanently silenced.[35]

In this quintessential persecution in which exterminating the intellect becomes as urgent as destroying the body, memory would endure for the medieval and early modern woman as a literal "prison house of language," a *metal* (not a *mental*) guardian of speech, a jailer of language.[36] The psychological axiom once cited by Friedrich Nietzsche that "a thing is branded on the memory to make it stay there; only what goes on hurting will stick" thus becomes an appropriate vocabulary for feminist rhetorical criticism: "there is perhaps nothing more terrible in man's earliest history than his mnemotechnics" (192).[37] Although Nietzsche writes that "whenever man has thought it necessary to create a memory for himself, his effort has been attended with torture, blood, sacrifice" (192–93), it seems that efforts to create a memory for women were even bloodier. If ever there were proof of Derrida's suggestion that "life is already threatened by the origin of the memory which constitutes it" (*Writing and Difference*, 202), it lies in Kramer's memory and the early modern brank. Similarly, when Gilles Deleuze and Félix Guattari extrapolate from Nietzsche that societies record their essence in the violent operations of "tattooing, excising, incising, carving, scarifying, mutilating, encircling, and initiating" with the design of "creating a memory for man" (*Anti-Oedipus*, 144–45), the vast sociocultural cruelty of which they speak applies more compellingly still to women.

In the learned Middle Ages and Renaissance, a woman cannot have a voice if she does not have a memory. But once she does have a voice, the likes of Kramer find a way to trace it back to the memory that she does not really have. They then efface that voice along with its nonexistent origins. Their own re-membering of what they have dis-membered resonates with Teresa de Lauretis' suggestion that "once a connection is assumed between violence and rhetoric, the two terms begin to slide, and, soon enough, the connection will appear to be reversible" (*Technologies of Gender*, 32). The medieval rhetorician and the early modern inquisitor already had at their disposal an epistemological model in which that commingling was enacted for better or, as in the case of so many brutalized women, for worse. It was the memory.

224 | Jody Enders

NOTES

1. These statements are all cited by Günther Jerouschek in his introduction to the *Malleus*, xxi; and have been culled from the following works: Soldan/Heppe find it "barbaric" and "disgusting" in *Geschichte der Hexenprozesse* (1911); S. Riezler calls it the most damaging book in history in *Geschichte der Hexenprozesse in Bayern* (Stuttgart, 1896); and the epithet "unglaubichen Monstrum voll geistiger Sumpfluft" is from J. Hansen, *Zauberwahn, Inquisition und Hexenprozess im Mittelalter und die Entstehung der grossen Hexenverfolgungen* (Munich, 1900).

2. See also Russell's discussion of the *Malleus*, which was written in 1485 or 1486, and appeared in 1486 with the *Summis desiderante* of Innocent VIII as a preface (*Witchcraft in the Middle Ages*, 230–34). Authorship of the *Malleus* has often been attributed jointly to Kramer and Jakob Sprenger; but historians have largely determined that the latter's participation was relatively minimal. Unfortunately, while German translations of the *Malleus* abound, access to the Latin edition is not as easy as one might think. For that reason, I refer here to the most readily available English and Latin versions: English citations are from Kors and Peters, eds., *Witchcraft in Europe*, who follow the much less accessible translation of Montague Summers; Latin citations are from the Brussels reprint of the 1949 edition of the *Malleus*, 2 vols. (rpt. 1969). Volume 1 contains the *Malleus*; and vol. 2 the *Mallei maleficarum tractatus aliquot.*

3. J. W. R. Schmidt, *Der Hexenhammer (Malleus Maleficarum)* (Munich, 1983), as quoted by Jerouschek, xxi.

4. For a converse perspective from seventeenth-century Russia, where the majority of accused witches (75%) were male, see Valerie Kivelson, "Through the Prism of Witchcraft."

5. For other rich treatments of memory in the *Malleus*, see, for example, Kramer's definition of *phantasia:* "est enim Phantasia, seu imaginatio quasi thesaurus quidam formarum per sensus acceptarum" (1:49; also 65). Several compatible sections of Weyer provide an interesting comparison, especially "Concerning the Imagination," "How the Devil Corrupts the Imagination," and "Concerning the Imaginary" (*Witches, Devils,* 186–94); as does a passage from Gratian's *Decretum* reproduced in Kors and Peters, *Witchcraft,* 29. Excellent historical analyses of the gendered ramifications of the prosecution of women in the Middle Ages include Prevenier; Cohen; and Hanawalt.

6. Here I invoke the title of Trevor-Roper's chap. 3 of *Crisis of the Seventeenth Century,* "The European Witch-Craze of the Sixteenth and Seventeenth Centuries."

7. Exemplary introductions to the art of memory include Yates; Carruthers; Coleman; Caplan; Zumthor and Roy; Clanchy; and Walter J. Ong, *Rhetoric,* chap. 4. For the classic general histories of rhetoric, see Murphy; Kennedy; and, more recently, Conley.

8. For the history of memory in a pedagogical context, see Riché, "Rôle de la mémoire." For mnemonic violence in that context, see Enders, "Rhetoric, Coercion"; Gibson; Irvine; Woods; and implicitly in Jed, chap. 1.

9. For a fascinating discussion of concomitant developments in medicine about the structure of the brain, see editor Mora's discussion of Weyer's "Memorative Function of the Brain," in Weyer, *Witches, Devils*, 728–31.

10. I discuss the virtual performativity of memory in detail in *Rhetoric and the Origins of Medieval Drama*, 44–54.

11. See also Eden's illuminating discussion of Plato's *Laws* (*Poetic and Legal Fiction*, 29–30); and for various discussions of medieval communities (textual or otherwise), see Stock, *Implications of Literacy*, chap. 2 (esp. 88–92); and David Aers, *Community, Gender*, introduction.

12. According to the widely circulated legend, mnemotechnics was born when Simonides was called away from a banquet, only to see the entire building collapse on top of the guests once he was safely outside. His story appears in numerous rhetorical treatises, including Cicero's *De oratore*, book 2, sections 351–55; Martianus Capella, *De Nuptiis*, 177g; and Quintilian, *Institutio oratoria*, book 11, chap. 2, sections 11–16. It has been discussed by Yates, *Art of Memory*, 1–2; Carruthers, *Book of Memory*, 147; and in my "Rhetoric, Coercion," 26–28. D. Vance Smith also treats the "dark underside" of memory in "In Place of Memory."

13. Some notable exceptions include D. Vance Smith, "In Place of Memory"; Carruthers, *Book of Memory*, 130–38; Eugene Vance, *Mervelous Signals*, 24–26, 53–55; Solterer, "Dismembering,"; Lynn Worsham "Eating History"; and David Farrell Krell, *Of Memory*.

14. This is also a principal difference between Kramer's tortured witches and the female saints of hagiography, who often take comfort in their torture, are exempted from feeling pain through divine intervention, and are habitually depicted as intelligent. For a rich introduction to this topic, see Cazelles, ed., *Lady as Saint*, chap. 1.

15. Emphasis mine. As Peters duly notes of the history of torture, the concepts of interrogation, testing, and punishment (*quaestio* and *tormentum/tortura*) became synonymous (*Torture*, 28; see also duBois, *Torture and Truth*, 21–25). Compare this passage from the *Malleus*, e.g., to Plato's advice in the *Laws* that "the good legislator will use noble and laudable phrases to persuade him—and, failing persuasion, he will compel him . . . to compose poems aright" (659d–660). In *The Medieval Theater of Cruelty*, I explore the interrelations of these phenomena by arguing that an ideal of Truth in torture is substituted for the unreliable and verisimilar criteria of drama (chap. 1).

16. For disenfranchisement, see also the story of Anne Marie Georgel and Catherine, wife of Delort of Toulouse (Kors and Peters, *Witchcraft*, 93–97). Catherine is persecuted for persecuting her aunts "whose heir she was" by means of another physical concretization of a classic memory image—the waxen block. She heats "waxen figures dressed in one of their blouses over a slow fire, so that their unfortunate lives wasted away as the waxen figure was melting in the brazier" (96–97).

17. For helpful introductions to torture and witchcraft, see Paster, *Body Embar-*

rassed, 244–60; Bartlett on their ordeals, *Trial by Fire*, 144–52; Peters, *The Magician, the Witch, and the Law* and his more general works *Inquisition* and *Torture;* and for an important feminist analysis of torture, see duBois, *Torture and Truth*, esp. chap. 14, "Women, the Body, and Torture."

18. This is similar to the female-on-female violence attributed to Catherine Delort (note 16). Moreover, to "justify" the conduct of medieval witches, Michelet falls back on the topos of a rapacious female sexuality. Dissatisfied in their marriages and questing after bizarre and unnatural unions, women gravitated toward the unnatural: "moins en avait l'union, et plus on l'eût voulue profonde. L'imagination déréglée la cherchait en choses bizarres, hors nature et insensées" (1:124–25; "The less actual intercourse was possible, the more profound the longing for a symbolic union. This a morbid fancy sought to find in all sorts of extravagances, equally unnatural and unreasonable," *Satanism and Witchcraft*, 96).

19. Except, of course, for the male-identified corrupt girl helping the somehow "incorruptible" men. I discuss these claims at much greater length in chap. 2 of *The Medieval Theater of Cruelty*.

20. Here, I allude deliberately to Foucault's work of the same title: *Discipline and Punish*.

21. This was the subject of the recent conference paper "Archives of Knowledge" by Daniel L. Smail; see also Patrick Geary, *Phantoms*, 63–73.

22. Both the *Metaphysics* and the *Poissance* are discussed in Solterer, *Master and Minerva*, 52–53, 82. The veritable explosion of interest in misogyny is a topic too vast to be treated adequately here: but two helpful introductions to the stakes of the debates are Bloch, *Medieval Misogyny*, and Burns, *Bodytalk*.

23. Additional early evidence to that effect may be found in Davidson and Ward, *Sorcery Trial of Alice Kyteler* (1324), the record of which begins with a bishop's discovery that "in the town of Kilkenny there had been for long time, and still were, very many heretical sorceresses (*haeretici sortilegae*) who practiced all kinds of sorceries (*sortilegiis*) and were well-versed in all kinds of heresies" (26). See also Russell and Wyndham, "Witchcraft and the Demonization of Heresy"; and Brown, "Society and the Supernatural."

24. For convenience, I cite from Brian P. Levack's readily accessible reprint edition, *Articles on Witchcraft;* see also Murray's discussion of the contestatory nature of medieval education in *Reason and Society*, chap. 10. Another important figure who would participate in the sixteenth-century continuations of the discussions about memory and violence is Thomas Murner, who is analyzed extensively by Kramer in the *Malleus*, 2:54–65. Not coincidentally, Murner is the author of both an *Ars memorativa* and of an antisemitic tract on *Die Entehrung Mariae durch die Juden*. He is discussed briefly by Walter J. Ong in *Rhetoric*, 125, and at greater length in his *Ramus*, 83–91; in my "Rhetoric, Coercion," 39–41; and in Po-chia Hsia, *Myth of Ritual Murder*, 25–28. While the disturbing topic of antisemitism lies outside the scope of this essay, it is worth noting that the intersection of gender, memory, and antisemitism recalls the same problematic nexus that has recently been explored by Biddick, "Genders, Bodies" (1993).

25. Even in the *Jeu* or *Mystère d'Adam*, Eve is the origin of the Fall, but because of her successful persuasion of her husband (205–315), she is also the first human rhetorician (the Devil being the first "divine" one). In operation here is the same assimilative phenomenon that Caroline Walker Bynum has identified in her work on clerical authors who "sometimes said explicitly that women were too weak to be women" ("And Women," 269). For general work on the scapegoat, see Girard, *Violence and the Sacred*, esp. chap. 4, and Frazer, *The Scapegoat.*

26. On Abelard's violent pedagogy of Heloise, see Kamuf, *Fictions*, esp. chap. 1; Irvine, "Literate Subjectivity"; Enders, "Rhetoric, Coercion," 42–43.

27. For the full discussion, see Andrews, *Old-Time Punishments*, 38–64. I am indebted to Caroline Clerc for sharing her work on branks with me.

28. Marlowe's Tamburlaine (pt. 2, 4.2.107–8); cited by Cunningham, "Renaissance Execution," 214.

29. Gregory, *Oratio* 6.6, *Patrologia Graeca*, 35:728; cited by Brown, *Power and Persuasion*, 50.

30. Smith's description appears in the *Archaeological Journal* of September 1856 and is cited by Andrews as an enhancement "far more formidable than branks" (*Old-Time Punishments*, 60).

31. See also Marie-Christine Pouchelle on this passage, *Body and Surgery*, 148.

32. The story of Saint Christine appears in Cazelles, ed., *Lady as Saint*, 138–50, although she summarizes rather than translates that particular section (149) from the original source, Gautier de Coinci. Christine's legend also appears in Christine de Pizan, part 3, chap. 10, 1001–10. For the violence of hagiography in general, see Cazelles, 43–61; and for Philomela, see, for example, Burns, *Bodytalk*, chap. 3.

33. For a discussion of this passage from her *Causae et curae*, see Pouchelle, 149.

34. Here, I borrow the resumé of Scarry's thesis (51–56) as offered by Herbert Blau, *The Audience*, 165.

35. Estimates on this "gynocide" vary from historian to historian and place to place. But Kors and Peters assert, e.g., that, for the period from the fourteenth through the seventeenth centuries, "few begin guessing below the range of 50,000–100,000" (*Witchcraft*, 13).

36. Here I suggest a literal meaning for two metaphoric book titles: Fredric Jameson's *Prison-House of Language* and R. A. Kaster's *Guardians of Language.*

37. For an intriguing discussion of Nietzsche, see Poulakos, "Nietzsche and Histories of Rhetoric."

WORKS CITED

Abelard, Peter. *Historia Calamitatum*. Ed. by J. Monfrin. Paris: Vrin, 1967.

Aers, David. *Community, Gender, and Individual Identity: English Writing 1360–1430*. London and New York: Routledge, 1988.

Andrews, William. *Old-Time Punishments*. London: Simpkin, Marshall, Hamilton, Dent, 1890.

Aristotle. *Metaphysica Aristotelis: Translatio anonyma sive "media."* Ed. by Gudrun Vuillemin-Diem. Leiden: E. J. Brill, 1976.

Augustine of Hippo. *The City of God Against the Pagans.* Ed. and trans. by George E. McCracken. 7 vols. Loeb Classical Library. Cambridge: Harvard University Press, 1957.

Bartlett, Robert. *Trial by Fire and Water: The Medieval Judicial Ordeal.* 1986; rpt. Oxford: Clarendon, 1988.

Biddick, Kathleen. "Genders, Bodies, Borders: Technologies of the Visible." *Speculum* 68 (1993): 389–418.

Blau, Herbert. *The Audience.* Baltimore: Johns Hopkins University Press, 1990.

Bloch, R. Howard. *Medieval Misogyny and the Invention of Western Romantic Love.* Chicago: University of Chicago Press, 1991.

Brown, Peter. *Power and Persuasion in Late Antiquity: Towards a Christian Empire.* Madison: University of Wisconsin Press, 1992.

———. "Society and the Supernatural: A Medieval Change." *Daedalus* 104 (1975): 133–51; rpt. in Levack, vol. 2, 97–115.

Burns, E. Jane. *Bodytalk: When Women Speak in Old French Literature.* Philadelphia: University of Pennsylvania Press, 1993.

Bynum, Caroline Walker. "'. . . And Women His Humanity': Female Imagery in the Religious Writing of the Later Middle Ages." In *Gender and Religion: On the Complexity of Symbols.* Ed. Bynum, Stevan Harrell, and Paula Richman, 257–88. Boston: Beacon, 1986.

Caplan, Harry C. "Memoria: Treasure-House of Eloquence." In *Of Eloquence: Studies in Ancient and Medieval Rhetoric,* 196–246. Ithaca: Cornell University Press, 1970.

Carruthers, Mary. *The Book of Memory.* Cambridge: Cambridge University Press, 1990.

Cazelles, Brigitte, ed. *The Lady as Saint: A Collection of French Hagiographic Romances of the Thirteenth Century.* Philadelphia: University of Pennsylvania Press, 1991.

Christine de Pizan. "The *Livre de la Cité des Dames* of Christine de Pisan: A Critical Edition." Ed. Maureen Cheney Curnow. Ph.D. diss., Vanderbilt University, 1975.

[Cicero]. *Ad C. Herennium.* Ed. and trans. Harry Caplan. Loeb Classical Library. 1954; rpt. Cambridge: Harvard University Press, 1977.

Cicero. *De oratore.* Ed. and trans. E. W. Sutton and H. Rackham. 2 vols. Loeb Classical Library. 1942; rpt. Cambridge: Harvard University Press, 1976.

Clanchy, M. T. *From Memory to Written Record: England, 1066–1307.* Cambridge: Harvard University Press, 1979.

Cohen, Esther. *The Crossroads of Justice.* Leiden: Brill, 1993.

Coleman, Janet. *Ancient and Medieval Memories.* Cambridge: Cambridge University Press, 1992.

Conley, Thomas. *Rhetoric in the European Tradition.* 1990; rpt. Chicago: University of Chicago Press, 1994.

Copeland, Rita, ed. *Criticism and Dissent in the Middle Ages.* Cambridge: Cambridge University Press, 1996.

Cunningham, Karen. "Renaissance Execution and Marlovian Elocution: The Drama of Death." *PMLA* 105 (1990): 209–22.

Davidson, L. S., and J. O. Ward, ed. and trans. *The Sorcery Trial of Alice Kyteler: A Contemporary Account (1324).* Binghamton, N.Y.: Medieval and Renaissance Texts and Studies, 1993.

Deleuze, Gilles, and Félix Guattari. *Anti-Oedipus: Capitalism and Schizophrenia.* Minneapolis: University of Minnesota Press, 1983.

Derrida, Jacques. *Writing and Difference.* Trans. Alan Bass. Chicago: University of Chicago Press, 1978.

duBois, Page. *Torture and Truth.* New York: Routledge, 1991.

Eckstein, Barbara J. *The Language of Fiction in a World of Pain: Reading Politics as Paradox.* Philadelphia: University of Pennsylvania Press, 1990.

Eden, Kathy. *Poetic and Legal Fiction in the Aristotelian Tradition.* Princeton: Princeton University Press, 1986.

Enders, Jody. *The Medieval Theater of Cruelty.* Ithaca: Cornell University Press. Forthcoming.

———. *Rhetoric and the Origins of Medieval Drama.* Rhetoric and Society, 1. Ithaca: Cornell University Press, 1992.

———. "Rhetoric, Coercion, and the Memory of Violence." In *Criticism and Dissent in the Middle Ages,* ed. Rita Copeland, 24–55. Cambridge: Cambridge University Press, 1996.

Foucault, Michel. *Discipline and Punish: The Birth of the Prison.* Trans. Alan Sheridan. New York: Pantheon, 1977.

Frazer, Sir James George. *The Scapegoat.* Vol. 6 of *The Golden Bough.* 3d ed. 1913; rpt. London: Macmillan, 1920.

Geary, Patrick J. *Phantoms of Remembrance: Memory and Oblivion at the End of the First Millennium.* Princeton: Princeton University Press, 1994.

Gibson, Joan. "Educating for Silence: Renaissance Women and the Language Arts." *Hypatia* 4 (1989): 9–27.

Girard, René. *Violence and the Sacred.* Trans. Patrick Gregory. Baltimore: Johns Hopkins University Press, 1977.

Hanawalt, Barbara. "Violent Death in Fourteenth and Early Fifteenth-Century England." *Comparative Studies in Society and History* 18 (1976): 297–320.

Hugh of Saint Victor. *The Didascalicon of Hugh of St. Victor.* Trans. Jerome Taylor. 1961; rpt. New York: Columbia University Press, 1991.

Irvine, Martin. "Literate Subjectivity and Conflicting Gender Positions in the Writing of Abelard and Heloise." In *Criticism and Dissent in the Middle Ages,* ed. Rita Copeland, 87–114. Cambridge: Cambridge University Press, 1996.

Jameson, Fredric. *The Prison-House of Language: A Critical Account of Structuralism and Russian Formalism.* Princeton: Princeton University Press, 1972.

Jed, Stephanie. *Chaste Thinking: The Rape of Lucretia and the Birth of Humanism.* Bloomington: Indiana University Press, 1989.

Jean de Meun. *Le Roman de la rose*. Ed. Daniel Poirion. Paris: Garnier-Flammarion, 1974.

———. *The Romance of the Rose*. By Guillaume de Lorris and Jean de Meun. Trans. W. Harry Robbins. New York: Dutton, 1962.

John of Salisbury. *The* Metalogicon *of John of Salisbury: A Twelfth-Century Defense of the Verbal and Logical Arts of the Trivium*. Ed. and trans. Daniel D. McGarry. Berkeley: University of California Press, 1955.

———. Ed. Clement C. J. Webb. Oxford: Clarendon, 1929.

Kamuf, Peggy. *Fictions of Feminine Desire: Disclosures of Heloise*. Lincoln: University of Nebraska Press, 1982.

Kaster, R. A. *Guardians of Language: The Grammarian and Society in Late Antiquity*. Berkeley: University of California Press, 1988.

Kennedy, George A. *Classical Rhetoric and Its Christian and Secular Tradition from Ancient to Modern Times*. Chapel Hill: University of North Carolina Press, 1980.

Kivelson, Valerie Ann. "Through the Prism of Witchcraft: Gender and Social Change in Seventeenth-Century Muscovy." In *Russia's Women: Accommodation, Resistance, Transformation*, ed. B. Clements, B. Engel, C. Worobec, 74–94. Berkeley: University of California Press, 1991.

Kors, Alan C., and Edward Peters, eds. *Witchcraft in Europe 1100–1700: A Documentary History*. 1972; rpt. Philadelphia: University of Pennsylvania Press, 1986.

Kramer, Heinrich (Institoris). *Malleus Maleficarum 1487*. Ed. Günter Jerouschek. Hildesheim, Zürich, New York: G. Olms, 1992.

———. *Malleus Maleficarum*. 2 vols. 1949 edition. Rpt. Brussels: Culture et Civilisation, 1969.

———. *Malleus Maleficarum*. Trans. Montague Summers. London: J. Rodker, 1928.

———. *Der Hexenhammer (Malleus Maleficarum)*. Ed. J. W. R. Schmidt. Munich: Deutscher Taschenbuch Verlag, 1986.

Krell, David Farrell. *Of Memory, Reminiscence, and Writing: On the Verge*. Bloomington: Indiana University Press, 1990.

Larner, Christina. "Witch Beliefs and Witch-Hunting in England and Scotland." *History Today* 31 (1981): 32–36. Reprinted in *Articles on Witchcraft, Magic and Demonology*, ed. Brian P. Levack, 12 vols., 7:250–54. New York: Garland, 1992–.

Lauretis, Teresa de. *Technologies of Gender: Essays on Theory, Film, and Fiction*. Bloomington: Indiana University Press, 1987.

Lea, Henry Charles. *Superstition and Force: Essays on the Wager of Law, the Wager of Battle, the Ordeal, Torture*. 2d ed. New York: Haskell House, 1971.

Levack, Brian P., ed. *Articles on Witchcraft, Magic and Demonology*. 12 vols. New York: Garland, 1992–.

Longinus. "On the Sublime." Ed. and trans. W. Hamilton Fyfe. In *Aristotle, Longinus, Demetrius*. Loeb Classical Library. 1927; rpt. Cambridge: Harvard University Press, 1946.

Martianus Capella. *De Nuptiis Philologiae et Mercurii*. Ed. Adolfus Dick. 1925; rpt. Stuttgart: Teubner, 1969.

Michelet, Jules. *La Sorcière*. Ed. Lucien Refort. 2 vols. Paris: Marcel Didier, 1952.

Trans. A. R. Allinson as *Satanism and Witchcraft: The Classic Study of Medieval Superstition.* New York: Citadel, 1992.

Murner, Thomas. *Logica memorativa.* Nieuwkoop: Miland Publishers, 1967.

Murphy, James J. *Rhetoric in the Middle Ages: A History of Rhetorical Theory from Saint Augustine to the Renaissance.* 1974; rpt. Berkeley: University of California Press, 1981.

Murray, Alexander. "Medieval Origins of the Witch Hunt." *Cambridge Quarterly* 39 (1976): 63–74. Reprinted in *Articles on Witchcraft, Magic and Demonology,* ed. Brian P. Levack, 12 vols. 2:247–58. New York: Garland, 1992–.

———. *Reason and Society in the Middle Ages.* Oxford: Clarendon, 1978.

Le Mystère d'Adam (Ordo Representationis Ade). Ed. Paul Aebischer. Geneva: Droz, 1964.

Nietzsche, Friedrich. *The Birth of Tragedy and the Genealogy of Morals.* Trans. Francis Golffing. Garden City, N.Y.: Doubleday, 1956.

Ong, Walter J. *Ramus, Method, and the Decay of Dialogue.* 1958; rpt. Cambridge: Harvard University Press, 1983.

———. *Rhetoric, Romance, and Technology: Studies in the Interaction of Expression and Culture.* Ithaca: Cornell University Press, 1971.

Paster, Gail Kern. *The Body Embarrassed: Drama and the Disciplines of Shame in Early Modern England.* Ithaca: Cornell University Press, 1993.

Peters, Edward. *The Magician, the Witch, and the Law.* Philadelphia: University of Pennsylvania Press, 1978.

———. *Inquisition.* Berkeley: University of California Press, 1989.

———. *Torture.* New York: Basil Blackwell, 1986.

Plato. *Laws.* 2 vols. Loeb Classical Library. 1926; rpt. Cambridge: Harvard University Press, 1942.

Po-chia Hsia, R. *The Myth of Ritual Murder: Jews and Magic in Reformation Germany.* New Haven: Yale University Press, 1988.

La Poissance damours dello Pseudo-Richard de Fournival. Ed. Gian Battista Speroni. Pubblicazioni della Facoltà di Lettere e Filosofia dell'Università di Pavia 21. Florence: La Nuova Italia, 1975.

Pouchelle, Marie-Christine. *Corps et Chirurgie à l'apogée du Moyen-Age.* Paris: Flammarion, 1983. Published in translation as *The Body and Surgery in the Middle Ages.* Trans. Rosemary Morris. New Brunswick: Rutgers University Press, 1990.

Poulakos, John. "Nietzsche and Histories of Rhetoric." In *Writing Histories of Rhetoric,* ed. Victor Vitanza, 81–97. Carbondale: Southern Illinois University Press, 1994.

Prevenier, Walter. "Violence against Women in a Medieval Metropolis: Paris around 1400." In *Law, Custom and the Social Fabric in Medieval Europe: Essays in Honor of Bryce Lyon,* ed. B. Bachrach and D. Nicholas, 263–84. Studies in Medieval Culture, 28, Kalamazoo, Mich.: Medieval Institute Publications, 1990.

Quintilian. *Institutio oratoria.* Ed. and trans. H. E. Butler. 4 vols. Loeb Classical Library. 1920; rpt. Cambridge: Harvard University Press, 1980.

Riché, Pierre. "Le Rôle de la mémoire dans l'enseignement médiéval." In *Jeux de mémoire: Aspects de la mnémotechnie médiévale,* ed. Paul Zumthor and Bruno Roy, 133–48. Paris: Vrin, 1985.

Russell, Jeffrey Burton. *Witchcraft in the Middle Ages.* Ithaca: Cornell University Press, 1972.

Russell, Jeffrey Burton, and Mark Wyndham, "Witchcraft and the Demonization of Heresy." *Medievalia: A Journal of Medieval Studies* 2 (1976): 1–21.

Scarry, Elaine. *The Body in Pain: The Making and Unmaking of the World.* 1985; rpt. New York: Oxford University Press, 1987.

Smail, Daniel L. "Archives of Knowledge and the Coming of the Black Death." Paper presented at International Congress of Medieval Studies, Kalamazoo, Michigan. 5 May 1994.

Smith, D. Vance. "In Place of Memory: Remembering Practices after 1348 and 1983." Paper presented at International Congress for Medieval Studies, Kalamazoo, Michigan. 5 May 1994.

Solterer, Helen. "Dismembering, Remembering, and the Châtelain de Couci." *Romance Philology* 46 (1992): 103–24.

———. *The Master and Minerva: Disputing Women in Old French Literature.* Berkeley: University of California Press, 1995.

Stock, Brian. *Implications of Literacy: Written Language and Models of Interpretation in the Eleventh and Twelfth Centuries.* Princeton: Princeton University Press, 1983.

Trevor-Roper, H. R. *The Crisis of the Seventeenth Century: Religion, the Reformation, and Social Change.* 1956; rpt. New York and Evanston: Harper and Row, 1968.

Vance, Eugene. *Mervelous Signals: Poetics and Sign Theory in the Middle Ages.* 1986; rpt. Lincoln: University of Nebraska Press, 1989.

Vinsauf, Geoffrey of. *Poetria Nova.* In *The* Poetria Nova *and its Sources in Early Rhetorical Doctrine.* Trans. Ernest Gallo. The Hague: Mouton, 1971.

Weyer, Johan. *Witches, Devils, and Doctors in the Renaissance: Johann Weyer, De praestigiis daemonum.* Ed. George Mora. Binghamton, N.Y.: Medieval and Renaissance Texts and Studies, 1991.

Woods, Marjorie Curry. "Rape and the Pedagogical Rhetoric of Sexual Violence." In *Criticism and Dissent in the Middle Ages,* ed. Rita Copeland, 56–86. Cambridge: Cambridge University Press, 1996.

Worsham, Lynn. "Eating History, Purging Memory, Killing Rhetoric." In *Writing Histories of Rhetoric,* ed. Victor Vitanza, 139–55. Carbondale: Southern Illinois University Press, 1994.

Yates, Frances. *The Art of Memory.* Chicago: University of Chicago Press, 1966.

Zumthor, Paul, and Bruno Roy, eds. *Jeux de mémoire: Aspects de la mnémotechnie médiévale.* Paris: Vrin, 1985.

Contributors

Jean Blacker is associate professor of French at Kenyon College. She has published numerous articles on Wace and historical writing, as well as *The Faces of Time: Portrayal of the Past in Old French and Latin Historical Narrative of the Anglo-Norman Regnum* (Texas, 1994). She is currently preparing an edition of the decasyllabic and alexandrine prophecies of Merlin for the Anglo-Norman Text Society Plain Text Series, and *Wace: An Annotated Bibliography* for Research Bibliographies and Checklists (Grant and Cutler).

Jane Chance is professor of English at Rice University. She is the editor and coeditor of six collections, including *The Mythographic Art: Classical Fable and the Rise of the Vernacular* (Florida, 1990) and *Gender and Text in the Later Middle Ages* (Florida, 1996); the translator of Christine de Pizan's *Letter of Othea to Hector* (Focus, 1990); and the author of many articles on Chaucer, women in medieval literature, medievalism, and other topics. Her books include *The Genius Figure in Antiquity and the Middle Ages* (Columbia, 1975), *Woman as Hero in Old English Literature* (Syracuse, 1986), *Medieval Mythography: From Roman North Africa to the School of Chartres* (Florida, 1994), and *The Mythographic Chaucer: The Fabulation of Sexual Politics* (Minnesota, 1995).

Carolyn Dinshaw is associate professor of English at the University of California, Berkeley. She has published numerous articles on Chaucer and is the author of *Chaucer and the Text: Two Views of the Author* (Garland, 1988), *Chaucer's Sexual Poetics* (Wisconsin, 1989) and *Getting Medieval: Sexualities and Communities, Pre- and Postmodern* (Duke, forthcoming).

Deborah S. Ellis is associate professor of English at Southwestern University in Texas. She has published numerous articles, mostly on medieval

women, in such journals as *Exemplaria, Chaucer Review* and *College English.*
She has recently completed a book manuscript entitled *Negotiable Securi-
ties: Medieval Women at Home,* with a focus on medieval Jewish women.

Jody Enders is professor of French at the University of California, Santa
Barbara. Among her articles on rhetoric and mnemonics is "Music, Deliv-
ery, and the Rhetoric of Memory in Guillaume de Machaut's *Remède de
Fortune"* (*PMLA,* 1992). Her book *Rhetoric and the Origins of Medieval Drama*
(Cornell, 1992) was honored by the Inaugural Aldo and Jean Scaglione
Prize in 1993. Her second book, *The Medieval Theater of Cruelty,* is forthcom-
ing from Cornell University Press.

Laurie Finke is director of Women's and Gender Studies at Kenyon College. She is the coeditor of three collections, including *Medieval Texts and
Contemporary Readers,* which she edited with Martin Shichtman (Cornell,
1987), and the author of numerous articles on English theater, feminist
theory, and pedagogy. Her books include *Feminist Theory, Women's Writing*
(Cornell, 1992). She is now working on *The Subversion of History* (with Martin Shichtman).

Shari Horner is assistant professor of English at Pennsylvania State
University, Mont Alto. She has published "Spiritual Truth and Sexual Violence: The Old English *Juliana,* Anglo-Saxon Nuns, and the Discourse of
Female Monastic Enclosure" (*Signs,* 1994) as well as other articles on
women in Old English poetry. She is currently working on a book-length
study of gender and female monasticism in Anglo-Saxon literature.

Madeleine Jeay is professor of French at McMaster University in
Canada. She has published numerous articles on sexual practices in medieval literature and culture and has edited the *Evangiles des Quenouilles,* a
fifteenth-century collection of popular beliefs. Her most recent book,
*Donner la parole. L'histoire-cadre dans les recueils des nouvelles des XVe–XVIe
siècles* (Montréal, CERES, 1992), focuses on the interaction between oral
and written narrativity.

Anne Laskaya is assistant professor of English and director of composi-
tion at the University of Oregon. She is the author of *Chaucer's Approach to
Gender in the Canterbury Tales* (D. S. Brewer, 1995) and coeditor of *The
Middle English Breton Lays* (Medieval Institute Publications, Western
Michigan, 1995).

Anna Roberts, the volume editor, is assistant professor of French at Miami University. She is the author of studies on medieval French literature and has contributed articles to *Les propos spectacle: Etudes de pragmatique théâtrale* (Peter Lang, 1996).

Martin Shichtman is professor of English at Eastern Michigan University. He has published numerous articles on Arthurian romance and has coedited collections including *Medieval Texts and Contemporary Readers*, with Laurie Finke (Cornell, 1987), and *Culture and the King: The Social Implications of the Arthurian Legend*, with James P. Carley (SUNY, 1994). He is currently working on *The Subversion of History* (with Laurie Finke) and on *Hitler's Arthur, Arthur's Hitler: Fascism in the Arthurian Legend*.

Angela Jane Weisl is assistant professor of English at Seton Hall University and the author of *Conquering the Reign of Femeny: Gender and Genre in Chaucer's Romance* (D. S. Brewer, 1995).

Index